An Understanding of Judaism

AN UNDERSTANDING OF JUDAISM

John D. Rayner

Berghahn Books
Providence • Oxford

First published in 1997 by
Berghahn Books

© 1997 John D. Rayner

Library of Congress Cataloging-in-Publication Data

Rayner, John D.
    An understanding of Judaism / John D. Rayner
        p.   cm. -- (Progressive Judaism today)
    ISBN 1-57181-971-1 (alk. paper). -- ISBN 1-57181-972-X (pbk. :
alk. paper)
        1. Jewish sermons, English.   2. Bible.   O.T.   Pentateuch--Sermons.
    3. Festival-day sermons, Jewish.   4. Reform Judaism.   I. Title.
    II. Series.
    BM740.2.R38   1997
    296.4'7--dc21   97-38773
                                                                    CIP

British Library Cataloguing in Publication Data

A catalogue record for this book is available from the
British Library.

Printed in the United States on acid-free paper.

CONTENTS

Part One
AN UNDERSTANDING OF SCRIPTURE

Part Two
SEASONS OF THE JEWISH YEAR

Season of Freedom

Season of Revelation

Season of Sorrow

Season of Repentance

Season of Atonement

LIST OF ABBREVIATIONS

ARN	Avot d'Rabbi Natan ('Fathers of Rabbi Nathan', 'Minor Tractate')
Ber.	Berachot ('Benedictions', Mishnah/Talmud Tractate)
Bik.	Bikkurim ('First Fruits', Mishnah/Talmud Tractate)
BM	Bava M'tzi'a ('Middle Gate', Mishnah/Talmud Tractate)
Cant.R.	Canticles Rabbah ('Great' Midrash on the Song of Songs)
Deut.	Deuteronomy
Deut.R.	Deuteronomy Rabbah ('Great' Midrash on Deuteronomy)
Exod.	Exodus
Exod.R.	Exodus Rabbah ('Great' Midrash on Exodus)
Ezek.	Ezekiel
Gen.	Genesis
Gen.R.	Genesis Rabbah ('Great' Midrash on Genesis)
Isa.	Isaiah
IT	Itturey Torah ('Ornamentations of the Torah', interpretations of the Pentateuch, ed. Aaron Jacob Greenberg, 6 vols, Tel-Aviv, 1976)
J.	'Jerusalem' Talmud
Jer.	Jeremiah
JPS	Jewish Publication Society of America
Kid.	Kiddushin ('Betrothals', Mishnah/Talmud Tractate)
Lam.	Lamentations
Lam.R.	Lamentations Rabbah ('Great' Midrash on Lamentations)
Lev.	Leviticus
Lev.R.	Leviticus Rabbah ('Great' Midrash on Leviticus)
LJS	Liberal Jewish Synagogue (St John's Wood, London)
Macc.	Maccabees
Mal.	Malachi
Meg.	Megillah ('Scroll', Mishnah/Talmud Tractate)
MHG	Midrash ha-Gadol ('Great Midrash' on the Pentateuch)
Num.	Numbers
Num.R.	Numbers Rabbah ('Great' Midrash on Numbers)
O.Ch.	Orach Chayyim ('Path of Life', Part 1 of Shulchan Aruch)

Pes.	Pesachim ('Passovers', Mishnah/Talmud Tracate)
PRE	Pirkey d'Rabbi Eliezer ('Chapters of Rabbi Eliezer', Midrashic/ethical work)
PRK	Pesikta d'Rav Kahana ('Sections of R. Kahana', Homiletical Midrash)
RH	Rosh Hashanah ('New Year', Mishnah/Talmud Tractate)
Sam.	Samuel
San.	Sanhedrin ('High Court', Mishnah/Talmud Tractate)
Shab.	Shabbat ('Sabbath', Mishnah/Talmud Tractate)
Suk.	Sukkah ('Booth', Mishnah/Talmud Tractate)
Taan.	Ta'anit ('Fast', Mishnah/Talmud Tractate)
THQ	*The Treasury of Humorous Quotations,* ed. Evan Esar & Nicolas Bentley, 1962
TJQ	*A Treasury of Jewish Quotations,* ed. Joseph L. Baron, 1956
ULPS	Union of Liberal and Progressive Synagogues

GLOSSARY

Aggadah	'Narrative' (non-legal Rabbinic literature)
Akedah	'The Binding of Isaac' (Gen. 22)
Al Chet	'For the sin' (liturgical confession of sins)
Aleph	First letter of the Hebrew alphabet
Amora, pl. Amora'im	'Speakers' (Palestinian and Babylonian Rabbis 200-500 CE)
Avinu Malkenu	'Our Father, our King' (penitential prayer)
Avot	'Fathers' (Mishnah Tractate)
Baraita	'External' (Tannaitic teaching not in Mishnah)
Bar'chu	'Bless' (invitation to public prayer)
Bat Kol	'Daughter of the Voice' (Echo, Heavenly Voice)
Chanukkah	'Dedication' (festival commemorating rededication of Temple)
Davka	'Exactly', 'Of all things' (Hebrew and Yiddish)
Dayan, pl. Dayanim	'Judge' (member of Rabbinic court)
Demai	'Doubtful' (whether tithed; Mishnah/Talmud Tractate)
Erev	Eve (of)
Gaon, Geonim	'Excellency' (heads of Babylonian Rabbinic academies in the post-Talmudic period
Gittin	'Divorce Writs' (Mishnah/Talmud Tractate)
Haftarah	'Dismissal' (public reading from the Prophets)
Haggadah	'Narration' (book containing Seder liturgy)
Halachah	'Law' (Rabbinic Law; legal content of Rabbinic literature)

Ha Lachma Anya	'This is the bread of affliction' (Aramaic passage in Haggadah)
Haskalah	'Enlightenment' (18th-19th centuries secularising movement)
Kaddish	'Holy' (Aramaic prayer)
Kasher or kosher	'Fit' (especially to be eaten)
Kedushah	'Holiness' (doxology)
Kohelet	'Preacher'? (Ecclesiastes)
Kol Nidre	'All the vows' (Aramaic annulment of unfulfillable vows)
Makkot	'Stripes' (Mishnah/Talmud Tractate)
Matzah	Unleavened bread
Mechilta	'Measures', 'Hermeneutic Rules' (Tannaitic Midrash on Exodus)
Meshugge	'Crazy' (Hebrew/Yiddish)
Midrash	'Exposition' (Rabbinic Bible interpretation)
Midrash Psalms	Midrash on the Book of Psalms
Mishnah	'Teaching' (compendium of Oral Torah, c. 200 CE)
Mishneh Torah	'Recapitulation of the Torah' (comprehensive codification of Jewish law by Moses Maimonides, 1177, Egypt)
Mitzvah, pl. Mitzvot	'Commandment' (law, religious observance, good deed)
Omer	'Sheaf' (measure of barley offering)
Oneg	'Delight' (cf. Isa. 58:13)
Parashah	'Division' (weekly Torah portion)'
Pesach	Passover
Pesikta	'Section' (title of two collections of homiletical Midrashim: 'Rabbati', the 'Great' one, and d'Rav Kahana (of Rabbi Kahana)
Piyyut, pl. Piyyutim	Religious poem
Purim	'Lots' (festival based on the book of Esther)
Rashi	Acronym of Rabbi Solomon ben Isaac (1040-1105, France)
Rosh Hashanah	'Head of the Year' (New Year festival)
Seder	'Order' (Passover Eve celebration in the home)
Shabbat	'Sabbath'
Sh'mini Atzeret	'Eighth Day of Conclusion' (festival following seventh day of Sukkot)

Shofar	'Ram's horn' (sounded on Rosh Hashanah and at conclusion of Yom Kippur)
Sforno	Obadiah Sforno (Bible commentator, c. 1475-1550, Italy)
Shechitah	'Slaughter' (of animals for food, as prescribed)
Shema	'Hear' (Deut. 6:4-9, 11:13-21, Num. 15:37-41, liturgically recited)
Shulchan Aruch	'Set Table' (Jewish law-code by Joseph Caro, 16th century, Palestine)
Sifra	'Book' (Tannaitic Midrash on Leviticus)
Sifre	'Books' (Tannaitic Mirashim on Numbers and Deuteronomy)
Sivan	Third month of the Hebrew year
Soferim	'Scribes' ('Minor Tractate')
Sotah	'Woman suspected of adultery' (Mishnah/Talmud Tractate)
Sukkah, Sukkot	'Booth' (as used during Sukkot)
Sukkot	'Booths' (festival of Tabernacles)
Talmud	'Teaching' (huge elaboration of Mishnah) (Babylonian: c. 500 CE)
Targum	'Translation' (Aramaic Version of the Bible)
Tav	Last letter of the Hebrew alphabet
Tish'ah b'Av	'Ninth of Av' (fast day)
Tishri	Seventh month of Hebrew year
Tosefta	'Supplement' (Collection of Baraitot arranged as Mishnah)
Yalkut Shim'oni	'Collection' (Midrashic collection attributed to Shim'on ha-Darshan, Simon the Preacher, 13th century)
Yerushalmi	'Jerusalemite' (Palestinian Talmud, early 5th century)
Yeshivah	Academy of Talmudic study (in medieval-scholastic manner)
Yom Kippur	Day of Atonement
Yoma	'The Day (of Atonement)' (Mishnah/Talmud Tractate)

To Susan, with all my love

FOREWORD

In the United Kingdom, Liberal Judaism (close in spirit and ideology to the American Reform movement) is the most radical and innovative expression of modern Jewish belief and practice. The Jewish Religious Union, as it was originally called, was founded in 1902 in order to halt the drift away from organised religion, and to invest Judaism with contemporary relevance. Its early leadership included prominent scholars and lay people like Claude Montefiore, Israel Abrahams and the Hon. Lily Montagu, and their programme, daring for its time, of sexual equality in religious worship with men and women sitting together, prayers in the vernacular, the use of organ accompaniment, and a theology that emphasised universalism, biblical scholarship, the primacy of truth over tradition and ethical conduct above ritual observance – soon attracted a growing number of followers.

The decision to form a congregation was taken in 1910, and The Liberal Jewish Synagogue was founded a year later. In 1912, Rabbi Israel Mattuck, a graduate of Harvard University and the Hebrew Union College, Cincinnati, was inducted as the synagogue's first minister. While the LJS, as it is popularly known, has always remained Liberal Judaism 'flagship' synagogue, today it has thirty sister congregations in the United Kingdom and Eire, all of them affiliated to an umbrella organisation that in 1944, to reflect its growth, was re-named the Union of Liberal and Progressive Synagogues.

As Liberal Judaism looks towards its centenary in 2002, the movement's rabbinic and lay leadership decided that it was an opportune time to review and re-formulate Liberal Jewish thought for the new millennium. We recognise that a movement which advocates Enlightenment values, stresses the informed conscience above legalism, and unlike Orthodoxy, will grant Jewish status to the child of a Jewish father and a non-Jewish mother who is brought up as a Jew – that such a movement is unlikely to command majority support in essentially conservative Anglo-Jewry. Nevertheless, our role at the cutting edge of Judaism, and readiness to stand by our convictions, ensures that Liberal Judaism has a voice and importance far beyond its numbers.

A scholarly, intellectually rigorous rather than sentimental approach to the teaching and transmission of Jewish values has always characterised Liberal Jewish thought. For the last forty years its most consistent and respected exponent has been John Rayner, now Rabbi Emeritus of The Liberal Jewish Synagogue. It has been my privilege and good fortune to be his colleague at the synagogue since 1975. In that time we have written books, articles and pamphlets together, tried ideas and arguments on each other, been jointly pilloried but ultimately vindicated over a host of controversial issues such as Zionism and the State of Israel, a Jewish response to homosexuality, or interfaith relations, and have been each other's sternest critics.

Once an association had been formed between the Union of Liberal and Progressive Synagogues and Berghahn Books, I was invited to become General Editor of a series of proposed centenary publications. It seemed altogether appropriate to begin our series with three volumes of John Rayner's writings. Their publication will be partly subsidised by the Peggy Lang Publications Fund of the LJS and a generous donation from Mr Franz D. Lucas.

This, the first volume, contains a selection of John Rayner's sermons delivered (mainly) at the LJS between the years 1953 and 1996. Eloquent, reasoned, demanding unwavering standards of the Judaism and the Jewish people he loves, insistent on ethical rectitude but lightened by flashes of humour, these sermons not only provide a major anthology of Jewish teachings applied in a modern context and to contemporary issues, but demonstrate that the largely lost craft of homiletics still has at least one outstanding Jewish practitioner.

This volume will be followed by a second on *A Jewish Understanding of the World* and a third on *Jewish Religious Law: A Progressive Perspective*. They will constitute an important statement of Liberal Judaism's beliefs, principles and practices. Together with proposed titles from other Liberal rabbis and scholars, our intention is to produce a comprehensive library of modern Jewish thought for the Progressive movement and beyond, as creative and challenging as were the writings of our founders almost a century ago.

David J. Goldberg
Senior Rabbi, The Liberal Jewish Synagogue

PREFACE

This is the first of two volumes of collected sermons and extracts from sermons given, mostly at the Liberal Jewish Synagogue, St John's Wood, London, in the forty-plus years between the mid-1950s and the mid-1990s.

They appear here much as they were delivered, with only minor changes so as to make them less time-and-place-bound or more readable. The earlier ones have also been stylistically revised in favour of gender-sensitive language – a *desideratum* which, I must confess, has impressed itself on me only in recent years.

They may be described as the testament of a disciple of the founders of the Jewish Religious Union (now Union of Liberal and Progressive Synagogues) who has wrestled with the conflicting claims of tradition and modernity during almost the entire second half of the twentieth century.

Part One applies that approach – of reverence for the Jewish past combined with a spirit of free inquiry and critical evaluation as demanded by the present – to the interpretation of Scripture; Part Two applies it to the interpretation of the Jewish festivals.

The indefinite article of the title, *An Understanding of Judaism*, is meant to indicate both a disclaimer and a claim: that what is presented in this volume is not the only possible understanding of Judaism, and that it is a valid one.

I want to thank all those who have helped and encouraged me: first and foremost, my wife Jane; then my teachers in Cambridge and Cincinnati; the congregations I have been privileged to serve in Streatham, Columbus and St John's Wood; my friend and successor Rabbi David J. Goldberg, editor of the series which this volume inaugurates; those organisations and individuals, named in his Foreword, whose generosity has made it feasible; and Marion Berghahn, its publisher.

John D. Rayner
London, 1997

Part One

❖   ❖   ❖

AN UNDERSTANDING OF SCRIPTURE

The Myth of the Garden of Eden
Shabbat B'reshit, 20 October 1979

The story of Adam and Eve in the Garden of Eden raises a number of difficulties. But before we examine it in detail, let us be clear about three things.

First, that it is largely aetiological: concerned with the origins of things. For though the Bible is mainly a history of the Jewish people, it begins with the history of humanity as a whole. Therefore, in these opening chapters all the most fundamental facts of human life need to be explained: why it is that human beings, like animals, go through a cycle of birth, procreation and death; and why it is that, unlike animals, they till the soil, wear clothes, do wrong, and feel guilty. Secondly, we need to remember that our story is mythological. The author had no access to prehistoric records; indeed, by definition, no such records exist. Nor is he interested in 'facts' as we normally understand that term; the subject-matter of myth is truth in a much deeper sense than the purely historical. And thirdly we need to realise that the author did not draw merely on his own imagination, nor only on that of his own people, but on oral traditions of great antiquity which were current in the folklore of the Near East as a whole. In particular, he drew heavily on ancient Babylonian mythological traditions, such as the Gilgamesh Epic; and though he reworked these legends from his own standpoint, he did not *invent* them, and was to some extent restricted by them. Therefore we should not be surprised if we find in the narrative elements of a primitive, pre-Hebraic outlook which have not been entirely erased.

With these preliminaries out of the way, let us now look at the story as we have it. The chief symbol it employs is a tree which is sometimes called the 'tree of life', and sometimes the 'tree of knowledge of good and evil'. What *kind* of a tree was it? According to Christian tradition, an apple tree; but that is only due to the linguistic coincidence that in Latin the word *malum* for 'evil' is also the word for 'apple'. Jewish tradition suggests various species; among them, for obvious reasons, the fig tree. But of course all these identifications are quite beside the point since the tree is essentially a mythological one.

The real question is: what does the tree symbolise? And about
that there are four possibilities. First, let us take the 'tree of life'. That
would mean: the one that bestows *eternal* life. And as soon as we say
that, we recognise that we are in the presence of a *motif* which runs
all through human literature: the quest for immortality. In the Gilgamesh Epic it is the central theme, and the hero, after a long search,
discovers a sea-plant which, though it does not actually make him
immortal, as he had hoped, at least rejuvenates him. In another
Mesopotamiam epic the substance that confers immortality is a mag-
ical kind of bread and water. In Egyptian mythology it is a sycamore
tree. In Greek mythology it is the food of the gods called ambrosia,
which actually means 'immortality'. In Indian mythology it is a plant
juice called 'soma'. European literature speaks of the elixir of life.
And in Christian tradition eternal life is conferred by the eating and
drinking of the sacramental bread and wine of the Eucharist.

Since it is so universal, it is hardly surprising that this myth should
have also found its way into the Hebrew Bible. But see what happens
to it! God *forbids* Adam and Eve to eat the fruit of the tree. Moreover,
although they defy God and do eat it, nevertheless they do *not*
become immortal. Here we have, indeed, one of the internal contradictions of the story; and in order to resolve it the narrator or editor suggests that there were really two trees, the tree of knowledge,
whose fruit Adam and Eve did eat, and the tree of life, whose fruit
they did *not* eat. That becomes explicit at the end of the chapter,
where God says: 'Behold, the man has become like one of us, knowing good and evil; and now, lest he put forth his hand and take *also*
of the tree of life, and eat, and live for ever' (Gen. 3:22), whereupon
he is expelled from the Garden of Eden. But whatever we may make
of the contradiction, the essential point is that Adam and Eve remain
mortal. In other words, the Hebrew Bible sets its face against the
whole concept of the quest for immortality; it declares it to be a vain
quest. Why? Partly because of its monotheism. For in ancient times
to become immortal meant to become divine, whereas Hebraism
insists that there is only One God. And partly because of its realism.
Human beings *are* mortal, and we had better face the fact. Rather
than indulge in illusory hopes, let us accept our limitations and seek
fulfilment within them. That is what the Bible seems to be saying;
but it must be added that it is perfectly compatible with the belief in
a purely spiritual immortality which came into Judaism in a later age.

So much for עץ החיים, 'the tree of life' (Gen. 2:9). But it is also
called עץ הדעת טוב ורע (ibid.), and that phrase is grammatically very
strange: so much so that it looks suspiciously like a combination of
two originally separate terms of which the first is simply עץ הדעת, 'the

tree of knowledge'. That would mean that to eat its fruit is to become omniscient. But once again, God forbids it. In other words, God does not desire human beings to become omniscient. And how is that to be understood? It may be yet another case of Hebraic realism. We are *not* omniscient, and we had better recognise our limitation. But there is more to it than that. For knowledge is power, and power can be used for good or evil. Therefore the quest for more and more knowledge can be positively dangerous unless it is accompanied by a corresponding growth in moral responsibility. Perhaps that, too, is what the Bible is trying to tell us. If so, it should strike a responsive chord in our minds, for if ever an age illustrated that danger, it is surely ours.

However, the Hebrew word דעת also has another connotation: not only knowledge in general, but also 'carnal knowledge' in particular, as when the Bible says that 'Adam knew Eve'. So here we have a third *motif* which we must recognise, even if it doesn't appeal altogether to our way of thinking. In this interpretation the fruit of the forbidden tree had an aphrodisiac property; it aroused sexual desire. That is obvious from the fact that immediately after eating it Adam and Eve become aware of their nakedness; that is to say, their sexuality. It is perhaps also implied by the figure of the serpent; for in addition to symbolising immortality, because of the way it casts off its skin and grows another, the serpent is also a universal symbol of sex; and in our story that point is further reinforced by the pun on the word *arum* meaning 'shrewd' or 'crafty', a proverbial quality of the serpent, and *erom* or *arom*, meaning 'naked'. Why then should the 'tree of carnal knowledge' be forbidden? We might say: because sexuality does tend to produce guilt feelings. Why that should be so, is yet another question. The causes may be partly irrational, and they may be wrongly exaggerated by an over-prudish morality; but equally, the sex drive, because it is so powerful, is a major source of selfish, inconsiderate and cruel behaviour. However that may be, guilt is what Adam and Eve feel, and it is symbolised in our story by the need they feel to cover their nakedness. Nevertheless, the point should not be pressed too far; for the Bible doesn't *always* moralise; sometimes it just describes. And to a large extent what it is doing here is merely to note the fact that in the life-cycle of every individual there comes a stage of sexual awareness, and then to transfer that process, as it were, to the childhood of humanity as a whole.

Finally, we come to the 'tree of the knowledge of *good and evil*'. Now it is possible that this doesn't mean what it is usually taken to mean; that it should really be translated 'good and bad' or 'pleasant and unpleasant', and that it is merely a Hebrew idiom, which occurs elsewhere in the Bible, for 'everything' (Deut. 1:39, II Sam. 14:17, 19:35, 24:50, 31:24, 29). In that case we are of course back with omniscience. But if the terms do have a moral connotation, then we must ask: why should God want to prevent Adam and Eve from eating the fruit of the tree? Surely discrimination between right and wrong is precisely what God does desire! Is not the major purpose of the Bible to inculcate just that?

One possible answer is that what is here condemned is not genuine moral perception but the false and arrogant claim which human beings, especially those in positions of power, are apt to make that they 'know' what is right and what is wrong, without reference to any Divine Will, that they are themselves the arbiters of morality, and that they are therefore entitled to impose their will on others. That theory was advanced a few years ago in a book entitled *The Art of Political Deception* by Charles Napper; but I can't say that I am entirely persuaded.

It seems to me more likely that what really matters in the story is not the nature of the tree and the kind of knowledge it was able to confer, but simply the fact that God, for whatever reason, gave a command which Adam and Eve promptly proceeded to disobey. The point then is that any moral code involves restrictions, requires us to restrain our greed, and that, being human, we are always liable to resent these restrictions, to disregard them, and to violate them. If so, the story merely points to another fact of life, namely the fact of sin, and tries to explain it.

Although the explanation may not be entirely satisfactory as regards the *cause* of sin, it is certainly masterly in its description of the *consequences*. First, the sense of shame, represented once again by the impulse which seizes Adam and Eve to cover their nakedness. Then the desire to lessen the guilt by sharing it with others, for it is to be noted that Eve does not eat the forbidden fruit alone but persuades Adam to eat it with her. Then the tendency to 'pass the buck', for Adam blames Eve, and Eve blames the serpent; it is always somebody else's fault! Then the lies to cover up what has happened, as when Adam tells God that he has been hiding because of his nakedness, not because of his guilt. And finally the sense of alienation – from God, from one's better self, and even from nature – which sin produces and which is symbolised in our story by the expulsion from Paradise. All these details are brilliantly depicted.

And yet we must return to the meaning of the story as a whole. In Christian tradition it is known as the 'Fall of Man', and that interpretation has profoundly influenced European literature. But it is hardly to be found in Jewish sources (exceptions: II Esdras 7:118,

Sira 25:24; cf. Romans 5:12, 18). As Chief Rabbi Dr J. H. Hertz wrote, 'Instead of the Fall of Man ... Judaism preaches the Rise of Man; instead of Original Sin, it stresses Original Virtue ... The Golden Age of Humanity is not in the past, but in the future' (*The Pentateuch and Haftorahs*, p. 196).

How is that view to be squared with the plain sense of our story? By seeing it as symbolising a transition. Just as there is in the life of every individual a transition from sexual unawareness to sexual awareness, which our story retrojects into the childhood of humanity, so there is a transition from moral unawareness to moral awareness, which is likewise retrojected. Of course neither must be taken literally. In the history of humanity there never was a stage of complete innocence, either sexually or morally. What happened was a growing awareness of the possibility of choice, and that is an ascent, not a descent.

Admittedly, with the awareness of choice comes the opportunity, and the temptation, to choose wrongly. But the possibility of choosing rightly nevertheless exists. Far from being taken away from us by Adam's sin, as Christianity has often taught, it is symbolically dramatised by it. God 'created Adam in the beginning, and left him in the power of his own inclination. If you will, you can keep the commandments, and to act faithfully is a matter of your own choice' (Sira 15:14f). That is what Judaism emphasises. And this principle holds within it the possibility that one day human beings, both individually and collectively, will learn to use their freedom rightly, for good and not for evil. Then they will enter the Garden of Eden, and it will be much more glorious than the mythical Paradise of Genesis. That is the hope of Judaism. It is in this sense that the Golden Age of Humanity lies in the future. And to work towards it is the task which gives meaning and purpose to our lives.

❖   ❖   ❖

Cain and Abel
Shabbat B'reshit, 20 October 1973

The story of Cain and Abel is tantalisingly cryptic. Presumably the biblical writer drew on a much more elaborate folk tale but omitted everything that seemed to him inessential. So one is left wondering what the fuller version might have contained, and what prompted the story-teller to select from it what he did. Nevertheless the essentials are clear.

First, that it is a story of two brothers: a fact which the Bible emphasises by using the word 'brother' no less than seven times in the space of ten verses (Gen. 4:1-10). Secondly, that, although they were brothers, they had little in common. Indeed, they represent two different types of civilisation. Cain is a farmer, Abel is a shepherd.

Furthermore – and this is the most puzzling aspect of the story – Abel is favoured by God: his offering is accepted, whereas Cain's is rejected. On the face of it, this is a case of divine favouritism. Are we to suppose that this didn't bother the narrator? That he had not yet attained the concept of an impartial God as expressed in Abraham's rhetorical question, 'Shall not the Judge of all the earth do justly?' (Gen. 18:25).

That is indeed a possibility. On the other hand, the mere difference in occupation may imply a moral judgment, for in the oldest strata of the Bible there is a tendency to equate the nomadic life with moral sobriety and the more sophisticated life of an agricultural society, as represented by the Canaanites, with licentiousness. Alternatively or additionally, there may be in the story an implication that Cain and Abel brought their offerings to God in a different spirit. Cain was niggardly, and brought only a handful of grains. Abel was generous; he offered, in Speiser's translation, 'the finest of the firstlings of his flock'.

So the differential treatment they received may have had a moral justification. And indeed the sequel seems to confirm this. For one would expect brothers, however different, to love each other. But in reality that isn't always what happens. Sometimes there is hatred between brothers, either mutual or one-sided. And in the case of Cain and Abel it is entirely one-sided. There is nothing in the story to suggest that Abel harboured any ill-will towards Cain. The hatred is entirely on Cain's side. The occasion for it is Abel's good fortune, but the real cause must lie in Cain himself. He is the sort of person who nurtures jealousy, resentment and aggression.

At this point God says to him in so many words: 'Why are you so angry? If your conscience is clear, you should be cheerful; but if not, then, far from venting your spleen on somebody else – on your innocent brother – you should take a good look at yourself, and strive to overcome the evil within you.' But Cain rejects this chance of rehabilitation which has been offered to him, and proceeds to commit the world's first murder.

What follows is the Bible's condemnation of that crime, all the more poignant because expressed, not in any moralistic generalisation, but in the form of a conversation. God says to Cain: 'Where is Abel your brother?' God asks this question, not because God doesn't know the answer but, as Rashi sensitively suggests, to give Cain a chance to confess his sin. But far from doing that, Cain answers, 'How should I know? Am I my brother's keeper?', and thereby shows that in killing his brother he has also killed the last vestiges of brotherly feeling within himself. Then comes the great arraignment: 'What have you done? Your brother's blood cries out to me from the ground.' Now it so happens that the Hebrew word for blood is in the plural, and on the basis of that fact the ancient Rabbis made a remarkable comment, which is also found in the Koran (Sura 5:30). The comment is that to kill a single human being is to kill all the posterity he might have had as well; and indeed, since every human being is infinitely precious, it is tantamount to destroying the whole world (San. 4:5).

So understood, what may seem at first a quaint, primitive and morally dubious story becomes one of the greatest passages in all of literature about, negatively, the evils of jealousy, hatred and murder, and, positively, the virtues of mutual caring, and the sanctity of life.

❖ ❖ ❖

Never Again?
Shabbat Noach, 4 November 1989

The long and fascinating story of the Flood reaches its climax in the eighth chapter of Genesis. But not only in the sense of 'journey's end', that the rain finally ceases, and the waters subside, and the dove returns with an olive branch, and the ark at long, long last comes to rest, and the passengers, human and animal, disembark. That is exciting enough, and worthy of the conclusion of a great novel; but there is more to it than that. For the story isn't just a story. It is that, of course, and though the biblical writer didn't invent the plot but took it from an ancient Babylonian myth, he re-wrote it so superbly that he created a masterpiece of literature in its own right; and there is every reason why we should enjoy it on that level.

But the writer didn't want *only* to tell a good story. He wanted to *use* the story to raise a big issue – indeed, the biggest of all issues: *Will humanity survive?* And on this level, too, the story reaches its climax with God's promise: 'I will never again curse the ground because of humanity, for the imagination of the human heart is evil from their youth; neither will I ever again destroy every living creature as I have done. While the earth remains, seedtime and harvest, cold and heat, summer and winter, day and night, shall not cease' (Gen. 8:21f). The answer to the question, whether humanity will survive, is apparently a resounding, reassuring 'Yes!'

Can we accept the reassurance? Certainly former generations accepted it. The Second Isaiah, for instance, had no doubt: 'As I swore that the waters of Noah should no more go over the earth ...' (Isa. 54:9). Former generations accepted the assurance because there was no compelling reason to doubt it. But we are different. We know that much in the Bible derives from human speculation rather than divine revelation; so we can't always be sure that it is right. And we know that there are in the present world situation dangers which *really could* destroy humanity. I need not spell out what they are, since we hear about them daily. But we should perhaps pause to reflect that one of the dangers – which has come to the fore just as the danger of nuclear war has, thank God, receded – is the much talked-about 'greenhouse effect', that is to say, the warming of the earth's atmosphere, which could raise the level of the oceans, which in turn could produce just the kind of flood that underlies the biblical narrative! How then can we be sure that it won't happen? The answer, to be honest, is: we can't. There is no certainty that what the Bible says is always literally true. There is no certainty that there will be no major disasters in the future. There is no certainty that the *ultimate* disaster will not happen, that humanity will not destroy itself. There are no certainties at all! That is what distinguishes the modern age from all previous ages. We live in an age of uncertainty – of chronic, inescapable, irreversible uncertainty. It is a heavy burden, especially for young people to bear, and we sympathise with them. But that is the harsh reality, and the fundamentalists, who think otherwise, only delude themselves.

But if that is so, then what value, other than as great literature, does the Flood story have for us? Let me suggest that it has at least *three* immensely important lessons to teach us.

The first is, quite simply, *hope*. So, all right, the biblical author went a little too far in saying: 'Never again'. But in saying it he expressed a fervent optimism which we can share. For though ours is an age of unprecedented uncertainty and danger, it is also an age of unprecedented possibility and opportunity. More than ever before, and in ways unimagined by previous generations, it lies within our power to achieve for human life on this planet conditions of hitherto undreamt-of physical security, material abundance, social harmony and cultural excellence.

Secondly, whether or not that hope is realised is a *moral* question. That is perhaps the *main* point of the biblical Flood story, and what distinguishes it most sharply from its Babylonian prototype, which doesn't even bother to raise the question of *why* the Flood occurred, and lets it be thought that it was simply a whim of the gods which had no rhyme or reason. But what is totally absent from the Gilgamesh Epic is *of the very essence* of the biblical narrative, which is first and foremost an attempt to interpret human history in *moral* terms. Why did the Flood happen? Because, as we are told at the very beginning of the story, ותשחת הארץ לפני האלהים, ותמלא הארץ חמס, 'the earth was corrupt before God, for the earth was full of violence' (Gen. 6:11).

When it says that 'the earth' was corrupt, of course it doesn't mean that literally. Those who know the little children's book, based on the Flood story, *The Log of the Ark* by Kenneth Walker and Geoffrey Boumphrey, may recall that it begins: 'Many many years ago, the world was all new and clean, and like most new things, it worked very well – much better than it does today'. There was nothing wrong with the earth as such, just as there is nothing wrong with it now. The earth was not corrupt; it was human beings who 'corrupted' it, who spoilt it. How? By their חמס, by the violence they did to each other – and perhaps to it. It is noteworthy that the Hebrew for 'was corrupt', ותשחת, literally means 'destroyed itself' and is the same verb used in the Deuteronomy law (20:19) לא־תשחית, 'You shall not destroy', referring there to the fruit trees of a besieged city but later taken as a prohibition against *any* wanton destruction. Perhaps, therefore, there is just a hint of that – greedy over-exploitation of the environment, the very tendency which could bring on another flood! – in the biblical story. But whatever the precise sin of the antediluvians may have been, that is why the Flood occurred. What happens to humanity on earth, for good or ill, depends on how humanity conducts itself, depends on the extent to which it submits itself to the Moral Law or (which is another way of putting it) the Divine Will. That is the standpoint of the biblical narrative, and its applicability today is crystal-clear.

There is indeed a little problem I must raise before I come to my last point. There is something very odd about the verse I quoted at the beginning, in which God says, 'I will never again curse the ground because of humanity, for the imagination of the human heart is evil from their youth'. Surely that is a *non-sequitur*. If human beings were really so evil, surely that would be a reason for destroying the earth, not *against* destroying it! To that puzzle I have found only one plausible answer, by Hillel Zeitlin, a Russian-born Hebrew writer who went through a stage of scepticism but ultimately became deeply religious, and died, wearing *tallit* and *tefillin*, on the way to Treblinka, on the eve of Rosh Hashanah, 1942. He emphasises the word מנעוריו, 'from their youth', and takes it to mean that in the days of Noah humanity was still in its youth, still relatively undeveloped and uneducated; that, as it matures, it will grow in wisdom and understanding; and that therefore God decided to give humanity another chance (IT, I, p. 74).

That observation actually links my first two points: that there is hope for humanity, and that the realisation of the hope depends on morally responsible behaviour. The third lesson which the biblical Flood story plainly teaches is that in this matter *a single individual may make all the difference*. For why, if the earth was corrupt and full of violence, did humanity nevertheless survive? Because of Noah! Because, as we are told at the very beginning of the story, 'Noah was איש צדיק, a righteous man, upright in his generation' (Gen. 6:9). One person can save humanity! A single individual can turn the tide – literally or metaphorically – of human destiny! That is perhaps the most striking message of the Flood story.

❖   ❖   ❖

The Tower of Babel
Shabbat Noach, 30 October 1976

The story of the Tower of Babel is set in prehistoric times, of which the author could not have had any knowledge. Therefore it rests on imagination. But not necessarily the author's alone. In all probability he merely gave the final shape to a legend that had already been told and re-told for many generations, so that it is quite impossible to know who contributed what. All we can do is to identify the various motifs.

One motif is what is known as aetiology – the explanation of origins. Human beings have always been curious to know how things began, and to satisfy that curiosity is one of the functions of story-telling. Indeed, if I may permit myself an aetiological conjecture, I suspect that story-telling began with the attempts of parents to answer the questions their children put to them about the facts of life. In the Tower of Babel story the facts of life to be aetiologically explained are chiefly two. First, the Tower itself, which was one of the wonders of the ancient world. As a matter of fact, there were in Babylonia many temples, each with a pyramid-like structure called *ziggurat*; but the one in Babylon was the most colossal and famous of them all. How then did it come to be built? The story answers that question. And the other fact of life is the diversity of languages. Why is it that every people speaks a different language, so that they can't communicate with each other except through interpreters? That is another puzzle, and one which even today has not been satisfactorily solved. The Tower of Babel story is an early attempt to solve it.

A second motif, barely disguised, is anti-Babylonianism. In the centuries during which the story must have evolved Babylonia was the most thriving centre of civilisation. It was a prosperous and sophisticated society which represented the height of human achievement in the arts and sciences. During the same period the Hebrews were a tiny nomadic people struggling against the elements to subsist on sheep-raising and against the world empires to maintain some kind of independence. They might well have been inclined to feel inferior when they compared themselves with the Babylonians. Very likely, therefore, they would have tended to boost their morale by saying, in so many words, 'All that glitters is not gold': by debunking Babylonian civilisation as a dazzling façade covering up a seething inner turmoil. The Tower of Babel story serves that purpose by another piece of aetiology, when it disparagingly explains the very name Babel as derived from the verb *balal*, 'to confuse'.

A third and closely related motif is the contempt, mingled with envy, which one often finds among country folk for city life. From the point of view of a shepherd, or a farmer, a city is a place of luxury, licentiousness and all manner of vice. Some of this disdain seems to underlie the Tower of Babel story. It is therefore a disdain, not just for Babylonian civilisation in particular, but for civilisation in general. As a matter of fact the very word 'civilisation' comes from the Latin for 'city'.

This negative view of civilisation is not indeed typical of the Bible, or of Judaism as a whole. But it is quite marked in these opening chapters of Genesis; it re-appears in some later books, such as Ecclesiastes; and there are touches of it elsewhere, for instance in the story of Sodom and Gomorrah and in the Prophets' denunciations of the evils of city life, contrasted with their nostalgia for 'the good old days' of the wilderness period.

How far this pessimism about civilisation is justified, is an intriguing question. But we are hardly likely to dismiss it altogether. On the contrary, our own modern experience of urbanisation and its concomitant evils – congestion, pollution, loneliness, violence and crime – should make us rather sympathetic towards it. We are certainly more conscious than previous generations of the danger of civilisation getting out of hand. And to point out that danger seems to be one of the purposes of the Tower of Babel story.

But what is the particular evil which the Tower of Babel story associates with civilisation? That, unfortunately, is not quite clear. But perhaps there is just a hint in the amount of detail with which the story, considering its extreme brevity, describes the building materials used in the construction of the tower – the bricks that served as stone, and the bitumen that served as mortar. In other words, the evil which the story, as its fourth motif, condemns may be what we would call materialism. And if that seems far-fetched, it gains credibility when we take into account how the Rabbis interpreted the story, for a Midrash relates that when, during the construction work, a man fell and died, his co-workers paid no attention, but when a brick fell they fasted and wept (PRE 24; MHG 11:3). Has there ever been a more damning indictment of materialism than this Midrash, which seems to be saying that what it ultimately leads to is a society in which things are valued more highly than persons? And are there not plenty of danger signals of just such a tendency in the contemporary world?

Even so, what the Tower of Babel story more obviously condemns is not so much materialism as – in a bad sense of the word – humanism. It is the overweening pride of human beings as a species when they become too self-satisfied and self-confident, when they become inebriated with the sense of their own power, convinced that they can do whatever they wish and that there is no power in heaven or earth to prevent them. Indeed, this is surely the *predominant motif* of the Tower of Babel story: that human beings are, so to speak, getting too big for their boots and, for their own good, need to be taken down a peg or two, reminded who is the Boss.

This is a theme we encounter elsewhere in the Bible and, once again, especially in the opening chapters of Genesis. Adam, for instance, is banished from the Garden of Eden because he has eaten the fruit of the forbidden tree. This tree is described in two ways. Sometimes as 'the tree of the knowledge of good and evil'; in that case the implication is that human beings are claiming omniscience and, in particular, the right to be the sole arbiter of what is right and what is wrong. And sometimes the tree is called 'the tree of life', with the implication that immortality is what humans aspire to. That implication is present also in the Tower of Babel story, when it says, 'Come, let us build a city, and a tower with its top in the sky, *that we may make a name for ourselves*' (Gen. 11:4), for clearly an *imperishable* name is meant. In any case, both of these attributes, omniscience and immortality, belong to God; and therefore both stories, that of the Garden of Eden and that of the Tower of Babel, illustrate the presumption of humans pretending, or aspiring, to be divine.

The same point is of course also made outside the Bible, and outside Judaism; for instance in the Sumerian Gilgamesh Epic, where the hero sets out on a long journey to discover the secret of immortality; in the recurring theme of the elixir of life, which is found in many literatures; and in the myth of Prometheus who steals the fire from Zeus and is grievously punished for his audacity. Regarding that, we need to remember that in those days the ability to make fire was one of the most startling evidences of humanity's growing mastery over nature; a modern equivalent might be their ability to manipulate nuclear energy.

Not the least of the powers which the invention of fire-making conferred was the ability to produce better building materials, such as bricks; and on this there is more than a little emphasis in the Tower of Babel story when the people say, 'Come, let us make bricks, נשרפה לשרפהו, and burn them till they are burnt hard' (Gen. 11:3).

But the main feature of the story, symbolising humanity's bid for divinity, is the Tower itself, וראשו בשמים, with its top in the sky. It is the *height* of the tower that is emphasised, and since this serves no utilitarian purpose, the only motive behind it is evidently to challenge the gods. To scale the heavens, to ascend higher than has ever been done before, has always been a human dream, and I suspect that there has always been in it an element of Prometheanism. It features in folklore; for instance in the tale of Jack and the Beanstalk. It features in architecture; for instance in the pyramids of ancient Egypt and in the skyscrapers of modern New York. It motivates the sport of mountaineering, culminating in the conquest of Mount Everest. And in recent years it has achieved its most spectacular success with the conquest of outer space.

There is nothing intrinsically wrong with the pursuit of technology, with the extension of humanity's control over their environment. But there are two provisos. First, that it is done with caution and prudence, and especially with due regard for the possible harmful side-effects and long-term consequences; otherwise, as we are now beginning to discover, nature has a way of hitting back in all sorts of unsuspected and potentially catastrophic ways. And secondly, that the advancement of the frontiers of technology does not absorb a disproportionate amount of human energy compared with the attention given to the more immediately urgent and morally significant tasks of perfecting human behaviour, or creating a just and compassionate society. It is when this order of priorities is reversed, when technological progress outstrips moral and social progress, that civilisation gets out of hand. And it is perhaps chiefly this lopsidedness, and the perils which it holds, that the Tower of Babel story warns against.

But if that is the essence of the matter – if the error of the builders of Babylon is essentially lack of prudence and a wrong scale of priorities, a matter of mis-directed ambition and energy – then their sin, though serious, is something less fundamental than downright wickedness. Therefore one would expect their punishment to be correspondingly mild. And that is exactly what we find, for they are merely scattered. And this is all the more striking because the story follows immediately on the story of the Flood, which involves the destruction of all humanity with the exception of a single family. The contrast did not escape the Rabbis. It is the basis of a famous Midrash which says that the generation of the Flood were destroyed because they practised every kind of injustice and oppression, but the generation of the Tower were only scattered because, although they defied God, there was unity among them, a unity implied in the biblical phrase (Gen. 11:1) that 'they were of one language and one speech' (Gen.R. 38:6; MHG 11:9).

This divine lenience towards the builders of the Tower enables us, too, to end on a note of hope. In spite of all the evils of the present-day world, and even in spite of the widespread denial of God, most human beings mean well; and most societies are making slow progress towards a better social order. The predominant sin of contemporary humanity is not so much wickedness as folly. It is imprudence in the reckless exploitation of nature, and an underdeveloped sense of priorities in that we concentrate too much on technological achievement and economic growth and too little on the cultivation of those virtues which make for happiness and peace.

If that is not too optimistic a diagnosis, then, though we need urgently to pay attention to the warning which the Tower of Babel story sounds, the change required of us is not so fundamental as to lie beyond the bounds of possibility. 'All your children shall be taught of the Eternal One, and great shall be the peace of your children' (Isa. 54:13). On that verse the Rabbis commented: 'Read not *banayich*, your children, but *bonayich*, your builders' (Ber. 64a). Our task is indeed to build; but it is not primarily to build higher towers or mightier machines: it is to build better human beings and a more harmonious society.

❖   ❖   ❖

Abraham and Sodom

Shabbat Va-yera, 22 October 1983

The first thing that strikes us when we read the story of Abraham's extraordinary plea for Sodom and Gomorrah is the intimacy – one might even say the impertinence – with which he addresses the Creator of the universe. Abraham is seen in our tradition as a man of faith: a faith so profound, so firm, so unclouded, that he can converse with the Creator of the universe as naturally as ordinary human beings talk to one another.

Yet this is not what our tradition chiefly emphasises about Abraham. Christianity differs here from Judaism. The verse Christianity stresses is that Abraham 'believed in the Eternal One, who reckoned it to his merit' (Gen. 15:6). It portrays him first and foremost as a believer, a man of faith. Not so Judaism. A modern commentator, Rabbi Nathan Finkel, known as 'the Grandfather of Slobodka' (1849-1927) draws attention to the phrase in our story, 'I have known him to the end that he may enjoin his children and his household after him to keep the way of the Eternal One by doing righteousness and justice' (Gen. 18:19), and makes this comment, drawing both on the biblical account and on rabbinic legend: 'Abraham was only three years old when he became the first human being to recognise his Creator, and to realise that the Eternal One alone is God and there is no other; he was condemned to death by burning for his faith; he taught all humanity the unity of God and converted many persons to God and God's Torah. Nevertheless all the praises and descriptions of Abraham refer only to his acts of kindness and not to his greatness in the matter of faith ... From this we may infer that Abraham's loving kindness was the true essence of his personality' (IT, I, p. 140). Judaism, in other words, has chosen to emphasise the ethical rather than the devotional side of Abraham's character, his conduct rather than his belief, his works rather than his faith; and that speaks volumes about the ethical emphasis characteristic of Judaism generally.

That, in turn, is of course a consequence of the Jewish belief that God is a moral Being, that righteousness is of the very essence of God's nature; and nowhere is that point more succinctly made than in the key phrase of our story, when Abraham protests against God's announced intention to destroy the cities of Sodom and Gomorrah by saying: השופט כל־הארץ לא יעשה משפט, 'Shall not the Judge of all the earth do justly?' (Gen. 18:25). Abraham never doubts, as Judaism never doubts, that God is just; he merely has difficulty, as we often have difficulty, in reconciling that not-to-be-questioned fact with the actual happenings of history.

That problem – how to square divine justice with human suffering – is known as theodicy, and theodicy is what our story has often been said to be about. Yet that is not how Jewish tradition has generally seen it. It does not set out to debate a philosophical puzzle but to teach a moral lesson. Once again, the ethical emphasis is paramount.

The chief point of the story is the contrast it paints between two kinds of behaviour: that of the people of Sodom and that of Abraham. What exactly was the sin of the Sodomites? Sexual perversion is what the Bible hints at. And that is how Christian tradition understands it; hence the connotation of the word sodomy. But once again Judaism differs. What it emphasises is something quite different, something mentioned already in the book of Ezekiel but more fully elaborated in the Rabbinic Aggadah. The Ezekiel passage occurs in a blistering condemnation of Judah and reads: 'Behold, this was the iniquity of your sister Sodom; pride, fullness of bread, and prosperous ease was in her hand and in her daughters', neither did she strengthen the hand of the poor and needy' (Ezek. 16:49). Taking their cue from that verse, the Rabbis, in Midrash after Midrash, describe how the people of Sodom, although they lived in an extremely fertile plain, of which the Bible itself says that it was 'like the garden of the Eternal One' (Gen. 13:10), and though most of them were therefore prosperous to the point of wallowing in luxury (it is said, for instance, that their streets were paved with gold) – how in spite of that fact, or perhaps because of it, they were callous and cruel to their own poor, and totally lacking in friendliness or compassion towards any strangers who entered their city. One tradition relates that they flooded the approaches to their city so as to keep strangers away (PRE 25) – a form of immigration control which modern nations practise in more sophisticated ways!

So the sin of the Sodomites, or the aspect of it which Jewish tradition has chosen to emphasise, was not sexual but social. It was above all a total absence of hospitality. And it was on this account that they incurred God's anger. Rabbi Gunther Plaut sums up: 'Social evil, then, caused Sodom to perish. The Bible thus takes the old story of the physical destruction of the plain and turns it into a moral tale that carries its warning to all ages: affluence without social concern is self-destructive; it hardens the conscience against repentance; it engenders cruelty and excess. The treatment accorded to newcomers and strangers was then and may always be considered a touchstone of the community's moral condition' (Plaut, *The Torah, A Modern Commentary*, pp. 134f).

That is one side of the contrast. The other is Abraham. What is Abraham's outstanding virtue according to Jewish tradition? Why, of course hospitality, the very quality which the Sodomites so conspicuously lacked! The contrast could not be more sharply drawn. It is all the more striking because immediately before the story of the destruction of Sodom and Gomorrah, in the same eighteenth chapter of Genesis, Abraham has demonstrated that very quality of hospitality by giving the most generous welcome to the three strangers who turn out to be messengers of God. And the Aggadah enlarges on the theme. It tells us, for instance, how Abraham built hotels along the caravan routes through the desert, not for profit but for the sole purpose of providing rest and refreshment for weary travellers.

Furthermore, Abraham displays that virtue, not only by his wayside inns, but by the very act of pleading for the people of Sodom. He has every reason to detest them, from what he has heard about them and perhaps experienced of them, and from the fact that their way of life is the very antithesis of his. They are town-dwellers (the word 'city' is repeatedly stressed in our story), debauched, depraved, corrupt and cruel; he is a man of the desert, accustomed to solitude, dignified, upright and generous. Abraham might well have responded with glee when he was told that Sodom was about to be destroyed; but he did the very opposite. As Rabbi Nathan Finkel comments, 'If Abraham had rejoiced over the destruction of Sodom, that would in itself have shown something of the character of the Sodomites. But Abraham's aim in life was to do good to his fellow human beings, not to see them destroyed. His desire was that sin should cease, that evil should pass away, not that the people should perish' (IT, I, p. 142). It is not only hospitality to wayfarers and kindness to strangers, but also compassion for evildoers which are revealed in this story about Abraham, and therefore about the system of values that is Judaism.

The *fact* that Abraham pleads for the people of Sodom: that, rather than the exact content of his dialogue with God, is what matters. And yet of course great stories can be appreciated on a variety of levels, and there is indeed great interest in the argument as well. Most intriguing of all is the question of why it stops after the number ten. Are we to suppose that there were no innocent people at all in Sodom, not even a single one? That seems unlikely; it is contrary to experience. Is it suggested, then, that ten good people suffice to save a city but nine do not? That would be much too literal an interpretation. No, the message is surely a more general one: that when a society becomes permeated with evil, a point may well be reached when the minority opposed to the general trend becomes too small, too frightened, too ineffectual, to halt the decline, and in the end disaster must ensue and engulf the good and bad alike. When that happens, it is not a refutation of God's justice but a manifestation of it; for God's justice applies to human society rather than to individuals. That is a hard lesson to learn, and in our story, though that is not its main point, Abraham learns it, and through him, Judaism invites us to accept it. Innocent Sodomites died in the fall of Sodom, as innocent Romans died in the fall of Rome, and innocent Germans in the fall of the Third Reich; but the collapse, sooner or later, of societies that flout God's will is nevertheless a proof, not a disproof, of God's justice. That, at any rate, is one interpretation of the way the argument ends. It assumes that if the argument had gone one stage further it would have ended in this fashion: 'Then Abraham said, What if five be found there? And God answered, For the sake of the five I would spare the city if I could, but I cannot, because justice must prevail.'

Perhaps it is as well, however, that the story doesn't end like that, that it ends, rather, in a great silence; for in that silence lies the whole mystery of theodicy for which there are no glib solutions, which will haunt, baffle, mystify and challenge human thought, including Jewish thought, for endless ages to come.

❖   ❖   ❖

Ishmael my Brother
Shabbat Va-yera, 2 November 1985

The birth of Isaac, related in the twenty-first chapter of the book of Genesis, has a prehistory which goes back to the fifteenth, where Abraham, like a typical Jewish father, begins to wonder whether he will ever have a son and heir, and God assures him that he will (Gen. 15:2ff). But when the promise has remained unfulfilled for ten years, his wife Sarah proposes that her Egyptian slave Hagar should become his concubine (Gen. 16:1ff). The proposal may seem strange to us, but historically, concubinage has been practised in many societies, and it is known that according to Hurrian law, which forms much of the background of the Patriarchal stories, a barren wife was actually *obliged* to provide her husband with a concubine, and it would therefore seem that Sarah merely acted in accordance with contemporary custom (E.A. Speiser, *The Anchor Bible, Genesis,* pp. 120f).

Her action nevertheless has unforeseen circumstances. For as soon as Hagar conceives, she feels superior to her infertile mistress, and ceases to treat her with respect (Gen. 16:4). Sarah, in return, is furious and would like nothing better than to demote Hagar back to the rank of an ordinary slave and then sell her to some passing caravan. But she knows that Abraham would not approve, and we know from the Code of Hammurabi that it would not have been allowed in law. So she does what unscrupulous landlords do to sitting tenants: she makes life so miserable for Hagar that she leaves of her own accord (Gen. 16:6).

God has pity on Hagar and sends an angel to comfort her. She will have a son, he tells her, and his name will be *Yishmael*, meaning that 'God has heard' her affliction, and he will become the progenitor of a great nation (Gen. 16:7-11). It is true that the angel goes on to say some uncomplimentary things about the child-to-be. 'He shall be a wild ass of a man, his hand against every man, and every man's hand against him' (Gen. 16:12). But here the angel is merely prefiguring a hostility that will exist in later times between Israelites and Ishmaelites. It is also true that the angel tells Hagar to go back home and put up with Sarah's ill-treatment (Gen. 16:9). This, however, is only a literary device necessitated by the fact that the story of Hagar's departure has come down to the editor in two versions. Hagar has to be brought back home in chapter 16 so that she may reappear in chapter 21.

During the interval Ishmael is duly born and named (Gen. 16:15f). But God informs Abraham that he will have another son, this time by Sarah, and he, being a hundred years old, takes the information as a joke, and laughs, and prays that God will look after the son he already has. God, however, repeats the improbable promise and, in allusion to Abraham's laughter, tells him that the baby-to-be is to be called *Yitzchak*, from the verb *tzachak*, 'to laugh'. At the same time God responds to Abraham's plea on behalf of Ishmael. 'Behold, I will bless him and make him fruitful and multiply him exceedingly; he shall be the father of twelve princes. But I will establish My covenant with Isaac, whom Sarah shall bear to you at this season next year' (Gen. 17:15-21). All of this happens in chapter 17, and in chapter 18 the divine promise is repeated yet again. This time it is three angels who convey the message to Abraham, and it is Sarah who, overhearing the conversation, takes it as a joke, and laughs (Gen. 18:1-15).

The story that concerns us is then interrupted by the account of the destruction of Sodom and Gomorrah, and one or two other episodes, and resumes only in chapter 21. Isaac is duly born and circumcised, and the fear of Sarah, aged ninety, that people will laugh at her, provides yet another variation of the pun concerning the name *Yitzchak*. Next, Isaac is weaned, presumably at the age of two, and a feast is held to celebrate the occasion (21:1-8). Then, in verse 9, we catch a momentary glimpse of the two boys, thirteen years apart in age, playing together. Actually, the text says that Ishmael is laughing – *m'tzachek*, that same verb again! But why? In view of the sequel, namely that the laughter angers Sarah, some translations assume that it is a *contemptuous* laughter. Thus the Authorised and Revised Versions both render the word 'mocking' and the older JPS Bible has 'making sport'. But *m'tzachek* could just as well mean *innocent* laughter, or even 'playing'; and playing together is just what the two boys were doing according to the Revised Standard Version and the new JPS Bible. It is a pleasanter and more natural interpretation, which brings to mind how white and black children play together spontaneously, as long as their minds have not been poisoned with prejudice by their parents.

Why then does Sarah react as she does? Because of the very prejudice I have just mentioned! So deep is her hatred of Hagar and Ishmael that she cannot even bring herself to pronounce their names! Instead, she says to Abraham: 'Cast out this slave woman with her son; for the son of this slave woman shall not be heir with my son Isaac' (Gen. 21:10).

Once again Abraham, though he gives in to Sarah, shows a generous impulse. 'The thing was very grievous in Abraham's sight on account of his son' (Gen. 21:11). Once again God reassures him that, though Isaac will be his heir, Ishmael will have an honourable future (Gen. 21:12f). Then Abraham gets up early – just as he will get up early in the next chapter for an even more macabre purpose – and provides mother and son with food and drink to sustain them on their way. There follows a scene in which Hagar deposits Ishmael under a shrub, presumably with the intention of abandoning him. (The editor has seemingly forgotten that by this time he is fifteen years old!) Then somebody weeps. According to the Hebrew text it is Hagar, but according to the Septuagint it is Ishmael, which accords better with the information that immediately follows, that 'God heard the voice of the lad' (Gen. 21:17). It also explains once more the name *Yishmael* and demonstrates yet again God's compassion for the boy as well as his mother, for 'God opened her eyes, and she saw a well of water' (Gen. 21:19). The story ends with yet another assurance that Ishmael survived, and married, and lived more or less happily ever after.

What can we learn from the story? Many things, but let me single out two. First, who comes out of it well? The answer is: nobody, really. Certainly not Sarah, consumed with jealousy, who doesn't care what happens to Hagar or Ishmael; and certainly not Hagar, who gloats at her mistress's expense and is prepared to abandon her own son. Ishmael is perhaps all right, except for the prediction about his future, that he will be at daggers drawn with everybody. With Isaac, still a baby, it is too early to tell. And even Abraham, though well intentioned, is somewhat weak What emerges therefore is a *true* picture! That is what human beings are like! We are not black or white but various shades of grey. We are none of us paragons of virtue. We are all flawed. Therefore we had better practise a little tolerance towards one another.

That is one lesson. The other lesson is that Ishmael and Isaac are not just individuals: already in the biblical narrative they are identified as the progenitors of great nations. They personify Jews and Arabs, and therefore the very juxtaposition of their names makes one think of all the mistrust, and worse, which has marred their mutual relations from time to time, and not least in the last fifty years. Here, too, because we are emotionally involved, we tend to see a black and white picture. 'We – that is to say, the Jewish people, the State of Israel and all who support it – are all right. They – that is to say, the Arabs, the Palestinians and all who support them – are all wrong'. And between them and us there is an unbridgeable chasm. There are, moreover, on both sides of the chasm those who want to keep it that way, who demand from the other side nothing less than total surrender, and since that is unlikely to be forthcoming, are willing to contemplate a never-ending conflict.

When, therefore, a little dialogue takes place across the chasm, all right-minded people should rejoice. And of course it *has* happened, at all levels, from the highest to the lowest, officially and unofficially, from time to time. Let us hope that it will happen increasingly, and help to create an atmosphere conducive to compromise and peace. In the words of Shin Shalom, one of Israel's leading poets (quoted in the Reform Synagogues of Great Britain's *Forms of Prayer for Jewish Worship*, Vol. III, p. 891):

Ishmael, my brother
How long shall we fight each other?

My brother from times bygone,
My brother – Hagar's son,
My brother, the wandering one.

One angel was sent to us both
One angel watched over our growth –
There in the wilderness, death threatening through thirst,
I a sacrifice on the altar, Sarah's first.

Ishmael, my brother, hear my plea:
It was the angel who tied thee to me ...

Time is running out, put hatred to sleep.
Shoulder to shoulder, let's water our sheep.

The Birthright of a Jew
Tol'dot, 7 December 1956

In ancient times the birthright was inherited by the eldest son and entailed certain well-defined legal privileges. But the story of how Jacob obtained the birthright from Esau (Gen. 25:27-34) should also be understood symbolically. It is not only the inheritance of property that is at stake, but the privilege of being the progenitor of the Jewish people, of being the unique link between the Patriarchs and the Israelites of later times – a privilege which Jacob craved and Esau despised.

The birthright of a Jew is the privilege of continuing the Jewish 'Chain of Tradition', and every Jew should regard himself or herself as if he or she were, like Jacob, the sole link in that chain. Every Jew, therefore, needs to ask himself or herself: how much does my birthright mean to me? How highly shall I value it? Shall I cherish it or shall I sell it for a mess of pottage? Shall I make sacrifices for it or shall I throw it away in favour of material benefits?

The question devolves with special force on Jewish parents. They are today in a happier position than Isaac. They are not obliged to restrict the birthright only to the eldest son. They have more than one blessing to bestow. They can bless all their children, sons and daughters; they can feed them all with the heritage of Jacob (Isa. 58:14). But how do they acquit themselves? How much care, thought and effort do they expend on their children's religious education?

Most Jewish parents, it seems, prefer their children to become successful hunters for material prosperity and professional advancement. Most Jewish children, therefore, leave their childhood well equipped to earn a living but ill equipped to live, well qualified to be a social success but ill qualified to be a Jewish success. Their Jewishness is skin-deep, and hopelessly inadequate for the responsibilities which their birthright places on them. The situation is reversed. Isaac believed that he could confer the birthright only on one child; modern Jewish parents all too often withhold it from all of their children. Today's Jewish children, if only they knew what they were being deprived of, would say to their parents: 'Bless me, even me also' (Gen. 27:34). For there is no greater blessing we can bestow on our children than this: to make them fit to inherit and exercise their birthright: to serve God and humanity in the name, and under the inspiration, of their ancestral faith.

❖ ❖ ❖

Israel and Edom
Shabbat Tol'dot, 2 December 1978

One of the pleasures of Bible study is to find unsuspected significance in seemingly insignificant details of the text. Take, for instance, the phrase, ויתרוצצו הבנים בקרבה, 'The children struggled within her' (Gen. 25:22). What is the purpose of it? Not merely to inform us that Rebekah had a difficult pregnancy, but to prepare us mentally for what is to come, much as a musical composition will often announce in its opening bars the major theme that is to be developed subsequently. And the major theme, in this instance, is the conflict between the two brothers. Their pre-natal struggle foreshadows their post-natal struggle.

Moreover, it is not merely a struggle between two individuals. Rather, they typify the two ethnic groups which are to spring from them. That theme, too, is announced at the beginning, when Rebekah learns from a divine oracle: 'Two nations are in your womb, two distinct peoples shall come out of your body' (v. 23).

Who are these two peoples? That question, too, is answered for us, at least by implication, from the beginning. For by telling us that the elder of the twins was hairy, the narrative makes a double pun. It explains the name Esau – in Hebrew *esav* – by its assonance with the Hebrew word *se-ar* for 'hair', and it alludes to the further assonance between *se-ar* and Seir, Seir being the name of a mountainous region to the south of the Dead Sea which in biblical times was the home of the Edomites. And in case the subtlety of this clue should have escaped us, it offers us a second clue by informing us that Esau came out reddish, for which the Hebrew is *admoni*, another allusion to Edom. And just to clinch the point, it goes on to tell us that Esau sold his birthright for a plateful of soup which is described as *ha-adom ha-adom ha-zeh*, 'that red, red stuff' (v. 30). Indeed, this time it tells us explicitly that for this reason Esau was also called Edom.

As for the other twin, we are told that at the moment of his birth his hand was clutching his brother's heel, and that he was therefore called Jacob, a play on the Hebrew words *akev* for 'heel' and *ya-akov* for 'Jacob'. Once again, the detail has an anticipatory purpose, for the implication is that already at the embryonic stage Jacob had tried to overtake Esau so as to gain the privilege of the first-born. But that is incidental. The main point is that twin number two was Jacob who, as every Bible reader knows, was later re-named Israel and so became the progenitor of the Jewish people.

So the identity of the two peoples is clearly established: Edom and Israel. But why the struggle between them? To some extent this theme was imposed on the story-teller. For there was an ancient tradition that of the twin brothers, Jacob was the younger but nevertheless the more privileged. How could this have come about? To that question we know an answer which the biblical writer did not know. It has to do with a people called Hurrians who, in the days of the Patriarchs, lived in that part of Mesopotamia from which Abraham came. Indeed, their name may have been derived from the city of Haran which features so prominently in the Patriarchal narratives. What we know from recently discovered inscriptions is that, according to Hurrian law, a father was permitted, if he so chose, to confer the right of inheritance on a younger son in preference to an older one. In all probability, therefore, Isaac merely exercised that prerogative. But, as I said, the biblical story-teller didn't know that. On the contrary, he knew that according to Israelite law a father may *not* bequeath his property to a younger son (Deut. 21:16). Hence his tortuous explanation of how it happened: how Esau sold his birthright to Jacob, and how Jacob later cheated Esau out of their father's death-bed blessing.

But the need to account for Jacob's pre-eminence is only a subsidiary motif. A more important one is the enmity which actually existed in the writer's time between the two peoples. This derived partly from historical memories of past encounters, for instance how the Edomites had refused to allow the Israelites to pass through their territory, after the Exodus from Egypt on their way to Canaan (Num. 20). But it was also due to the fact that the Edomites were pagans and idolaters; and because of their close relationship to the Israelites, this fact, that they did not worship the same God, rankled all the more. Consequently there is in the Bible a curious ambivalence towards the Edomites. On the one hand we read in Deuteronomy: 'You shall not abhor an Edomite, for he is your brother' (23:7). On the other hand the Edomites are often portrayed as Israel's worst enemy. The prophet Ezekiel, for instance, devotes a whole chapter (number 35) to a condemnation of them. And Malachi states the paradox bluntly: 'Is not Esau Jacob's brother? says the Eternal One. Yet I have loved Jacob but I have hated Esau' (Mal. 1:2f.)

Not surprisingly, therefore, Esau is portrayed unsympathetically. Not indeed as an outright villain, any more than Jacob is portrayed as a saint. There is good and bad in both of them. Nevertheless, the comparison which the reader is supposed to draw is always in Jacob's favour. 'When the boys grew up,' we read, 'Esau became a skilful hunter, a man of the fields; but Jacob was a quiet man, who preferred to stay at home' (Gen. 25: 27). Implied in this factual statement is a moral judgment. It is a case of brawn versus brain, might versus right, cruelty versus gentleness. Esau is the pagan type. As such, he is not necessarily bad, but one never knows what he is going to do, for he has no moral scruples. He is hard, self-seeking, this-worldly, materialistic, and if he has to kill to achieve his ends, he does not let any soft sentimentality stand in his way. Jacob, on the other hand, is the Hebrew type. He may not always behave as he should; he can be devious and deceitful; but he would never *really* hurt a fellow human being, for he has a conscience, and he is fundamentally decent and compassionate.

So when Esau sells his birthright for a bowl of soup, the implication is that he cares more for the body than for the soul, and the narrator clinches the point by saying: 'So Esau despised his birthright' (Gen. 25: 34). It is true that Jacob took advantage of Esau's weakness in persuading him to sell it, and to that extent acted ignobly; but the clear implication is that this is incidental. It only explains *how* it happened, not *why* it happened. The real reason is that Esau did not care, that he had no desire to bear the responsibility of continuing the Abrahamic tradition, and that he would therefore have proved himself unworthy of his birthright anyhow.

Once again, though, we must see in all this not only a judgment of Jacob versus Esau, but of Israel versus Edom, and more generally, of Hebraism versus Paganism. And if in the Bible that is merely implicit, it becomes explicit in the interpretation of the Rabbis. By that time the Edomites had ceased to exist as a distinct people, for one of the Hasmonean rulers, John Hyrcanus, had conquered them and converted them to Judaism. The Number One enemy of the Jewish people was now Rome, and it is with Rome that Edom is commonly identified in Rabbinic literature. How this came about is not quite clear. The similarity of the two names may have been a contributory factor. Another may have been the fact that Herod the Great was of Edomite stock, for though he was already a second-generation Jew, he ruled Judea largely in the Roman interest and so came to symbolise Rome in Jewish eyes, and of course Rome represented for the Jews all that they most hated: polytheism, idolatry, arrogance, immorality and cruelty.

At any rate, the identification enabled the Rabbis to express their contempt for Rome by so interpreting the biblical references to Esau and Edom. For instance, on the verse with which I began, that 'the children struggled within her', they commented that whenever Rebekah passed a synagogue or a school, Jacob struggled to get out of her womb, so eager was he, even as an embryo, to worship God and to study Torah; but whenever she passed a Pagan temple, Esau struggled to get out in order to practise idolatry (Gen.R. 63:6). Likewise, on the verse that 'when the boys grew up, Esau became a skilful hunter, a man of the fields, but Jacob was a quiet man, who preferred to stay at home', they commented: 'The case may be compared to a myrtle and a wild rose bush which grew side by side; when they were full-grown and blossomed, one put forth its fragrance and the other its thorns. Likewise, for thirteen years the boys went to school together. But after thirteen years, one went to the houses of Torah study and the other to the houses of idol-worship' (Gen.R. 63:10).

Another case in point is the well-known Midrash of how God offered the Torah to all nations, but all except Israel refused it. The Edomites, for instance, on learning that the Torah included the commandment, 'You shall not murder', declined it on the ground that precisely this was their stock-in-trade, since their ancestor Esau had been told, 'By your sword shall you live' (Gen. 27:40; Mechilta to Exod. 20:2).

But now a postscript. In the fourth century, Christianity became the official religion of the Roman Empire, and Rome became the capital of Christendom. From that time onwards, therefore, Jews tended to make a three-stage identification, to say in so many words: for Esau read Edom, for Edom read Rome, and for Rome read Christendom. And not without reason. For *superficially* Christianity had some of the appearances of another pagan religion: with its deification of Jesus, with its doctrine of the Trinity, with its Eucharist, and with the use of images in its worship. Above all, it soon succeeded Rome as Israel's chief enemy, for it persecuted the Jewish people with a ferocity that increased from age to age.

Understandably, therefore, Jewish attitudes to Christianity were often bitter. And even today it is not easy for Jews to view Christianity objectively, respectfully and sympathetically. For Christian anti-Semitism still persists. Two books, both published in 1978, sadly remind us of that fact. One is a paperback by Charlotte Klein, a member of the Roman Catholic Sisters of Sion, entitled *Anti-Judaism in Christian Theology*, which shows that the text-books studied by Christian theological students in Germany, and to a lesser extent in France, are full of all the old prejudices against the Pharisees, and against Judaism generally, as if the authors had learnt nothing at all either from modern scholarship or from modern history. The other book is *Anti-Semitism in the New Testament* by Professor Samuel Sandmel. As its title implies, it does not deal with modern times. But it reminds us how difficult it is to eradicate Christian anti-Semitism because it is rooted in the Christian Scriptures themselves, so that only those who have the courage to take a radically critical view of the New Testament are likely to be unaffected by it; and they, unfortunately, are still few and far between.

Nevertheless, both the books I have mentioned end on a hopeful note. For at least in the English-speaking world there has been a change of attitude to Judaism which is little less than a revolution. Much of that, as Professor Sandmel points out, is due to the pioneering work of one American scholar, George Foot Moore. And on the Jewish side there has been a corresponding re-appraisal of Christianity, in which Claude Montefiore played a leading part. Therefore Professor Sandmel ends his book by saying: 'This generation of Jews and Christians, receptive to each other, has an opportunity for reconciliation that is without precedent'.

Let us hope that he is right, and that the opportunity will be taken. But it must be taken by *both* sides. We too must play our part. And we must read the literature of Judaism, as of Christianity, with understanding, realising that it reflects the animosities of bygone ages which need not be perpetuated. It is of historical interest to know what Jews thought of Esau, of Edom, of Rome and of Christendom. But it is of present importance that we should stress the injunction of Deuteronomy: 'You shall not abhor an Edomite, for he is your brother'.

❖   ❖   ❖

Jacob's Ladder
Shabbat Va-yetze, 5 December 1981

Just as a ladder has many rungs, so the story of Jacob's dream at Bethel can be interpreted on many levels. To begin with the most down-to-earth (so to speak!), the conventional image of the ladder is almost certainly wrong. Why? Because the Hebrew word translated 'ladder' comes from a verb which means 'to heap up' and therefore suggests a ramp, or a solid stairway, rather than a ladder.

What makes it all the more likely is that just such a ramp-like stairway was a characteristic feature of the ancient Mesopotamian temples. It led all the way from ground level to the top of the temple tower, or ziggurat, where there was a platform which was regarded as the most sacred part of the building, the place where humans could communicate with God. Now Jacob's family came from Mesopotamia; so he would certainly have heard about these ziggurats, which were indeed among the wonders of the ancient world. Moreover, he was on his way to Mesopotamia, where he hoped to find shelter among his relatives from the vengeance of his brother Esau; so it is entirely natural that, as he lay down to sleep, he should have conjured up in his mind in anticipation the sights he was likely to see when he reached his destination.

If now we step up to level number two, we must remind ourselves that Jacob's state of mind was not only one of eager anticipation; it was also one of fear and apprehension. After all, he was leaving his home for the first time in his life, and had no means of knowing for how long. In the event, as *we* know, it would be twenty years. And not only was he leaving his home, but his country, the land he had been taught to regard as holy, as having a special relationship with the God of his people. How could he be sure that, in leaving his land, he was not leaving the domain of his God, like an astronaut travelling beyond the gravitational pull of the earth, and therefore venturing into unknown territory full of unforeseeable hazards? The thought must have worried him greatly, and the dream, understood on this level, provided the assurance he needed.

How? In various ways. Partly because, whatever the exact interpretation of the dream, it was clearly a religious experience, and therefore God's way of allaying his anxiety. It was all the more reassuring because it was so unexpected. And here we must dwell a little on the phrase, ויפגע במקום, 'He came upon a certain place'. The Rabbis read all sorts of cryptic meanings into that word מקום. They saw in it an allusion to Mount Sinai, or to the Temple, or even to God. But in the biblical narrative itself no such implications are present. On the contrary, we are probably meant to understand that it was a very ordinary, nondescript place. There was nothing there: no shrine, no building, no human habitation, just a few stones lying around; a God-forsaken place, as it might well have seemed to Jacob. Therefore, if God nevertheless appeared to him there, of all places, then God must indeed be accompanying him on his journey.

An ancient Midrash makes the same point, more specifically, in relation to the angels who are said to be עולים ויורדים בו, 'going up and down', on the stairway. On the face of it, the order seems odd. Angels, since their habitat is heaven, should come down before they go up! However, says this charming Midrash, the reference is to two different companies of angels: those who have been accompanying Jacob until now, in the land of Israel, and who are now returning to heaven because their task is done; and those who are coming down to take over from them because their assignment is to accompany Jacob outside the land of Israel (Gen.R. 68:12). It is a kind of changing of the guard!

If God is sending angels to escort Jacob to Mesopotamia, then indeed he may feel reassured. But how can this be? Only if God's sovereignty extends beyond the borders of Israel. And therefore Jacob's dream, in addition to reassuring him about his personal safety, contains for him a lesson about the nature of God: that God is indeed, as the Prophet Malachi was to say, 'great beyond the borders of Israel' (1:5): a universal as well as an omnipresent God; and to say that brings us to a paradox which lies at the very heart of Judaism.

The paradox is this. The grander your conception of God, the greater is the danger that God will seem remote. Judaism took that risk. It refused to have any truck with Paganism, which brings its gods down to earth by identifying them with particular things or places or animals or persons. Judaism pushed its conception of God to the limits of human thought and beyond; a grander, more transcendent God than the God of Judaism is not humanly conceivable. Yet Judaism has always taught that God is also immanent and therefore accessible to human beings. That is the paradox. But if we think about it, it is not as paradoxical as it seems. On the contrary, it is because God is transcendent that God is also immanent. For instance, because God transcends time, therefore God also permeates it, and can be encountered in any moment of it. And because God transcends space, therefore God also pervades it, and can be encountered in any location. Only a universal God can be omnipresent; and a God who is omnipresent must be universal. That truth, too, dawned on Jacob, we may surmise, that night at Bethel.

Mind you, the fact that God is omnipresent doesn't mean that there are not some places where, because of their associations, the sense of God's presence may come to us more readily than elsewhere. We have all had that experience, have we not, when we have entered some synagogue or church: the feeling that because here so many generations of good people have prayed so devoutly, therefore God's presence lingers in it almost tangibly. Well, this idea, too, can perhaps be found in our story. For when Jacob wakes up and says, 'Surely God is in this place, and I did not know it', there is possibly an implication, not only that God can be encountered anywhere, but that this particular place has a particular association with the worship of God of which Jacob was previously unaware. Indeed, the Bible tells us in an earlier chapter that Bethel was the very place where, long ago, Jacob's grandfather Abraham had already built an altar (Gen. 12:8, 13:4). We must imagine, therefore, that subsequently, with the passage of time, the altar had crumbled and disappeared in the sands of the desert, so that there was nothing left of it when Jacob stumbled upon it; yet his unconscious mind sensed something of God's lingering presence and helped to induce his dream.

But now let us move on to just one more level of interpretation. When Jacob lay down to sleep at Bethel, he was concerned not only about his future safety, or whether his God was capable of affording him protection beyond the borders of his home country. There was something else on his mind. Jacob was ambitious, and the ladder – or stairway – was in one sense a symbol of his ambition. We, too, speak of climbing the ladder of success. But Jacob's idea of success was not a materialistic one. It was his brother Esau whose aim in life was virtually limited to food and drink. Jacob's ambition was above all to become his father's heir in the spiritual sense and so to become the vital link between past and future, between the Patriarchs and the Jewish people yet to be. He aspired, if you like, to the role of leadership. That is why, long ago, he had bought from his elder twin brother the birthright, and why he had just obtained from his father Isaac the paternal blessing reserved for the first-born. Both these things he had done by means which throw an unpleasant light on his character. In mitigation, several things could be said; for instance, that Jacob was merely acting out what he believed to be a divine plan, and that it would indeed have been disastrous for that plan if Esau had been cast in the role of transmitter of the tradition. But the chief point to be made is that Jacob was as yet immature. He was not yet Israel. That was to happen twenty years later. He still had a long way to go, a lot of growing to do. And his dream at Bethel was a growing experience.

Until now he had no doubt thought of the role of leader of his people as a privilege, an honour, a status symbol. And we can easily imagine how worried he must have been, as he fled from Esau, whether that ambition, after all his scheming, might not come to nothing. There were so many uncertainties. He might be killed on the way to Haran; he might not find a wife; she might not bear any children; it might never become safe for him to return to the land in which his ambition was to be realised. The dream reassured him on that score, for in it God says to him: 'The land on which you are lying I will give to you and to your descendants ...' But it also changed his ideas.

For if the God of the Patriarchs was indeed the universal God, who holds sway in the most distant lands, then what can it mean to be the founder of a people with a special relationship to such a God? It can only be to render some service to all humanity. That is why, in his dream, he hears God saying to him: 'Through you and through your descendants all the families of the earth shall be blessed'. What he realises at this point is that the birthright he has always craved is, after all, not so much a privilege as a responsibility.

❖ ❖ ❖

Esau's Kiss
Shabbat Va-yishlach, 22 November 1980

'And Esau ran to meet him, and embraced him, and fell on his neck, and kissed him; and they wept' (Gen. 33:4). In this verse there is something peculiar: over the word וישקהו, 'and kissed him', there is a series of dots.

What is the significance of these dots? The specialists in the study of the Masorah, the transmission of the text of the Hebrew Bible, tell us that they are called *puncta extraordinaria*; and extraordinary they certainly are, for they are found only in fifteen places in the entire Bible (Otto Eissfeldt, *The Old Testament, An Introduction*, p. 686). But what exactly do they mean? That, unfortunately, is not at all certain; but in all probability these dots are a device employed by the ancient scribes to call attention to the fact that they suspected that the word in question was wrong: either that it shouldn't be there at all, because it was missing in the best manuscripts, or that it was incorrectly spelt. In our case, for instance, the scribes may have thought that the word should be in the plural, saying that 'they kissed each other', since the verse goes on to say, in the plural, 'and they wept' (Arnold Ehrlich, *Mikra Kifshuto*, Vol. I, pp. 93f)).

However that may be, these dots were interpreted in *another* sense, as casting doubt, not on the accuracy of the text, but on the exact meaning to be ascribed to it; and in our case, whether Esau's kiss was, or was not, sincere. This question is raised in the Sifre to the Book of Numbers, which is one of the oldest Midrashim we possess, dating perhaps from the third century. The passage reads: 'The word וישקהו has dots over it because Esau did not kiss Jacob בכל־לבו,

whole-heartedly. However, Rabbi Simeon ben Yochai commented that, although it is well known that Esau hated Jacob, nevertheless on this occasion his latent love for his brother was roused within him, and he did kiss Jacob בכל-לבו, whole-heartedly' (to Num. 9:10).

So there you have a difference of opinion which runs through all the subsequent interpretive literature: that Esau's kiss was, and that it was not, sincere. Which view shall *we* take? Let us consider the evidence.

Did Esau have cause to hate his brother? Indeed, he did! For Jacob had cheated him, first out of his birthright, and then out of the paternal blessing due to him as the first-born. And that was no small matter. It meant that the younger brother was to have authority over the elder. As Isaac had said in blessing Jacob, 'Be lord over your brothers, and may your mother's sons bow down to you' (Gen. 27:29); and though the Bible doesn't actually say so, we have no reason to doubt that Jacob relished, and perhaps gloated over, the superior status that had been conferred on him. Not surprisingly, therefore, Esau was furious, and resolved to kill his brother at the first opportunity. It was for this reason that Rebekah, who knew of Esau's plan, advised Jacob to flee to far-off Mesopotamia. There he would be safe from his brother's vengeance; and there, incidentally, he would also be able to find a wife for himself among his kinsfolk.

All that, admittedly, was twenty years before the episode that concerns us, for that is how long it took Jacob to obtain from his uncle Laban the privilege of marrying his two daughters and of acquiring enough wealth for the homeward journey. But throughout all these long years, Jacob has not forgotten what transpired before he left. His fear of Esau has continued to haunt him, and his feeling of guilt towards his brother has never ceased to prey on him. And now, as he approaches the old, familiar landscapes, these memories come back with ever increasing vividness, and his anxiety is further intensified when he receives news that Esau is actually on his way towards him, and not alone, but with an army of four hundred men. The moment of truth is fast approaching. All Jacob can do now is to pray for deliverance, and to take various precautions in case his prayer should go unanswered.

It is at this stage that Jacob has his dream, in which he wrestles with a mysterious being. Evidently the dream is an enactment of his fears; and when the dawn awakens him, there, on the horizon, is Esau with his four hundred men. Yes, Jacob has every reason to fear the worst; and when Esau comes running towards him, and hugs him and kisses him, it can only be a trick, a way of catching him off guard, a sinister prelude to the fatal stab.

That is one way of interpreting our verse, and it was reinforced in the minds of the Rabbis by the tradition that Esau was the ancestor of the Edomites, Israel's enemies in ancient times, and furthermore a symbol of Rome, the cruel, oppressive regime of their own time. Obviously, therefore, Esau is the villain of the piece and must have been ill-intentioned. One Midrash goes so far as to say that Esau's real intention was not to kiss Jacob but to bite him – this on the basis of the similarity in Hebrew between the word *nashak*, to kiss, and *nashach*, to bite; only, by a miracle, Jacob's neck became hard as marble, so that he was unable to do so! (Gen. R. 78:9).

But not all interpreters have taken this line. Some have recognised that the Bible is more objective than the Midrash; that it does *not* paint its characters in black and white; that Jacob, as portrayed in the Bible, is by no means all good; that he *had* behaved reprehensibly towards his brother; that he *had* employed trickery to gain personal advantage; and that, conversely, Esau is by no means depicted as all bad; he has his weaknesses, of course; his craving for food and material things, for instance; but within the limitations of his earthy way of life, he conducts himself with honour and dignity; therefore he may well be capable of magnanimity, and the kiss of brotherhood may be genuine.

There are other reasons for thinking so. One is the passage of time; for even if twenty years is not long enough for Jacob to get rid of his sense of guilt, it may be long enough for Esau to lose his thirst for revenge. After all, even the Pope's mule, in Daudet's story, saved up his kick of vengeance only for seven years! Another reason is that the description of the reconciliation sounds so authentic; it uses the language of spontaneity, not of intrigue. That is why Abraham ibn Ezra, the medieval commentator, rejects so contemptuously the Midrash, which Rashi still repeats, about Esau having intended to *bite* Jacob. 'It is all right', he says, 'for little children, but the plain sense of Scripture is that Esau did not mean to do any harm to his brother, and the proof of it is that it goes on to say that they both wept' (Rashi to Gen. 33:4).

But there is another and profounder reason. It is that Jacob has in fact changed. He is no longer the cunning trickster and the schemer for personal power he used to be. For the dream on the bank of the Jabbok has been a turning-point in his life. He has finally come to terms with himself; he has confronted, and struggled with, the evil within him, for that, according to one interpretation, is what his adversary symbolises; he has paid the penalty for his past misconduct, for that is presumably the meaning of the injury he sustains to his thigh; he has therefore expiated his guilt, and he is consequently able to face the future with a new maturity. His character has undergone a transformation; hence the change of name from Jacob to Israel.

Of the medieval Jewish commentators, the one who perceived this most clearly was Obadiah Sforno, who lived in Italy in the fifteenth to sixteenth centuries. 'All of a sudden', he writes, 'Esau's heart was changed as he beheld Jacob's self-abasement' *(ad loc.)*. But the point is even better made by a contemporary Jewish commentator, Rabbi Gunther Plaut of Toronto. This is what he says: 'In the brothers' fateful meeting all is suddenly changed – and hardly because of the gifts that Jacob brings, for Esau is a wealthy man in his own right. The reconciliation occurs because it is Israel, not Jacob, whom Esau meets, and Jacob is a new man who asks forgiveness, if not in words then in manner, who limps toward him with repentant air and not deceitful arrogance. He is not a man to be put to the sword, he is a man who can be loved as a brother. The essentially simple and uncomplicated Esau, who himself has matured, senses this at once and runs to kiss his newly found brother. The two are now at peace, and Jacob-Israel, who has no further need to flee from Esau's wrath, settles down and builds a house' (*The Torah, A Modern Commentary, Genesis,* p. 325).

Does this account ring true to you? It does to me; and therefore I am inclined to think that the kiss is sincere, and that the *puncta extraordinaria* are, to that extent, unnecessary. But now two brief postscripts. The first is that just as one strand in Jewish tradition has been reluctant to concede that Esau could possibly be sincere, so there are those today who find it hard to believe that Israel's erstwhile enemies, such as Egypt, could possibly mean what they say when they talk about peace, that in reality they only want to buy time before launching another war. They are the people of whom Abba Eban has said 'they won't take yes for an answer'. And I don't mean to imply that they are necessarily completely wrong. Of course it is prudent to be cautious. But even while maintaining caution, we must surely believe in the *possibility* of reconciliation and peace; and not only with the Egyptians but, sooner or later, with the Palestinians as well. That time, perhaps, is not yet; but if it is ever to come, then we must work towards it; and that means that there will have to be some changes, not just on the other side – that is obvious – but on the Israeli side as well. They will have to give up the simplistic view that all is black and white, that there are only heroes and villains, that right belongs entirely to one party in the conflict, and wrong to the other; they will have to become a little more humble, more self-critical, and therefore more mature; they will have to advance from being Jacob to being Israel.

And here is another afterthought. Inasmuch as Esau symbolises Edom, and Edom Rome, therefore the reconciliation scene of our Torah portion may be regarded as pointing to the ultimate reconciliation between the Jewish people and the Gentile world generally. That time *certainly* has not come, and in the twentieth century it seems as remote as ever. Perhaps, therefore, the dots over וישקהו need to be retained. They represent a question-mark; for there can be no certainty that the time will ever come. There can be no certainty because it does not depend on God alone; it depends also on human beings, on their co-operation with God which they are free to extend or withhold. But the *hope* that it will happen, surely we must maintain and cherish *that*. Surely that is what it means to be a Jew: to live and work in the hope for the ultimate reconciliation, which is the messianic age. Then the dots over וישקהו, the question-mark over the kiss of brotherhood, will be finally removed, for all will know that it is sincere.

❖   ❖   ❖

Life and the Use we make of it
Va-yiggash, 18 December 1953

Pharaoh, intrigued by Jacob, the venerable shepherd from the desert, asks him how old he is, and receives a curious answer: 'The days of the years of my sojourning are a hundred and thirty years; few and evil have been the years of my life' (Gen. 47:9). This answer so puzzles Pharaoh that he does not proceed with the interrogation. It has puzzled Bible commentators, too.

Perhaps the most helpful suggestion comes from Obadiah Sforno (c.1470 – c.1550, Italy). Jacob, he says, is drawing a distinction between *m'gurim* – sojourn on earth, mere existence, and *chayyim* – true living. His chronological age is 130. That may not be old by the standards of his father and grandfather, but it is a good span, and yet Jacob feels that his life has been short – not in terms of duration but of something else.

What is that 'something else'? Perhaps it is happiness. Perhaps Jacob means that he has suffered much. That is the view Sforno takes. Jacob's flight from his brother Esau, his twenty years' exile in Mesopotamia, his ill-treatment at the hands of his uncle Laban, his grief for his disappeared son Joseph, and the famine which has brought him to Egypt: all these might well have prompted such a reflection.

Yet Jacob also has much to be thankful for. He has, after all, the birthright and the paternal blessing. He is the head of a large family. He has acquired great wealth. He has been granted famine relief and permission to settle in Goshen.

Surely the truth is that Pharaoh's question has given Jacob a jolt and set him thinking, not about the duration of his life, nor about its content of happiness, but about the use he has made of it; and the reflection leaves him profoundly dissatisfied. No doubt he thinks of all the wrongs he has done and the opportunities he has missed. That is why he says: 'Few and evil have been the years of my life.' For only a good life deserves to be called *chayyim*, true living.

❖   ❖   ❖

The Ten Plagues
Shabbat Bo, 10 January 1981

What is it that troubles us about the story of the Ten Plagues? I suspect, three things. First, a nagging doubt as to whether they ever happened. Of course, if we were fundamentalists, that question would not arise. But since we are not, we have to reckon with the possibility that what we are dealing with in this section of the book of Exodus is legend rather than history, fiction rather than fact, or at any rate a mixture of the two.

There is, for instance, a theory that the historical kernel out of which the whole story grew was nothing more than the sudden death of a Crown Prince of Egypt, which the popular imagination then exaggerated, first, into the death of *all* the firstborn of Egypt, and then into the culmination of a whole series of plagues, each of which, it is alleged, was invented in allusion to one or another of the Egyptian deities: the Nile god Hapi, the frog-headed goddess Hekt, the sun god Re, and so forth.

A more moderate view suggests that the story derives from a series of natural disasters which did indeed take place, but over a long period of time, and which the story-teller then compressed into a few days. The propounders of this view point out some striking similarities between the Ten Plagues, as recounted in the Bible, and seasonal events of a kind which were and are a common occurrence in that part of the world. For instance, swarms of locusts are frequent there; the Nile tends to turn reddish-brown before it overflows its banks; and the *chamsin* raises sandstorms which destroy all visibility for hours on end.

A subtler suggestion was made by the late Professor Samuel Sandmel in his novel about Moses, *Alone Atop the Mountain,* namely that there was indeed a succession of natural disasters, but that these were reinforced by *human* initiative in the form of a series of acts of sabotage, meticulously planned and daringly executed by Moses in co-operation with a hand-picked group of Israelite leaders and Egyptian dissidents.

The most extraordinary theory of all is that of Immanuel Velikovsky, the author of *Worlds in Collision* and *Ages in Chaos,* to the effect that the planet Venus was once a comet which passed so near the earth that it caused colossal earthquakes, volcanic eruptions and tidal waves, and that reminiscences of these cataclysmic events, closely parallelling the biblical Exodus story, are to be found in ancient Egyptian records.

So, on the question of *'what really happened'* we have a large variety of theories to choose from, and we must admit that we have no means of knowing with any certainty just how much of the biblical narrative is history and how much is folklore. But does that really matter? Surely not. For it is likely enough that the story has a factual core; and even if it has not, it might still teach us a religious lesson of great significance, as other, purely fictional stories of the Bible, such as Ruth and Jonah, certainly do.

But if we now move on from history to theology, we run into other and perhaps even greater difficulties. For if the Ten Plagues were merely a series of natural disasters which, quite fortuitously, occurred at an opportune time, then there is no problem, for *any* philosophy must allow for lucky chance; and if Samuel Sandmel was right, and sabotage played a part, there is no problem either, since *no* philosophy would deny the possibility of human initiative. But of course neither of these views accords with the standpoint of the biblical author. On the contrary, the whole point of the story of the Ten Plagues, as he tells it, is that they demonstrate the power of *God.* They are neither freak events of nature nor humanly engineered, but a manifestation – one of the *supreme* manifestations – of God's providential, supernatural intervention in human history. And it is precisely here that we find ourselves sceptical. We must frankly confess that the biblical view is not ours, least of all when it speaks of God hardening Pharaoh's heart; that we do not think of history as 'manipulated' by a supernatural Being in that way. But then, what becomes of God's guidance of the historical process, and without such guidance, what religious significance is there to be found in the story of the Ten Plagues?

I suppose we have to take a more sophisticated view than the traditional one, perhaps along the following lines. Nature behaves according to unchanging laws. These laws emanate from God, who does not interrupt their working every now and then to produce what the film industry calls 'special effects'. But even unchanging laws can, in unusual conglomerations of circumstances, produce *unusual* effects. Such effects are therefore coincidental rather than providential, natural rather than supernatural. After all, even Velikovsky doesn't suggest that when the comet approached the earth, the laws of physics were suspended. On the contrary, he *adduces* the laws of physics to show how such an event *would* have produced earthquakes, tidal waves and the like. But when such an unusual event does occur, it is open to human beings to exploit it. Obviously, Moses did so. He saw in the catastrophic effect of the Plagues on the political and economic life of Egypt an opportunity to accomplish something which would not otherwise have been possible: the freeing of his fellow Israelites from Egyptian slavery.

On this interpretation, was the Exodus a miracle? Not in the conventional sense. And yet in another sense it was. The miracle was the willingness of Moses and those who followed him to seize the opportunity, in spite of all the risks that it entailed. The miracle was the *will* to freedom, and not just political freedom in the negative sense which every hackneyed slogan of every contemporary liberation movement calls for, but freedom for a purpose beyond itself, freedom to live on a higher plane, freedom to serve God. שלח עמי ויעבדוני, 'Let My people go, that they may serve Me' (Exod. 10:13): that, and not some demagogic demand for national self-determination, was the motto of Moses, to which the people responded. And in the proclamation of that ideal, as well as the response to it, we may well see the influence of God.

God, we may surmise, does not intervene either in the habitual course of nature or in the exercise of human freedom. But God does exert a moral pressure on human minds to which they can respond and which, if they do respond to it, releases a power that produces achievements far beyond the ordinary. Such a view sees the channel of God's guidance of the historical process, not in the realm of nature, but in that of the human mind which responds to the Divine Will; but the consequences are not therefore less remarkable.

In addition to the historical and theological questions we have discussed, the story of the Ten Plagues raises an ethical problem which is perhaps what troubles us most of all. Why does the Bible tell the story at such length and in such detail? Does it not, in doing so, betray a certain gloating over the discomfiture of the Egyptians which is less than generous? And is not that unworthy sentiment reinforced by the role the story plays in the Passover Haggadah?

Something like this, one suspects, motivated Claude Montefiore when he omitted the story from his *Bible for Home Reading*. 'It is not necessary', he explained, 'for us to hear much of the punishment of the Egyptians. It is better and pleasanter to fix our attention upon the deliverance of the Hebrews ' (Vol. I, p. 67). But that is precisely where we have travelled a long, long way from Montefiore's way of thinking. 'Not necessary'? Not if we want to live in a fool's paradise! 'Better and pleasanter'? Yes, indeed, if we want to shut our eyes to reality! But we have lived through the Holocaust and the many other catastrophes of the twentieth century. We know that human history has its ugly, sordid, painful, tragic side, which is not going to go away because of our wishful thinking. It is a permanent condition of our humanity, at least this side of the messianic age; and we had better be, and remain, aware of it.

Of course, much depends on what we *do* with the awareness. If we see evil only in our enemies and righteousness only in ourselves; if we are roused to compassion only by the suffering of our own people and not the suffering of others, then we are indeed at a primitive, sub-religious level of ethical discernment. But that is not how the story of the Ten Plagues need be, or should be, understood. On the contrary, the traditional custom of spilling one drop of wine at the mention of each Plague, in the Passover Seder, was interpreted by no less an authority than Don Isaac Abravanel as a symbol of sorrow, not glee, that the Egyptians suffered, in the spirit of the Proverbs verse, which indeed Abravanel quotes: 'Do not rejoice when your enemy falls' (24:17).

It is this, the most mature strand in the traditional Jewish understanding of the story of the Ten Plagues which should be our guide both when we read it in the Torah portion of the week and when we rehearse it in the celebration of the Seder.

❖   ❖   ❖

The Spirit of Nachshon
Pesach, 20 April 1987

The account of the crossing of the Red Sea – or more accurately the Sea of Reeds – is full of difficulties. We don't know where the Sea was; many different locations have been suggested. It is not clear whether the Sea was divided into two halves, leaving a dry corridor in the middle, or whether all of it was driven back by a unidirectional east wind; whether what happened, happened at God's command, or by a magic trick performed by Moses with his rod, or through a freak occurrence of nature. An angel, previously unmentioned, appears from nowhere. A pillar of cloud, which has been mentioned before, re-appears but plays an obscure role. Nor is it clear whether the Egyptians drown because their chariots lose their wheels or get stuck in the mud, or because they are surprised by the returning waves, or because they are frightened of the Israelites and, in their panic, flee into the Sea instead of away from it.

It is therefore pretty obvious that what we have in this chapter is a conflation of several traditions. But then the exact details of what happened don't really matter. What matters is how the event, in its totality, was understood, how the Israelites perceived it, and how that perception shaped the subsequent course of Jewish history.

And there we could leave the matter except that the scriptural account, precisely because of its peculiarities, gave rise to some interesting interpretations which are worth pondering in their own right.

We begin with God saying to Moses, 'Why are you crying to me? Tell the Israelites to go forward!' (Exod. 14:15). What was Moses crying about? We don't know, for nothing to that effect has been mentioned in what precedes the verse. Here then is another loose end. But never mind. What is of interest is a famous comment on the verse by Rabbi Eliezer. According to him, Moses was praying, and therefore God's rebuke to him was: 'My children are in trouble, with the Sea barring their way ahead and the enemy pursuing them from the rear, yet you stand there reciting long prayers!' And Rabbi Eliezer draws out the moral: יש שעה לקצר ויש שעה להאריך, that there are times for praying briefly and times for praying at length (Mechilta, B'shallach, 4).

Perhaps we might put it this way. Prayer is important. It is a way of focusing our minds on the right values. But it is only a preparatory exercise, and the purpose of the exercise is that we should implement these values in our lives. There is therefore an important sense in which religion begins at the door of the synagogue, not when we enter it but when we leave it, to put into practice outside the synagogue what we have learnt inside it. Contemplation versus action. Both are important, but contemplation is the means and action is the end.

Five verses on we read that there was a pillar of cloud but also darkness, yet that in some strange way the darkness lit up the night, ולא קרב זה אל זה כל־הלילה, 'and one did not come near the other all night' (Exod. 14:20). Which is the 'one' and which is the 'other', and what prevented their mutual approach? All that is quite obscure. But never mind. It is far more important that the phrase reminded the Rabbis of another, in the sixth chapter of Isaiah, which is the basis of the doxology known as the *K'dushah*, where, in the prophet's vision, the angels sing God's praise; for there we read: וקרא זה אל זה ואמר, 'One called to the other and said, קדוש קדוש קדוש, Holy, holy, holy is the God of hosts; the whole earth is full of God's glory' (v. 3). Obviously, therefore, it was the angels who were prevented from coming near each other! Who prevented them? God. And why? Because at that time the ministering angels wanted to sing a song of praise to the Holy One, ever to be blessed; but God restrained them, saying: 'My creatures are drowning in the sea, and you would sing before Me?'

The passage, by the way, occurs twice in the Talmud, in Tractate Megillah (10b) and in Tractate Sanhedrin (39b). Both of them state the general principle that אין הקדוש ברוך הוא שמח במפלת רשעים, 'God does not rejoice in the downfall of the wicked', with the implication, of course, that we humans ought not to do so either. Action is necessary, and sometimes, as when tyranny must be overthrown and freedom established, it may involve the infliction of suffering; but we need not feel good about it!

Two verses on we read: ויבואו בני ישראל בתוך הים ביבשה, 'And the children of Israel went into the midst of the sea on dry ground' (Exod. 14:22). Again the text is a bit obscure. Did they get wet or didn't they? But that doesn't matter nearly as much as the frame of mind in which they embarked on what must surely have seemed to them a highly dangerous journey, and about that we have two contradictory speculations, attributed to two Rabbis of the second century, Meir and Judah.

According to Rabbi Meir the twelve tribes vied with each other for the privilege of being the first to cross over, but while the rest of the tribes were standing there, debating the problem of precedence, and wasting precious minutes, the tribe of Benjamin, realising that it was a time for decisive action, not for debating protocol, jumped up and went ahead into the Sea (Mechilta, B'shallach 6; Sot. 36b).

According to Rabbi Judah, the Israelites were, on the contrary, terrified and said, one after another: 'I don't want to be the first to go down into the sea!' And while they stood there, dithering, one individual took his courage in both hands and jumped into the waves. And who was that individual? Nachshon ben Amminadav, not of the tribe of Benjamin, but of the tribe of Judah. And why he? The Bible doesn't even mention him in its account of the Sea of Reeds, so how could the Rabbis assign the role to him?

The answer in brief is that it was a case of type-casting. For in the book of Numbers the same Nachshon appears, first, as the repre-

sentative of the tribe of Judah who helped Moses with the census
(1:7) and then again as the first of all the princes to present an offering for the dedication of the altar (7:12). He was, in short, the volunteering type.

Do we know anything more about Nachshon ben Amminadav?
Well, yes, a little more; but before we come to that let me tell you
about an attempt to reconcile the two speculations: Rabbi Meir's
and Rabbi Judah's. It comes from a great Polish rabbi, Israel Joshua
Trunk of Kutno, who lived in the nineteenth century (1820-1893).
According to him both speculations are correct but must be understood as referring to two different moments in time. At first, while the
Israelites were still standing at some little distance from the shore of
the Sea, they were all eager, as Rabbi Meir rightly said, to make the
crossing, and boasted of their eagerness. But when the time came to
put their eagerness to the test, then, as Rabbi Judah rightly said, they
all got cold feet – all, that is, except one. In the words of Rabbi
Joshua Trunk, 'When the time for action came, they all began to hesitate and to vacillate, and one by one they slipped away, until
Nachshon came forward and jumped into the sea' (IT, II, p. 120).

It is one thing, therefore, to have the right ideas; it is another to
resolve to put them into practice; and it is another still actually to do
so, especially when it takes courage because we are confronted by
waves, if not of water, then of apathy, or prejudice, or popular dis-
approbation. Having good ideas is important; having good intentions is even more important; but it is only the third stage, of
implementation, of action, that puts to the test what we are made of.
To be truly religious, we must be prepared, like Nachshon ben
Amminadav, to get our feet wet.

About this Nachshon we have just two more significant pieces of
information. One is a passing mention in the sixth chapter of Exodus that he had a sister called Elisheba who married Aaron (v. 23).
In other words, he was Moses' brother's brother-in-law and therefore would certainly have been present at the crossing of the Sea of
Reeds and might very well have felt a sense of *noblesse oblige* to set a
good example.

The other piece of information comes, more surprisingly, from
the book of Ruth (4:20 f.) which tells us that Nachshon had a son
called Salmon who was the father of Boaz – the same Boaz who
married Ruth and by her became the great-grandfather of King
David, the ancestor, according to Jewish folklore, of the Messiah!
And why do I mention that? Partly because the festival of Pesach,
which we are about to conclude, looks forward to the Festival of
Shavuot, when, by tradition, we read the book of Ruth; and partly

because it looks forward, beyond Shavuot, to the Passover of the Future, that is to say, the Messianic Age; and therefore it will do us no harm to remind ourselves that if that hoped-for age is ever to come, a little of the spirit of Nachshon ben Amminadav – the spirit of volunteering, of *noblesse oblige* and of courage – is what we chiefly need to bring its coming nearer.

❖   ❖   ❖

Miriam and Deborah
Shabbat Shirah, B'shallach, 6 February 1993

Ever since Margaret Thatcher said 'The lady's not for turning', the Government – to its credit – has been making one U-turn after another. But not only the Government! A few weeks ago the Chief Rabbi of the United Hebrew Congregations, Dr Jonathan Sacks, intervened to stop a group of women members of a United Synagogue congregation in Stanmore from holding their own services. During the past week he – to *his* credit – has issued a statement *permitting* such services.

To do him justice, his interdict of a few weeks ago was only provisional. It was really a way of saying: Hold your horses – or your Rolls Royces, or whatever Stanmore ladies use (strictly on weekdays only, of course) to get about. For he needed time: to agonise, to consult and to cajole, and to overcome some mountainous obstacles, otherwise known as Dayanim.

And now that he has finished his labour, he has brought forth, not indeed a mouse, but a kosher animal of similar size. Henceforth United Synagogue women are permitted to pray: not indeed on behalf of the men, or even with them, but on their own, provided that they don't do it in the synagogue, and that they omit certain key prayers such as the *Bar'chu, K'dushah, Kaddish* and the statutory reading of the Torah.

For this remarkable act of magnanimity on the part of the men at the head of the United Synagogue, the women will no doubt be duly grateful: grateful enough to accept, without complaining, the restrictive conditions that have been laid down as well as their continuing inferior status in marriage and divorce. It is a concession we should certainly welcome and applaud. But if the truth be told, the Chief Rabbi's U-turn is not, as revolutions go, the most momentous in the history of humanity, or even of Judaism.

In Progressive Judaism women have sat and prayed together with men for nearly two hundred years; and seventy-five years ago, in this Synagogue, they were given permission to preach. Even in Judaism generally, they have not always been excluded to the extent commonly supposed. In his marvellous book, *Jewish Life in the Middle Ages*, Israel Abrahams wrote:

> The rigid separation of the sexes in prayer seems not to have been earlier ... than the thirteenth century ... By the end of the thirteenth century, and perhaps earlier, Jewish women had their own prayer-meetings in rooms at the side and a little above the men's synagogue, with which the rooms communicated by a small window or balcony. Or if the women had no separate apartments, they sat at the back of the men's synagogue in reserved places, screened by curtains ... In their own prayer-meetings the women were led by female precentors, some of whom acquired considerable reputation. The epitaph of one of them, Urania of Worms, belonging perhaps to the thirteenth century, runs thus: – *This headstone commemorates the eminent and excellent lady Urania, the daughter of R. Abraham, who was the chief of the synagogue singers. His prayer for his people rose up unto glory. And as to her, she, too, with sweet tunefulness, officiated before the female worshippers, to whom she sang the hymnal portions. In devout service her memory shall be preserved'* (pp. 39f).

Evidently, therefore, Traditional Judaism has been progressing so fast that it has just arrived where it was seven centuries ago! However, it has not yet caught up with where it was twenty-five centuries before that. For Miriam not only led the women in a triumphal song of praise but accompanied herself on a percussion instrument (Exod. 15:20). And in addition, as the same verse tells us, she was a prophetess: one of four women explicitly so described in the Bible (Exod. 15:20, Judges 4:4, II Kings 22:14, Nehemiah 6:14), while the Talmud makes the total number seven (Meg. 14a).

It should also be noticed that Miriam is described (ibid.) as אחות אהרן, 'the sister of Aaron'; and the commentators have debated endlessly why Moses is left out of that identification. My favourite explanation is by Judah Leib Graubart, a Russian Rabbi who emigrated to Toronto in 1920 and died there in 1937. It is, he said, because Aaron, as High Priest, offered sacrifices on behalf of all the people, men and women alike, whereas Moses taught Torah only to the men. Thus Miriam was the first woman – and note the pun on her name – המרימה דגל שוויון הנשים, 'to raise the banner of women's equality' (IT, III, pp. 128f). Miriam the suffragette – or, to bring out the pun, the *mirror-image* of Emmeline Pankhurst! I bet you had never thought of that!

And only a century or so after Miriam, there lived the heroine of our Haftarah (Judges 4-5), who was not only a prophetess but a judge to boot! Indeed, as the *Encyclopaedia Judaica* points out (Vol. 5, p. 1,430), she was the only judge who actually judged!

Deborah, we are told, was the wife of Lappidot, a name which means something like 'torch-bearer', although it is quite apparent that she, not he, bore the torch of women's liberation. In fact, according to the Midrash, he was something of a nincompoop. But about her there is a remarkable comment in a Midrashic work called *Seder Eliyahu Rabbah*. Why, it asks, was she, a woman, the Judge and Prophetess at a time when Phineas the High Priest, grandson of Aaron, was still alive? And to this silly question it gives the perfect answer: 'I call heaven and earth to witness that it makes no difference whether a person is Gentile or Jewish, man or woman, or even manservant or maidservant: according only to their deeds does the רוח הקדש, God's holy spirit, which is the spirit of prophecy, rest upon human beings' (Beginning of chapter 10; ed. Friedmann, p. 48).

❖　❖　❖

The Jews had Light
Shabbat Va-yak'hel, 9 March 1991

Let us explore the origin and significance of what is probably the most widely practised of all Jewish rituals: the kindling of the Sabbath lights.

How old a custom is it? Was it already observed in biblical times, for instance? To that question the answer is almost certainly no, not only because the Bible doesn't positively mention it, but because it contains a prohibition which could have been taken to mean, and by some Jewish sects *was* taken to mean, that to do any such thing was actually *forbidden*. It occurs in the thirty-fifth chapter of Exodus and reads לא תבערו אש בכל־מושבותיכם ביום השבת, which is usually translated: 'You shall kindle no fire in all your habitations on the sabbath day' (v. 3).

What would be the reason for such a prohibition? We tend to assume that it must be because of the *work* involved in kindling a fire in those ancient, pre-technological days, and to think of another passage, in the book of Numbers, about an unfortunate individual who was caught gathering sticks on the Sabbath, and put to death (15:32-36). But surely, making a fire wasn't *such* a laborious process! Boy scouts do it with the greatest of ease, and the sticks can always be gathered before Shabbat comes in. So there must be something more to it.

Probably the clue is to be found in pre-Jewish, pagan societies, such as Babylonia. For we know that they too had their rest days, though not regularly every week, which was a uniquely Jewish contribution to civilisation. They regarded these days with superstition, not as social institutions for the welfare of human beings, but as unlucky days on which one had to be extra careful not to offend the gods.

Now fire, because of its mysterious nature and extraordinary power, was looked upon with great awe, as something supernatural which comes from, and belongs to, the gods. We find this association in many cultures. Probably the best known is the myth of Prometheus in Greek mythology. There are two versions of the myth. In both of them fire is in the possession of Zeus, the chief god, but is stolen and brought down to earth by one of the Titans, Prometheus. The difference is in the way Prometheus is punished for his offence. According to one legend Zeus has him bound in chains and sends an eagle to eat his immortal liver. According to the other legend Zeus creates a woman called Pandora and sends her down to earth with a pitcher which she opens, with the result that evil, hard work and disease, like genies from a bottle, fly out to torment humanity, and only hope remains inside.

In the Bible, too, this association between fire and divinity is a recurring theme. Moses encounters God in a burning bush (Exod. 3:2). On their journey through the wilderness the Israelites are accompanied, as a symbol of God's protection, by a pillar of cloud which by night becomes a pillar of fire (Exod. 13:21). At the supreme moment of Revelation, Mount Sinai is covered with smoke, and God comes down upon it in fire (Exod. 19:19). In Isaiah's vision God's throne is surrounded by Seraphim, which means 'fiery angels', one of whom takes a live coal from the altar (6:6). Ezekiel's vision of the Heavenly Chariot is full of burning coals and torches, and an intense source of light called חשמל which in modern Hebrew has become the word for electricity (1:13, 27). Daniel, in one of his visions, sees נהר די־נור, a river of fire issuing from God's presence (7:10).

Obviously, therefore, the Hebrews too thought of fire as something associated with God, and therefore not to be used by human beings on a sacred day, except in the context of worship, for it is noteworthy that in the Temple the kindling of fire was permitted even on the Sabbath.

We may also put it in another, related way. Civilisation is, in one sense, a manipulation of nature and therefore a human encroachment on divine prerogative. Fire was the chief symbol of civilisation. It is an interesting fact that the Babylonian city from which Abraham came, and which was regarded as the cradle of civilisation, was called Ur, which means fire or light. And observance of the Sabbath required not just abstention from work in the sense of physical exertion, but specifically abstention from activities characteristic of civilisation. On the Sabbath one should *contemplate* God's Creation, not manipulate it.

Furthermore, לא תבערו אש doesn't *really* mean 'you shall not *kindle* a fire', but 'you shall not *burn* a fire', so that, if Jews had a fire burning on a Friday afternoon, they would have to *extinguish* it before the beginning of the Sabbath. And that is how the prohibition was *in fact* understood by the Samaritans and most probably by the Sadducees (see Jakob Z. Lauterbach, *Rabbinic Essays*, pp. 456f), with the result that on Friday night they would sit in darkness and, during the cold season, shivering: a pretty miserable way of spending Erev Shabbat!

It was the *Pharisees* who changed that. For they referred to the great speech in the fifty-eighth chapter of Isaiah about the wrong and right kind of fast, during the course of which the prophet says, וקראת לשבת עונג, 'you shall call the Sabbath a delight' (v. 13), the phrase from which, in modern times, the Hebrew poet Bialik derived the term *Oneg Shabbat*. If the Sabbath is supposed to be a day of joy, then on this day the Jewish home should be a place of light and warmth. Therefore the Pharisees deliberately interpreted the prohibition, contrary to its plain meaning, as forbidding only the *kindling* of fire on the Sabbath. As they put it, ביום השבת אי אתה מבעיר אבל אתה מבעיר מערב שבת לשבת 'You may not make a fire on the Sabbath, but you may make a fire on the eve of the Sabbath for the Sabbath' (Mechilta de-Rabbi Shim'on ben Yochai, Va-yak'hel, 3).

It was a pretty daring thing to do. But the Pharisees went even further! Not only did they allow a fire kindled before the Sabbath to be *kept burning*, they actually made the kindling *obligatory*. As they said, הדלקת נר בשבת חובה, it is a *duty* to kindle a Sabbath light. What the Sadducees considered forbidden they made into an obligatory religious ritual, and one to which they gave a place of central importance in Jewish domestic observance (Shab. 2:6, 7).

Did they also institute a *blessing* to be recited when performing the ritual? Apparently not, for no such blessing is mentioned anywhere in ancient rabbinic literature. It is first found in *Seder Rav Amram*, the earliest Jewish prayer book, which was compiled in Babylonia in the ninth century. And that is very interesting, because shortly before then another Jewish sect had sprung up in that part of the world, the Karaites, who, like the Sadducees of old, argued that the biblical prohibition should be understood literally.

The argument they used was, incidentally, quite ridiculous. They pointed out that both in the Fourth Commandment, when it says 'you shall do no work', and in the prohibition 'you shall not kindle', the verb begins with the letter Tav (which is hardly surprising in view of the rules of Hebrew grammar!) and inferred that, just as work is forbidden throughout the Sabbath, so having a fire is forbidden throughout the Sabbath (Leo Nemoy, *Karaite Anthology*, p. 17)!

This time, however, the defenders of mainstream Judaism, known as Rabbanites, decided to go one step further than their Pharisaic predecessors. Not only did they endorse the custom of kindling lights specifically for the Sabbath, but they instituted the blessing, אשר קדשנו במצותיו וצונו להדליק נר של שבת. From now on, every Friday night, in every Jewish home, what other Jewish sects had considered *forbidden* by God was to be declared to have been *commanded* by God! Snubs to you, Samaritans, Sadducees and Karaites!

So the Rabbanites completed the re-interpretation of Scripture begun by the Pharisees. It was an extraordinarily daring thing to do and, incidentally, as startling an example as any of what Claude Montefiore called 'Progressive Revelation'. For the assertion that what the Bible forbids God has commanded is a clear recognition that significant religious innovation and advance occurred in later as well as earlier times.

But there is also something more specific involved. In making a ritual of the kindling of Sabbath lights, the Pharisees turned their faces against the old Promethean myth. According to the Greeks, Zeus wants to *withhold* the gift of fire from human beings, and punishes them for getting hold of it. According to a Rabbinic Midrash, God, immediately after the first Sabbath, made a point of *teaching* Adam how to make a fire by rubbing two stones together (PRE 4, Pes. 54a).

The contrast could hardly be more startling, and it has tremendous implications. From a Greek point of view human beings are in *competition* with the gods, and civilisation is a *defiance* of them; from a Jewish point of view human beings are called upon to *co-operate* with God, and civilisation is a fulfilment of that demand.

Of course, like all other aspects of technology, fire is a two-edged sword. It can be used for good or ill, to illuminate or to destroy, and the point was never made more graphically than recently, when The *Independent* (7 March 1991) published on its front page an article by a journalist called Richard Dowden. He had just visited the site of the ancient city of Ur, in southern Iran and, following the Gulf War, found it a place of desolation, which prompted him to make this striking comment: 'It is, they say, where Western civilisation began … Standing on top of the Ziggurat [the ancient terraced temple, excavated by archaeologists], the scene looked more like the place where civilisation ended'.

We can use fire to give light and warmth, or we can use it to consume oil wells and pollute the atmosphere. We can use technology to improve the world or to destroy it. By saying that God has commanded us to kindle the Sabbath lights we declare that God wishes us to use the tools of civilisation for human welfare. It is an important point to make, especially in conjunction with the Jewish faith that *ultimately* human beings *will* learn to co-operate with God. For from a Jewish point of view hope is not kept stored away in Pandora's pitcher. It is our human heritage. ליהודים היתה אורה ושמחה, 'The Jews had light and gladness'. כן תהיה לנו, so may it be for us and for all humanity.

❖   ❖   ❖

Sacrifices
Shabbat Va-yikra, 31 March 1990

This is the time of the year when, paradoxically, just as we get ready to celebrate Pesach, we leave behind the book of Exodus, with its stirring account of the deliverance of our ancestors from Egyptian slavery, and turn to the very different book of Leviticus, which will provide our Torah readings for the next seven weeks.

It is a time which Jewish preachers don't particularly relish. For there is little in the book of Leviticus to inspire, to edify or even to interest a modern congregation. Of course there is the great nineteenth chapter with its lofty moral exhortations, such as 'Love your neighbour as yourself'. There is the 23rd chapter, about the festivals of the Jewish year, which still regulates our calendar. And there is the twenty-fifth chapter with its Utopian provisions for a just social order, including the Jubilee. But that makes only three chapters out of twenty-seven. The rest is almost entirely occupied with the priesthood and the sacrificial cult and the laws of ritual defilement and purification, particularly chapter after dreary chapter prescribing in minute detail the sacrifices to be offered day by day.

There is therefore a great temptation at this time of the year to choose the Torah readings with judicious selectivity. But that is the easy way out, and it leaves in our minds a lingering doubt about our honesty in ascribing to the Torah the value we do, if so large a chunk of it is such an embarrassment to us. Therefore let us take the bull by the horns (to use a metaphor which seems rather appropriate in the circumstances) and ask ourselves where we really stand in regard to the sacrificial cult.

Why do we feel so uncomfortable about it? Partly because the whole idea of killing animals, for whatever purpose, gives us a sense of unease; and that is because, as Rabbi Dr Bernard J. Bamberger remarks, although 'we eat much more meat than our biblical ancestors did ... it comes to us neatly prepared and packaged, and many of us do not even see it till it is ready for the table. The sights, sounds and smells of the slaughterhouse would be very upsetting to our squeamish generation' (*The Torah: A Modern Commentary*, Leviticus, p. 753).

But that is only part of it. Even if we could get rid of the squeamishness, I think we would still find the thought of killing animals to the glory of God disturbing. Slaughterhouses may be necessary, but the combination of slaughterhouse and temple seems incongruous and repugnant.

Of course, not all sacrifices involved animals. There were also cereal and drink offerings. But though the thought of them doesn't make us squeamish, it still seems absurd. If it isn't repulsive, it is ludicrous, because it seems to imply that God *needs* these things for sustenance. And that is, of course, the origin of the whole institution of sacrifice, which our Israelite ancestors didn't invent but merely carried on from where the Canaanites and other peoples of the ancient Near East left off. It goes back, in other words, to a time when the gods were thought of as physical, like human beings, and therefore in need of food.

Admittedly, there are not many traces of that remote, primitive, pagan origin of the sacrificial idea in the Hebrew Bible; but there are *some*, particularly in the recurring expression ריח־ניחוח, 'a sweet savour' or 'a pleasant odour'. Besides, the book of Leviticus goes on to refer to sacrificial offerings as לחם אלהים, 'the food of God' (21:6, 8).

Although these *expressions* are found occasionally in the Hebrew Bible, it is indeed true that the *beliefs* from which they evidently stemmed had long ceased to be taken seriously, at least by the biblical writers. In fact, the Psalmist goes out of his way to ridicule such beliefs, as when he says in God's name, 'Do I eat the flesh of bulls, or drink the blood of goats?' (50:13). And the very next Psalm goes even further and seems to suggest that God doesn't really want sacrificial worship at all. 'For You do not delight in sacrifice', it says; 'were I to bring a burnt offering, you would not be pleased. The sacrifice acceptable to God is a broken spirit' (51:16f).

So, too, the greatest of the Prophets expressed considerable doubt about the sacrificial cult. If they didn't reject it altogether, they certainly spoke about it with disdain, as having very little importance compared with God's moral demands, which, in their view, are what true religion is all about. Hosea summed it up most succinctly when he said in God's name, 'I desire love and not sacrifice, and the knowledge of God rather than burnt offerings' (6:6; cf. Amos 5:22-25; Jer. 7:22; I Sam. 15:22f; Isa. 1:11-13; Micah 6:6-8).

Therefore, when we read the sacrificial chapters of Leviticus, we are uncomfortably aware, on the one hand, that there clings to them a ריח which is by no means ניחוח, a far from pleasant smell of paganism, and on the other hand that the Prophets already felt uneasy about it; and therefore we ask ourselves: what then are we doing here, still reading about them two-and-a-half millennia later?

The problem is that after the great Prophets had spoken, the Pentateuch was canonised; the Torah, complete with its levitical legislation, was declared to be 'the word of God'; that principle became the very foundation of Rabbinic Judaism; and from that time onwards, whatever doubt individuals might have entertained about the sacrifices, they could no longer dismiss them as *merely* a bygone stage in the history of Jewish worship.

At best, what we find is *ambivalence*. The Rabbis, for instance, could say that the cessation of sacrifice with the destruction of the Temple was not as great a catastrophe as it might seem, since there were other means of atonement, such as prayer, repentance and good deeds. Yet the same Rabbis instituted prayers for the *restoration* of the Temple, and stressed the importance of *studying* the sacrificial laws as a substitute for observing them (e.g., ARN 4; Lev.R. 7:3).

There is even a fascinating Midrash, quoted by Bamberger, which seems to imply that sacrifices (unlike diamonds) are not 'for ever'. The Midrash tells the parable of a king's son who, as children will, rejects all parental authority and goes about eating forbidden food. So the king says: I will have him always at my own table, and so wean him from his bad habits. Similarly, says the Midrash, because the Israelites have been offering sacrifices at pagan shrines, God says: Let them offer sacrifices to Me at all times in the Tabernacle; so they will be weaned from idolatry (Lev. R. 22:8).

That Midrash, in turn, seems to have influenced Maimonides in his celebrated chapter in the *Guide of the Perplexed*, when he put forward the idea that the sacrificial cult of the Bible was nothing more than a temporary concession on God's part to a people that could not yet be expected to conceive of worship in any other way (III, 32). And yet the same Maimonides, in his other great work, the *Mishneh Torah*, not only reproduces all the sacrificial laws in the greatest detail, but states quite explicitly that in the Messianic Age they will be re-instituted (*Hilchot M'lachim*, 11).

The same ambivalence is characteristic of many Orthodox Jews today, in that, on the one hand, they recite prayers for the restoration of the Temple with its sacrificial cult, but on the other hand they don't really believe that it will happen or desire that it should.

From that ambivalence there are only two ways of escape. One is the way of the ultra-Orthodox, now growing in number, especially in Israel, who take the matter in dead earnest, who really believe and hope that the Temple will be rebuilt, possibly quite soon, and many of whom, especially if they happen to be *kohanim*, are busy studying the sacrificial laws so that they may be ready to resume the priestly duties where their putative ancestors left them off two thousand years ago. To them the book of Leviticus is no embarrassment at all but rather a source of pride.

The other way is the way of Liberal Judaism, which is to say quite openly and unequivocally that the sacrificial cult represents a stage in the development of Judaism which was left behind long ago, and has no place at all in our hopes for the future. We, too, can read the biblical account of the sacrificial cult without embarrassment, because we know exactly where we stand in regard to it.

Soon we shall be celebrating Pesach. Then we shall recite once more, 'We were slaves to Pharaoh in Egypt' and 'In the beginning our ancestors were idol worshippers'. That is to say, we shall recall our past, without any sense of shame but also without any desire that it shall be replicated in the future, rather as an act of retrospection and thanksgiving, like looking at childhood photographs and saying: 'That is how we once were, and this is how we are now'. We look to the past only to see how far we have travelled, and to understand more clearly where we must go, which is not 'back to square one' but forward to a better future, to a more mature kind of religious belief and worship.

❖   ❖   ❖

Loving the Stranger
Acharey Mot – K'doshim, 23 April 1994

It is eight weeks now since the Hebron massacre, the most appalling atrocity committed by a member of our people for many centuries. So horrific was it that we would dearly like to forget about it. But we may not let ourselves off so lightly. For it was not an individual case of criminal insanity. Baruch Goldstein acted out a particular philosophy which purports to be Jewish; a philosophy in which non-Jewish life counts for little or nothing; a philosophy explicitly stated by the rabbi who buried him when he made that infamous remark,

'One million Arabs are not worth a Jewish fingernail.' It is a philosophy shared in varying degree by many Jews who have praised Baruch Goldstein as a hero or condoned his action. And that is such a shattering fact that neither the passage of time since the incident, nor the brutal acts of revenge which it has predictably provoked, can excuse us from confronting the fundamental question it raises: What *does* Judaism teach about the proper attitude to non-Jews? The answer is not simple, but let us start digging.

We begin in the eighteenth chapter of Leviticus where God says, 'You shall keep My statutes and My ordinances אשר יעשה אותם האדם וחי בהם, by doing which humanity shall live' (18:5). I draw your attention to the word אדם, which refers to all who are descended from Adam and therefore to human beings generally. Judaism, it would seem, addresses itself not only to the Jewish people but to humanity as a whole: not indeed all the time – the rules of worship and ritual have a more limited application – but much of the time, and especially where right conduct is concerned.

Exactly that point was made in a famous comment by a fourth-century rabbi of the name of Jeremiah. He quotes first our verse, then several other verses of a similar kind, and about each of them he says that Scripture does not speak of Priests, Levites and Israelites but of human beings generally, and then delivers the punch-line: הא אפילו נכרי ועושה את־התורה הרי הוא ככהן גדול, 'It follows that a non-Jew who observes the Torah is equal to the High Priest' (Sifra 85b).

Now you might wonder, what sort of a non-Jew would observe the Torah? Surely only a proselyte! But that is not the meaning here. Rabbi Jeremiah is referring to a Gentile who has remained a Gentile. Such a person, admittedly, would not be likely to observe all the Jewish rituals. But that is not what matters! The Torah is not chiefly about ritual. It is chiefly about right conduct. And an unconverted non-Jew who observes that part – the more important, moral part – of the Torah is every bit as worthy in God's eyes as the High Priest.

A very enlightened view, but one which didn't go unchallenged! The view that prevailed was that God requires non-Jews only to observe the so-called 'Seven Laws of the Children of Noah', which are a very rudimentary code of conduct, and even then it was long debated whether Christians and Muslims are to be regarded as 'Children of Noah' or as idolaters.

So let us dig again, and this time go straight to the great commandment, ואהבת לרעך כמוך, 'You shall love your neighbour as yourself' in the next chapter (19:18). Surely that settles the issue, since 'your neighbour' obviously means 'your fellow human being', whether Jewish or non-Jewish. Yes, I think that is what the Torah does mean. But it doesn't follow that it was always so understood.

The earliest Midrash we have on the book of Leviticus records a famous debate. Rabbi Akiva says, 'Love your neighbour as yourself is the greatest principle of the Torah.' But Ben Azzai disagrees and proposes instead the Genesis verse beginning זה ספר תולדות אדם, 'This is the book of the descendants of Adam' (Sifra 89b, q. Gen. 5:1). What is Ben Azzai's point? It is twofold. First, if you despise yourself, then to love others only as yourself is to love them very little. But the Genesis verse precludes that because it goes on to say that all human beings were created in God's image. Once you recognise that, you are bound to hold yourself, and therefore your neighbour also, in the highest esteem.

And Ben Azzai's other point is precisely the fact that it *is* possible to take רעך, 'your neighbour', to mean 'your fellow Jew'. Not only is it possible but that is how it *was* taken by the Rabbis for halachic or legal purposes, just as every other ancient legal system legislated in the main for citizens rather than non-citizens. This is one respect, and not the only one, in which the Halachah is less liberal than the Aggadah, for I have no doubt that aggadically or 'non-legally', most Jews have always understood the commandment in an inclusive sense.

Still, there is that element of ambiguity, so let us dig again and go towards the end of the chapter, where we read: 'The strangers who live with you shall be to you as the natives among you, and you shall love them as yourself' (19:34). That surely clinches the point: non-Jews are to be treated in exactly the same way as Jews! Yes, that is without doubt what the text says and means. But the Rabbis were lawyers, and lawyers don't interpret texts in the same way as other people do, according to their plain sense. For legal purposes, they ruled, the word גר, here and in most places, means 'proselyte'.

If, then, your neighbour is a born Jew and the stranger is a Jew by conversion, where do non-Jews come in? The answer is that they don't very much because from a halachic point of view the Torah is essentially the constitution of a Jewish society. Of course the Halachah does go on to make special provisions for the treatment of non-Jews. In general, we may not hurt or defraud them. If they are in danger, we must rescue them. If they rule over us, we must obey their laws. We may even enter into business partnerships with them. And there is the famous passage in the Talmud that we support the poor of the Gentiles, visit their sick and bury their dead just as we do for fellow Jews מפני דרכי שלום, for the sake of peace (Gittin 61a; cf. J. Demai 4:6).

All that is pretty enlightened, considering the age from which it comes, and compares well with the attitude of other ancient religions and societies towards outsiders. But it falls short of the ideal. To say that we should do these things 'for the sake of peace' is, after all, to appeal only to our enlightened self-interest. How much nobler it would have been if it had said that we should do these things out of love for our fellow human beings, created, like ourselves, in God's image!

So let us go digging once more. The Bible does not always speak with the same voice. It is, after all, a literature spanning a thousand years. And there are some pretty harsh things said in it about idolaters. The policy it advocates towards the Canaanites is one of ethnic cleansing. Towards the Amalekites it is one of genocide. As a matter of fact, the execution of that policy, as carried out by King Saul, though not punctiliously enough to satisfy the prophet Samuel, is the subject of the last Haftarah Baruch Goldstein would have heard before he carried out the Hebron massacre. Was there a causal connection? Considering that in 1980 the Campus Rabbi of Bar Ilan University publicly identified the Palestinians as 'present-day Amalekites', there is, alas, little doubt about it.

But the Bible is also the source of the very noblest teachings about the respect due to non-Jews: teachings which are often obscured, or go unemphasised, in the later, Rabbinic Halachah. Our Parashah, as we have seen, affords at least three examples, for all of them – about the commandments that make for life, about the love of neighbour and of strangers – were originally meant to apply to human beings generally. And there are other examples, especially in the Prophetic literature, as when Isaiah says in God's name: 'Blessed be Egypt My people, and Assyria the work of My hands, and Israel My heritage' (19:25).

One of the most striking of all occurs in today's Haftarah, when Amos thunders: 'Are you not as the Ethiopians to Me, O children of Israel? says the Eternal One. Did I not bring Israel up from the land of Egypt, and the Philistines from Caphtor and the Arameans from Kir?' (9:7). A universalistic sentiment if ever there was one, but too much so for Rashi! Rashi contrives to turn even that into a particularistic statement: about the divinely engineered migrations of various peoples, yes, but only in order to emphasise the more strongly the uniqueness of God's relationship with Israel.

Judaism is not all of a piece. It is the record of a living community which has struggled for four millennia – sometimes more, sometimes less successfully – to interpret the mind of God. On the subject of the right attitude to non-Jews, as on other subjects, we can find in it higher and lower, broader and narrower teachings, advances and retrogressions. Our task – a task rendered more urgent by the Hebron massacre – is to select and emphasise *the best*.

The time has come – or, rather, as recent events have shown, it is overdue – to re-state clearly and unequivocally the simple and majestic truth taught long ago by the author of the Creation Story and of the nineteenth chapter of Leviticus, by Amos, Isaiah and Ben Azzai: that the God we Jews worship is the God of humanity; that all human beings, of all races, nations and religions, bear the imprint of the Divine Image, and that for that reason we are duty-bound to honour their right to life and liberty and dignity, to hold them in reverential respect, and to love them as we love ourselves.

❖   ❖   ❖

The Numbers Game
Shabbat B'midbar, 18 May 1991

The fourth book of the Torah is known in Jewish tradition as במדבר, 'In the Wilderness', but more generally, from the Greek translation of the Bible, as the Book of Numbers. That is because it begins with the numbering or census of the children of Israel.

What is the purpose of a census? According to the *Encyclopaedia Britannica*, before modern times, that is, before the seventeenth century, the purpose was 'to control particular individuals – for example, to identify who should be taxed, inducted into military service, or forced to work' (II, 678a).

And that describes well enough the purpose of the census of the Wilderness, at least in one respect. For the Bible makes it very clear that the main purpose was *military*. The journey through the Wilderness was hazardous, not only because of the climatic conditions, but because in and around it there were hostile tribes who might, and sometimes did, attack the Israelites. For that reason, and of course also in anticipation of the ultimate conquest of the Promised Land, it was important for Moses to know how many troops he could muster. Hence only males were to be counted, 'from twenty years and upwards, כל־יוצא צבא בישראל, all who are able to go forth to war in Israel' (Num. 1:3).

So, in an imperfect world in which one has to defend oneself against enemies, the census was legitimate. Nevertheless the actual *process* of counting evidently caused some unease. That can be seen already in the language used. It doesn't say straightforwardly, as you might expect, 'Count', but uses a circumlocution, שאו את־ראש כל־עדת בני־ישראל, literally, 'lift up the heads of the whole community of the children of

Israel' and then adds לגלגלתם, literally, 'according to their skulls'. You don't count persons: you count 'heads' or 'skulls'. Hence also the English word 'poll', which originally meant a head of hair.

What is the reason for this unease? It is evidently a very ancient, deep-seated and widespread superstition, related to the 'evil eye'. For a little elucidation of that concept, let us turn to the classic work on *Jewish Magic and Superstition* which was written by a London-born American Reform rabbi, Joshua Trachtenberg. The root of the idea, he says, 'is the pagan conviction that the gods and spirits are essentially man's adversaries, that they envy him his joys and his triumphs, and spitefully harry him for the felicities they do not share ... The attention of the spirit-world is cocked to detect the least word or gesture of commendation ... Such words and glances, in themselves perhaps innocent, constitute the evil eye, which brings swift persecution in its wake' (p. 54).

Hence, when something congratulatory or self-congratulatory is said, the tendency, in Yiddish, to add *kain ain hora*, which means 'no *ayin ha-ra*', 'no evil eye'.

To count your possessions is dangerously close to boasting of them and is therefore to tempt Satan to take them away. 'Don't count your chickens before they are hatched' is just a mundane expression of that fear. The peculiar fact that in Hebrew masculine numerals are used with feminine nouns and feminine numerals with masculine nouns may also be connected with the same superstition; it may have originated as a way of confusing Satan.

At any rate, to count human beings is particularly hazardous. Hence the various circumventions, such as the counting of heads. Another circumvention is to levy a tax and then count the money, which has the double advantage of not counting people and of raising revenue. And that is precisely how the census of the Wilderness was conducted, to judge from a passage in the book of Exodus which describes the procedure. There God instructs Moses to collect from every male Israelite a 'ransom' sum of half a shekel, and significantly adds, לא־יהיה בהם נגף בפקד אתם, 'that there may be no plague among them when you number them' (30:12).

The Second Book of Samuel tells of another census, conducted during the reign of King David. But this time no precautions are taken. There is no mention of heads rather than persons, and no collection of money. It is a straightforward count.

What is even more peculiar is that *God* instructs David to conduct the census in that way. *God* says to him לך מנה את־ישראל ואת־יהודה, 'Go, number Israel and Judah' (II Sam. 24:1). But it is made very clear that God does so *in anger*, in order to punish the people all the more severely. That is indeed, like the hardening of Pharaoh's heart, a feature of the story which, from our theological point of view, we must reject. And it is somewhat reassuring to note that the author of the Book of Chronicles experienced the same difficulty and therefore gives a different account of the same incident, in which it is *Satan*, not God, who instigates David to conduct the census (I Chron. 21:1).

Both versions are of course instances of externalisation. In reality the impulse comes from within David, and – here both versions agree – it is an *evil* impulse. Even Joab, David's nephew and commander-in-chief, perceives that there is something wrong with the plan, and tries to dissuade David from it (II Sam. 24:3). And as soon as it is done, David himself is smitten with remorse. חמאתי מאד אשר עשיתי, 'I have sinned greatly in what I have done', he says to God, and asks forgiveness (v. 10), but too late.

But what exactly is wrong with David's census? It is partly the taboo we have been talking about. Eight hundred thousand men are counted in Israel, and five hundred thousand in Judah: 1,300,000 in all. Quite an army to boast of! And immediately seventy thousand are swept away by a plague, just the kind of plague the book of Exodus had warned about. That's what comes of defying a taboo! And that aspect of the story we may dismiss as superstition.

Perhaps there is also a suggestion, implicit rather than explicit, that David was wrong, not only in his method, but also in his motive. He mustered his potential army in order to wage war. His policy was not a peace policy but one of military expansionism. And for that he was condemned. In the Chronicles version of our story he goes on to confess to his son Solomon: 'It was in my heart to build a house in the name of the Eternal One, my God. But the word of the Eternal One came to me, saying: You have shed much blood and made great wars; you shall not build a house in My name, because you have shed too much blood on the earth in My sight' (I Chron. 22:8).

What we may infer from this for our purpose is that the judgment on a census depends not only on the way it is conducted but also on the *purpose* for which it is conducted. The encyclopaedia article from which I quoted earlier makes it clear that since the seventeenth century population censuses, especially if repeated at intervals, have become increasingly important as a source of information about demographic trends and therefore as a basis for the formulation of social policy.

One more question needs to be asked: whether in this whole business of counting anything, but especially of counting human beings, there isn't a danger that we may become overly concerned with numbers, with size, with quantity, and tend to forget that every individual is unique, and uniquely precious.

Of course there is such a danger, and though it doesn't follow that we should actually *object* to enumerations, including population surveys and opinion polls of all kinds – they clearly serve a useful purpose – we should refuse to pay too much attention to them. As Jews especially we should be on our guard against the dangers of the 'numbers game'. Not only do we always carry with us the mental image of the concentration camp tattoos, to remind us what happens when human beings are reduced to numbers, but we are the heirs of a Tradition which, perhaps more than any other, has emphasised both the individuality and the preciousness of the individual. As the Mishnah says, 'We stamp many coins with one seal, and they are all alike, but God has stamped all human beings with the seal of Adam, yet not one of them is like another. Therefore every individual must say: The world was created for my sake' (San. 4:5).

❖   ❖   ❖

Eldad and Medad
Shabbat B'ha-alot'cha, 24 June 1989

Moses has been having a lot of trouble with the Israelites. They are a rabble of recently liberated slaves, always quarrelling, always complaining, interested in nothing but food and drink, materialistic, stiff-necked and incorrigible. Even for Moses the task of leading such a people is too much, and he asks to be relieved of it.

At this point God comes up with a solution which was previously proposed in another form by Moses' father-in-law Jethro (Exod. 18:13-26): *power sharing*. Let Moses appoint seventy elders to ease his work-load.

Why seventy? To which you might reply: Why not? It is a good round number. But remember that there were twelve tribes, so one would expect to have an equal number of elders – say six – for each tribe, making a total of seventy-two. So there is a discrepancy of two; and that may account for the seemingly supernumerary status of Eldad and Medad; which is indeed what the Rabbis suggested. According to them, Moses did select six men from every tribe, making a total of seventy-two, then conducted a ballot to eliminate two of the candidates, who, seeing that they had just been unlucky, would bear no grudge (San. 17a; Num.R. 15:19).

What sort of men is Moses to pick? The text says: אשר ידעת כי הם זקני העם ושטריו, 'whom you know to be elders of the people, and officers over them' (Num. 11:16). That is to say, they are to be established, experienced, sound and reliable administrators.

But while these qualifications may suffice for *tribal* leadership, when it comes to *national* leadership something more is needed: that requires vision, idealism, statesmanship, the ability to look beyond what is to what should be, the ambition to re-shape society according to a master plan; and of course in a Jewish context that means according to *God's* plan.

In biblical language, what the seventy elders need is רוח. That word has many meanings, including 'wind' and 'spirit'; but more particularly it refers to the gift of prophecy; that is, the ability to see the world as God sees it, to criticise it in God's name, and to bring it into closer accord with God's will.

So Moses gathers the seventy elders in front of the אהל מועד, the 'Tent of Meeting' or portable temple, for a kind of ordination ritual which is supposed to effect a transference of רוח, of prophetic authority, from Moses to them. And it works! Immediately, ויתנבאו, 'they prophesied' (11:25). But the text goes on, ולא יספו, and it is not certain what that means.

It *could* be taken from the root סוף, 'to come to an end', in which case the meaning would be that, having started to prophesy, they didn't stop but went on and on. But that seems unlikely, and most commentators take the word as coming from the root יסף, 'to add' or 'continue', in which case the phrase means just the opposite: that the elders prophesied only for a moment but did not go on. The newly acquired well of prophecy dried up almost immediately!

If that is how we are supposed to read it, the implication seems to be that the רוח transference worked only momentarily; that even God can't transform hard-headed, hard-bitten, petty politicians all of a sudden into prophets; that you have to be born that way or else work your way up to it; that the experiment therefore failed, and consequently Moses was not able, after all, to get much help from the seventy elders, except as civil servants, but had to continue to bear the burden of top-level leadership largely alone, which is indeed what seems to have happened, to judge from the rest of the Pentateuchal narrative.

But just at this point we are told, וישארו שני אנשים במחנה, that two men had stayed behind in the camp, with the implication that they – Eldad and Medad – should have attended the ordination ceremony at the Tent of Meeting but didn't; and this is confirmed by the information that they were בכתובים, 'among those who had been inscribed'.

Why then were they absent? Why did they disobey Moses's summons to appear at the Tent of Meeting? Was it to their credit or to their discredit? According to the Rabbis, it was to their credit! They were motivated by modesty! The others responded with alacrity. They were, after all, bigwigs in their own tribes, so it seemed to them only fitting that they should be elevated to national leadership. But Eldad and Medad, in their humility, thought themselves unworthy of so high an honour. So they crept away into the anonymity of the camp. And for their self-effacement, according to the Rabbis, they were actually commended and rewarded, for God says to them, אתם מעטתם את עצמכם, אני אגדל אתכם יותר מכולם, 'Because you have belittled yourselves, I will make you greater than all the rest of them' (Sifre Num. 95). And that is why, whereas the other elders acquired the gift of prophecy only for a moment and immediately lost it, Eldad and Medad retained it for the rest of their lives (Num.R. 15:19).

But this favourable view of Eldad and Medad was not shared by Joshua! He is positively *incensed* by the report that they are 'prophesying in the camp' and urges Moses to 'restrain them' or 'lock them up' (11:28). That, at least, is the usual interpretation of another doubtful word. A different interpretation, suggested in the Talmud, is 'finish them off'. How? By laying צרכי צבור, the cares of the community, upon them; that will finish them off in no time (San. 17a)!

What exactly does Joshua have against Eldad and Medad? About that, too, there are various suggestions in our literature. According to one, they are about to prophesy that Moses will die, and be succeeded by Joshua, before the Israelites reach the Promised Land, and he wants to spare Moses the anguish of hearing such a prophecy (San. 97a). According to another, Joshua resents, on Moses' behalf, the fact that Eldad and Medad have become prophets *all of a sudden*, whereas he, having 'ministered to Moses since his youth' (Num. 11:28), knows what spiritual struggles and purifications he had had to go through before attaining his status (Joseph Saul Nathanson in IT, Vol. 5, p. 65).

Surely, however, the best explanation is the obvious one! Joshua resents Eldad and Medad because they had absented themselves from the ritual at the Tent of Meeting. Therefore, Joshua assumes, the רוח has not been conferred on them. They have not been properly ordained. They have no accreditation, no title, no Ph.D.! How dare they speak as prophets in God's name? They are not authorised to do so! They are usurpers! They must be stopped.

If this is the true explanation, perhaps there lies behind it the age-old struggle between, on the one hand, kings, priests and professional, so-called 'cultic' prophets, who are inducted into office by some kind of sacramental rite, and, on the other, charismatic prophets, who derive their authority from nothing but their inner religious experience and conviction.

At any rate, Joshua reacts as most human beings would react. They accept, with or without good grace, the authority of those who have been duly installed, the Establishment figures, the bureaucrats, the apparatchiks, who behave in conventional, predictable ways. They suspect and resent the individualist, the eccentric, the maverick, who challenges accepted norms and demands from individuals and societies a 'quantum leap' to new and higher moral attitudes. But that is exactly what a true prophet is, for all the greatest prophets were charismatics, and it is to them that all moral progress has been due.

Moses understands that. That is why he says, ומי יתן כל־עם ה' נביאים, 'Would that all God's people were prophets' (Num. 11:29).

We don't have to be kings or priests or politicians to advance God's redemptive purpose: we only have to be responsive to God's spirit.

❖   ❖   ❖

The Cushite Woman
Shabbat B'ha'alot'cha, 19 June 1976

The twelfth chapter of the book of Numbers is a conflation of two traditions, relating to two separate incidents, which have somehow got mixed up: one to the effect that Miriam disapproved of a marriage contracted by her brother Moses, the other to the effect that both Miriam and Aaron challenged his leadership of the Jewish people.

What is the evidence? It is contained already in the first verse which reads: 'Then Miriam spoke – and Aaron too – against Moses on account of the Cushite woman he had married, for he had married a Cushite.' Even in English the words, 'and Aaron too', sound like an afterthought; and that is even more apparent in Hebrew where the verb 'spoke' – ותדבר – is in the third person singular feminine. Almost certainly, therefore, the reference to Aaron was inserted by the redactor to make sense of what follows, for the next verse continues in the plural: 'And they said: "Has God then spoken only through Moses? Has not God spoken also through us?"' Moreover, if both of them challenged Moses' leadership, one would expect both of them to be punished for their rebellion. Yet in the sequel only Miriam becomes leprous whereas Aaron apparently gets away scot free. Obviously, therefore, the leprosy incident belongs to the first tradition, involving Miriam alone.

Let us first consider the second tradition which is the more straightforward one. Moses, we must remember, was in an unenviable position. On the one hand he believed himself to be charged by God with the task of leading a motley crowd of fugitive slaves across long stretches of inhospitable and dangerous terrain to an unknown destination, a task which called for firm leadership and sometimes stern measures. On the other hand, he was not by temperament at all autocratic. On the contrary, he had a *penchant* for democracy, for power-sharing, as shown in the appointment of the seventy elders which immediately precedes our chapter. This inner conflict led to a certain amount of vacillation on his part between self-assertion and self-effacement. Inevitably, therefore, there were power seekers who resented what they saw as his arrogance, and at the same time took advantage of what they saw as his weakness, to challenge his leadership. The wilderness narrative recounts a whole series of such rebellions, and it is not hard to believe that Aaron and Miriam would have been involved in one of them. As Moses' elder brother and sister, they might well have been jealous of him, especially as God had indeed spoken through them as well, for Aaron had played a prominent part in the negotiations with Pharaoh, and was later appointed High Priest, while Miriam is described elsewhere as a prophetess.

Faced with this challenge from his own brother and sister, Moses apparently says nothing. That too is in keeping with his character, a fact which the Bible goes out of its way to emphasise precisely at this point by telling us that Moses was the humblest man who ever walked on earth. But though Moses pretends not to hear, 'God heard it' (v.2). And though Moses takes no action, God intervenes – 'suddenly,' (v.4) – by administering to Aaron and Miriam a severe reprimand, telling them that Moses, though not the only prophet, is in a class of his own, God's servant in a unique sense, enjoying God's full confidence, and that his authority is therefore not to be challenged. With this rebuke, the incident is closed, and Tradition Two ends.

But now let us return to Tradition One, which is much more problematic. Who was the mysterious Cushite woman whom Moses had married, and what did Miriam have against her? Mysterious, because the phrase, 'because of the Cushite woman,' seems to imply that the reader is already familiar with her, yet she has not been mentioned previously, which is why the redactor finds it necessary to add the explanatory gloss, 'for he had married a Cushite'. Mysterious also because the meaning of Cushite is not certain. The Bible does indeed mention Cush as the name of a land connected with the Garden of Eden by the river Gihon (Gen. 2:13), and again as one of the sons of Ham, the youngest son of Noah (Gen. 10:6-8), who was regarded as the ancestor of the African peoples. And to students of ancient history Cush is known as a kingdom in North East Africa, between the First and Sixth Cataracts of the Nile, which the Greeks called Nubia, and which corresponds to what we know as the Sudan. Traditionally, however, Cush is more commonly equated with Ethiopia. So the identity of the Cushite woman remains somewhat obscure. All we can say with reasonable assurance is that she was an African woman.

Yet even that view has not gone unchallenged, for in the Midrash there is a strong tendency to identify her with Zipporah, daughter of Jethro, the priest of Midian; and the Midianites were not exactly Africans, for they lived in the Arabian Peninsula, which strictly speaking belongs to Asia, and were probably Semites rather than Hamites. Indeed, it is not impossible that the term Cushite might have been used loosely, to include the Midianites. But the fact that Moses married Zipporah is already well known to the reader by the time the book of Numbers is reached, so it is hardly likely that the Bible would mention it at this point as a news item, and we must assume that the motive of the Midrash in identifying the Cushite woman with Zipporah is to avoid the implication that Moses married twice.

Besides what could Miriam possibly have had against Zipporah? That she was not a Jewess? But that fact passed without comment many scores of chapters ago, and it seems a bit late to raise the issue now. Moreover, Rabbinic interpretation assumes that Zipporah, like her father Jethro, converted to Judaism. Therefore, having got itself into this difficulty, the Midrash has to invent a rather far-fetched explanation to account for Miriam's complaint. According to this explanation, Moses had separated himself from Zipporah; had supposed, like so many other prophets, priests and mystics, chiefly in religions other than Judaism, that the most intensely spiritual life demanded sexual abstinence; and had therefore committed the sin of failing to satisfy his wife's conjugal rights. But if that charge was true, then there is no reason why Miriam should have been punished for making it. Which is why Samuel Sandmel, in his novel *Alone Atop The Mountain*, gives the story yet another twist by hinting that Miriam had been spreading false rumours about Zipporah's infidelity.

But there is really no good reason to go along with the identification of the Cushite woman with Zipporah. It is much more likely that according to the original tradition Moses did marry twice and that his second wife was African. As a matter of fact, Josephus, in his *Antiquities of the Jews* (II, 10), relates a legend which may be connected with this tradition. According to this legend, Moses, while still in Egypt, was made a general of the Egyptian army in the double hope that he would defeat the Ethiopians and that he would be killed in the battle. The Ethiopians withdraw to their capital Saba, which is an almost impregnable fortress, and while Moses besieges the city, the daughter of the Ethiopian king, a young woman called Tharbis, falls deeply in love with him, whereupon Moses marries her in return for the surrender of the city.

Let us then assume that the Cushite woman of our Parashah was Ethiopian or Sudanese, and therefore dark-skinned. As a matter of fact, in modern Hebrew *kushi* is simply the word for a black person. No doubt she was very beautiful, as so many black women are, a fact not unknown to the ancient Israelites, for you may recall the phrase in the Song of Songs, שחורה אני ונאוה which is usually translated 'I am black but comely' (1:5) but could as well be translated: 'I am black *and* comely.' And it is interesting that the Targum, the Aramaic Version of the Bible, evades the problem of the racial origin of the Cushite woman altogether by translating simply: אתתא שפירתא, which means 'a beautiful woman!'

But beautiful or not, the question remains: what did Miriam have against her? The truth is: we don't know. But because we don't know, we are free to speculate. One possibility, which I have already mentioned, is that Miriam might have thought it unfitting for the leader of the Jewish people to be a bigamist. But that is unlikely since there is no objection in the Bible to the polygamous marriages of other leading personalities, such as Jacob and Solomon. Another possibility is that Miriam objected to her brother marrying a foreigner. But that, as we have already seen, would have applied equally to Zipporah; and since we must assume that both of them became Jewish, the objection would have had no validity.

There is, however, a third possibility. Perhaps Miriam had a colour prejudice! That would explain why she could accept Zipporah but not the Cushite woman. Admittedly, we don't encounter any colour prejudice, as such, elsewhere in the Bible. Xenophobia, yes; but there is no evidence that the negative attitudes to foreigners that existed were related to the pigmentation of their skin. Nevertheless, colour prejudice is so widespread a phenomenon, and so deep-seated, that it is by no means unimaginable that it might have existed among the ancient Israelites. Moreover, if that is the explanation, it may throw some light on the nature of the punishment which Miriam receives. For this suggestion, I am indebted to David Daiches, who, in his book on *Moses: Man in the Wilderness*, writes: 'We have discussed earlier the significance of the traditions that Moses married a foreign wife. Here there are no details of any kind given, and we are not told whether the objection to the Cushite wife was her colour. But it is perhaps significant that God punished Miriam for this attack on Moses by turning her "leprous, white as snow" and her leprosy was cured only on Aaron's intervention ... Was this an example of divine irony? Perhaps the implication is: "She's too dark for you, is she? If you prefer whiteness, I'll make you whiter than ever."' (p. 164).

If that theory is correct, it brings us back with a bump from ancient legend to contemporary reality. For colour prejudice is, alas, very much a matter of the present as well as the past. In some respects the situation has indeed improved. Who would have dared to predict a few years ago that by this time both the Vorster regime in South Africa and the Smith regime in Rhodesia would be beginning to dismantle their discriminatory racial laws? And in this country, too, the absorption of hundreds of thousands of non-white immigrants has taken place, in view of the doom forecast by Enoch Powell and others, remarkably quietly.

Now I could of course go on to demonstrate that Judaism is opposed to racial discrimination. But I hope and believe that to do so would be to insult your intelligence. It is too obvious. It would be like saying that Judaism is opposed to sin. But since we have been talking about the Cushite woman, it would be appropriate to remind ourselves of the great declaration of the prophet Amos, 'Are you not as the children of the Ethiopians unto Me, O children of Israel? says the Eternal One' (9:7), where the Hebrew for 'Ethiopians' is כֻשִׁים, 'Cushites.' Nor would it do any harm to recall the famous Midrash which, noting that the Hebrew word for 'man', *adam*, is related to the word *adamah* for 'earth', relates that God made Adam from earth gathered in the four corners of the world, red and black and white and greenish, so that no land should be able to say to any race of human beings: 'You do not belong here; this soil is not your home' (Yalkut Shim'oni, B'reshit 1:13).

But it is not enough to be opposed to racial discrimination in theory. What Judaism demands of us above all is positive action; in favour of liberal immigration policies; in favour of the admission of the dependents of those already here, so that families may be reunited; in favour of the courteous and respectful treatment of all applicants by the immigration authorities; and in favour of the social integration of those who have chosen to make their home in this country, so that they may feel not only tolerated here, but welcome.

As I said at the beginning, the complaint against Moses on account of his Cushite wife was probably made only by Miriam, and the mention of Aaron in that context is an interpolation, due to confusion with another tradition. Yet this doesn't necessarily mean that

Aaron was altogether uninvolved. According to the medieval Jewish commentator, Abraham ibn Ezra, Aaron agreed with Miriam's complaint, or remained silent when she made it; therefore he too was guilty. Let *us* not incur the guilt of silence. As Moses prayed for the recovery of Miriam from her leprosy, saying אל נא רפא נא לה 'Heal her, I beseech You, O God', so let us pray that those who still suffer from the disease of colour prejudice may soon be healed. And as the prayer of Moses is commended in Jewish tradition for its brevity, reminding us that deeds are more important than words, so may the words of our mouths and the meditations of our hearts be speedily translated into action.

❖ ❖ ❖

The Spirit that Affirms
Sh'lach L'cha, 23 July 1973

The story of the Twelve Spies is full of puzzles. Why, for instance, did Moses send them out in the first place? According to the book of Numbers, he did so at God's command (13:1). The book of Deuteronomy tells us that when the Israelites reached Kadesh-Barnea, the logical vantage-point for an incursion into Canaan from the south, Moses was in favour of proceeding immediately (1:21) but the people got cold feet, and it was they who said, in so many words: 'Not so fast! First let us make sure that it is safe' (1:22). And for their lack of faith the Midrash castigates them (Sifre Deut. to Deut. 1:22) .It is true that the Deuteronomy account goes on to make Moses say: 'The thing seemed good to me' (1:23). But even here the Midrash, stressing the word 'me', comments that to Moses it seemed good, but not to God (Sifre Deut. to Deut. 1:23). In other words, God, far from having ordered the reconnaissance expedition, never approved of it at all! It was merely a concession on the part of Moses to a faithless people, and one which, in the event, proved futile. For the majority of the spies brought back an unfavourable report which so frightened the people that they abandoned the invasion and wandered in the wilderness for another generation before making another attempt.

And here is another puzzle. Why did the spies bring back a cluster of grapes? Surely if most of them wanted to dissuade the people, it was not in their interest. Here again the Midrash steps in and tells us that it was Caleb who insisted. He drew a sword and said to the others: 'If you want to stop me from taking these grapes, you will have to kill me first' (Num. R. 16:14).

Again, why did the majority admit that the land they had reconnoitred was 'flowing with milk and honey' (Num. 13:27)? Presumably because, with the evidence of the grapes, they could not very well deny it. But then, how could they go on to report that 'it is a land that devours its inhabitants' (Num. 13:32), which is usually taken to mean that it produced insufficient food to sustain its population, or else that it was so riddled with pestilence that only the sturdiest could survive there – hence the reference to giants? Perhaps the answer is simply that they were lying, and those who lie are liable to contradict themselves.

But the greatest puzzle of all is: how could twelve men, who performed a joint reconnaissance mission, and a pretty thorough one, lasting forty days, come back with two such disparate reports? Surely they had travelled the same roads and seen the same sights! Yet to Joshua and Caleb it seemed a fertile land, inhabited by ordinary people who, if they should resist, could easily be overcome; to the others it seemed an inhospitable land, populated by giants and studded with impregnable fortresses.

The answer is that, though the objective facts were the same for all, they *interpreted* them differently according to their subjective frames of mind. What then is it about people's mental orientation that causes some to see evil where others see good?

One cause is *fear*. It was a traumatic experience for the Israelites when they left Egypt. True, it was a great relief to be rid of their taskmasters. But the first flush of liberation soon wore off. In Egypt they had known a kind of security. As slaves, they had indeed been humiliated and oppressed; but they had had their daily rations and their daily routine. Now they faced an uncertain future, and the uncertainty filled them with a growing fear.

The ten spies who presented the majority report were of such a fearful frame of mind. They went into Canaan expecting their fears to be confirmed; and what one expects one finds. That is why they did not see the grapes, only the fortresses. That is why they saw the inhabitants of the land as giants, and themselves as grasshoppers. And their fear communicated itself, as fear does, to the people. Their report caused panic.

But fear does not remain fear. It soon turns into resentment against its supposed cause. That is why the Israelites repeatedly rebelled against Moses, blaming him for all their misfortunes. The ten spies clearly belonged to that rebellious element; therefore they went on their reconnaissance mission, not to prove Moses right but to prove him wrong. They looked for evidence that would discredit his whole plan, and, not surprisingly, they found it.

Such bitterness, moreover, doesn't remain confined towards those who can with some rationality be held responsible for one's perceived misfortune. It tends to be directed towards everybody, even past generations. The Talmud tells us that when the spies came to Hebron, Caleb visited the cave of Machpelah in order to pray at the tomb of Abraham, Isaac and Jacob; but the ten did not follow him; to them the grave of the Patriarchs meant nothing (Sotah 34b).

Finally, such hostility turns even towards God. According to the Deuteronomy version of our story, the Israelites, on hearing the majority report, exclaimed: 'It is out of hatred for us that God has brought us from the land of Egypt, to give us into the hand of the Amorites, to destroy us' (1:27). And as the Midrash points out, that was really a projection, and it quotes the proverb, 'What is in your mind against your neighbour is what you imagine to be in your neighbour's mind against you' (Sifre Deut. ad loc).

Fear, resentment, hostility: these are the negative attitudes which explain why ten of the twelve spies saw in the land of milk and honey, not a promise but a threat, not a blessing but a curse. And this tendency exists in all of us: to shy away from freedom, to see a difficulty in every opportunity, to cling to what is old and resist what is new, to prefer the security of routine to the insecurity of adventure, to be afraid of challenge, to hate ourselves for our fearfulness, and then to project our self-hate on to others; to resent those who would lead us forward into the unfamiliar; to see only the faults of others, not their virtues; to suspect their motives and belittle their achievements; to mock their hopes and despise the values they hold sacred; and then to see the world as so pervaded with evil that the God who created it must be malevolent or non-existent.

It is an evil spirit which Goethe, in reference to Mephistopheles, defined as *Der Geist der stets verneint,* 'the spirit that always denies' (Faust, Pt. 1, *Studierzimmer*). But the religious spirit affirms. It accentuates the positive. It is the spirit of Joshua and Caleb, which looks to the future and says: טובה הארץ מאד מאד, 'The land is very very good' (Num. 14:7).

❖   ❖   ❖

Controversies and Controversies

Shabbat Korach, 3 July 1976

The sixteenth chapter of the book of Numbers is a conflation of two originally unconnected traditions. One of them concerns yet another rebellion against the leadership of Moses. This time it is led by Dathan and Abiram of the tribe of Reuben. As usual, it is occasioned by the hardships of the wilderness, especially the shortage of food and drink, as well as the despondency generated by the 'evil' majority report of the spies, and we can well imagine that it might have occurred in the height of summer, when water was scarce, the sun scorching, and tempers frayed. For in those days as in ours, there was a tendency to 'blame the government' for the state of the economy, if not also for the weather, and Moses was the obvious target. Like other rebels before them, Dathan and Abiram say to him: 'Why did you bring us out of Egypt only to kill us in the wilderness?' (v. 13). And they add a bitter ironic touch by referring to Egypt – the 'house of bondage' the people have escaped from, not the Eldorado they are supposed to be heading for – as 'a land flowing with milk and honey' (ibid.)!

The other tradition relates to a rebellion led by Korach of the tribe of Levi and is really directed against Aaron rather than Moses, or if against Moses, then because he has conferred the priesthood on Aaron. This tradition is most probably a reading back into the wilderness period of a conflict that occurred several centuries later, in the days of the Monarchy, when the Levites, who were rather humble Temple servants and choristers, challenged the privileged status of the Kohanim, the Aaronide priests. The message is therefore plain. It is a solemn warning to the Levites against aspiring to the priesthood, reinforced by the object lesson of what allegedly happened to one of their tribe who did just that. For the sequel of the combined story is that all the rebels are wiped out by an 'act of God': some are swallowed up by the ground, some burnt to death. Perhaps this sequel owes something to yet another tradition, about an earthquake and a volcanic eruption, which became confused with the other two. At any rate, that Korach and his family were *not* completely annihilated, is attested by the fact that the Bible elsewhere mentions his descendants as one of the leading levitical families of later times.

A different kind of conflict lies behind our Haftarah (I Sam. 12:1-22). The First Book of Samuel preserves two opposing attitudes to the monarchy, one for, the other against. According to one tradition, it is God's will, revealed to Samuel, that a monarchy shall be established; when Saul, looking for his father's donkeys, comes to Samuel for advice, God tells him that he is the man, and Samuel immediately proceeds to anoint him. According to the other tradition, represented by our Haftarah, Samuel regards the people's demand for a king as tantamount to rebellion against God, resists it as long as possible, and then yields to it reluctantly. Obviously, therefore, there existed two schools of thought, pro-monarchical and anti-monarchical. Probably each had a valid case; for on the one hand the political situation demanded the kind of unity most likely to be achieved by a monarchy; on the other hand, in view of the tendency of ancient Near Eastern peoples to deify their kings, such a step held grave dangers for the religion of Israel. In the end, idealism gives way to realism. The monarchy is established, with consequences partly good and partly bad, and the old controversy becomes academic.

Another controversy worthy of note, or rather series of controversies, occurred a thousand years later between the schools of Hillel and Shammai. Here the protagonists were not motivated by ill-will towards the national enterprise, nor by personal ambition, nor by conflicting political theories, but merely by the desire, equally sincere on both sides, to interpret the will of God, which, because of differences in temperament as well as the general fallibility of human beings, sometimes led them to different conclusions. And about this controversy between the schools of Hillel and Shammai, the Talmud makes the beautiful comment: אלו ואלו דברי אלהים חיים, 'These and these are the words of the living God' (Eruvin 13b). What it presumably means is that there is something sacred about a sincere attempt to understand God's will, even if it is sometimes mistaken.

The Talmudic passage continues: 'Nevertheless, the Halachah is in accordance with the school of Hillel.' But, it goes on, if both are the words of the living God, how can that be? And the answer it gives is both charming and profound. The Hillelites, it says, deserved that their opinions should become the accepted law because they were gentle and humble; for instance, they always cited the opinions of their opponents as well as their own; indeed, they made a point of always citing the opinions of their opponents *first*. In other words, if you can't decide which of two opinions is right, because the case for the one seems as cogent as the case for the other, then judge by the character of the protagonists and plump for the one who is more modest, self-effacing, self-critical, courteous and conciliatory.

However, what is more important is that, regardless of who wins, a conflict conducted from the highest motives, which is not a power struggle but a single-minded endeavour to discover what is

right, has *intrinsic* value and is bound, in one way or another, to
be beneficial in its consequences. Precisely that is the point of
the great affirmation in the Ethics of the Fathers, when it says:
כל מחלוקת שהיא לשם שמים סופה להתקיים, ושאינה לשם שמים אין סופה להתקיים,
'Any controversy conducted for the sake of God will in the end vindicate itself; but any controversy which is *not* conducted for God's
sake will ultimately *not* vindicate itself' (5:17). And then the passage
continues: 'What is an example of the first kind of controversy? It
is the controversy between Hillel and Shammai. And what is an
example of the second? It is the controversy stirred up by Korach
and all his company.'

❖   ❖   ❖

The Mortality of Moses
Shabbat Chukkat, 25 June 1977

For forty years Moses led a fractious people through an inhospitable
wilderness towards the Promised Land. How he must have longed to
reach the destination! How he must have dreamed daily of that glorious moment which would be the crowning achievement of his life! But
it was not to be. Which is why the scene on Mount Nebo, when Moses
sees from afar the land he will never enter (Num. 27:12-14, Deut.
32:48-52, Deut. 34:1-4) is one of the most poignant in all of literature.

Ever since this tradition, that Moses died before the land was
entered, first became established, it has prompted 'The Question
Why'. What had Moses done wrong to deserve so tragic a fate?
Already the Bible attempts to answer this question in various places,
and nearly always it refers to the incident recorded in the twenty-sev-
enth chapter of the book of Numbers, where God says to Moses: 'Go
up this mountain of Avarim [apparently another name for Nebo]
and behold the land which I have given to the children of Israel.
And when you have seen it, you shall be gathered to your people, as
your brother Aaron has been gathered, because you rebelled against
My commandment in the wilderness of Zin, at the time of the strife
of the congregation, to sanctify Me in their sight in the matter of the
water, namely the water of Merivat-Kadesh' (vv. 12-14). Similarly,
the thirty-second chapter of Deuteronomy gives as the reason:
'Because you trespassed against Me among the children of Israel at
the water of Merivat-Kadesh, in the wilderness of Zin, in that you did
not sanctify Me among the children of Israel' (v. 51).

Two points emerge: that Moses, in association with his brother Aaron, was guilty of some kind of disobedience, and that, in consequence, he failed to sanctify God. But what exactly was the act of disobedience? The most obvious answer would seem to be that, whereas God had told Moses to *speak* to the rock, that is, to *command* it to bring forth water, Moses, in the event, *struck it with his rod*. In itself, that may seem a trivial enough offence, especially when we consider that, according to our narrative, God had in fact told Moses to *take* the rod, and it was therefore a natural assumption on his part that he was supposed to strike the rock with it, especially as he had done exactly that once before, and at God's explicit command, in an earlier incident, related in the seventeenth chapter of Exodus (vv. 1-7). Besides, why would God have ordered him to take the rod at all if not with the intention that he should use it?

One possibility which we might entertain here is that, in the telling of the story, the two incidents have become accidentally confused; that the divine command to take the rod belonged only to the earlier incident and was inserted here by mistake. And it is even possible that this was done deliberately, so as to make the sin of Moses seem less serious; for though there is sufficient evidence that the biblical writers and redactors did not wish to portray Moses as *perfect*, nevertheless it is to be assumed that they venerated him sufficiently to wish to tone down his shortcomings. In other words, they wanted to convey that Moses' misdemeanor was due to a mere misunderstanding of what God had intended him to do.

But in that case, the penalty seems all the more disproportionate. And even if we assume that in the original version of the story the divine command to take the rod did not feature at all, it is not easy to see why it should have been a matter of such gravity that Moses brought forth the water by one means rather than another. Of course, we have to understand what was involved. To bring forth water from a rock by a mere word of command would have been a miracle. To do so by striking the rock could have been construed as a natural event, since the impact might have dislodged some obstruction that had previously prevented the underground spring from gushing out. On this view, therefore, Moses had shown a lack of faith in God's power to perform miracles, which is indeed confirmed by the phrase 'because you did not believe in Me' (Num. 12:12), and had therefore missed an opportunity to demonstrate that power just when such a demonstration was urgently needed to reassure the disgruntled people.

And why would the effect of such a demonstration have been to 'sanctify' God? Well, we must not read too much into that, for the whole incident took place in an area called Kadesh, and it was evidently an incidental purpose of the story-teller to explain that place-name. Just as the exact location, Merivah, which can mean 'strife', is explained as the place where the people 'strove' over the lack of water, so the general area, Kadesh, is explained as the area in which Moses and Aaron failed *l'kaddesh*, to sanctify God.

Nevertheless, this explanation, which is, as I have said, the most obvious one, leaves us dissatisfied; for the sin of Moses, so understood, still does not seem of a sufficient magnitude to warrant the severity of the penalty. So we look for other possible explanations, as indeed the Jewish commentators have done through the ages. Nachmanides, for instance, drew attention to the words which Moses and Aaron addressed to the people as they stood in front of the rock: המן הסלע הזה נוציא לכם מים 'Shall *we* bring forth water for you out of this rock?' (Num. 12:10), from which he inferred that they meant to claim credit for themselves rather than for God. On this view, their sin was not due to any misunderstanding of God's command, nor to any lack of meticulousness in carrying it out, nor to any lack of faith in God's power to perform miracles, but a deliberate attempt at self-glorification. Such an explanation certainly comes nearer to justifying the severity of the penalty that ensued.

But our conscience still seems to demand that the offence should have been of a more plainly *moral* kind; and of this, too, there is a hint. It is contained in the contemptuous language used by Moses and Aaron when they say to the people: שמערנא המורים 'Listen now, you rebels' (20:10). Their sin, in other words, was a lack of that patience and courtesy which leaders should always show towards those they lead. This is a point made by Abraham ibn Ezra, basing himself on earlier commentators. Indeed, as he remarks, it is alluded to already in the Bible itself, namely in Psalm 106, where we read: 'They angered God at the waters of Merivah, and it went ill with Moses because of them; for they embittered his spirit, ויבטא בשפתיו and he spoke rashly with his lips' (v. 33). On this view, therefore, the fundamental fault of Moses was his anger, his hot temper; the same fault which he displayed when, exasperated by the people's worship of the Golden Calf, he broke the tablets of the Law; an anger which he usually managed to control but which sometimes, as on this occasion, got the better of him.

These, then, are the various interpretations of the Merivah incident. They are all to be found in the Jewish sources, for this is one of the beauties of Judaism, that in the area of Aggadah, as distinct from Halachah – of theory, as distinct from practice – it allows divergent interpretations to stand side-by-side, without any attempt to harmonise them; that it permits, and even encourages, free speculation.

But since that is so, let us speculate a little further. It has been suggested, for instance by Arnold Ehrlich (*Mikra kif-shuto* to Num. 12:12), that Moses' real sin was graver than the Bible, as we have it, indicates; for, as I have already hinted, the biblical authors or redactors, in their veneration of Moses, tended to gloss over his shortcomings. So Ehrlich says that the Bible is silent about the sin of Moses, just as it is silent about the circumstances of his death. But the exact opposite has also been asserted, that his sin was indeed very slight, and consisted in nothing but a seemingly minor misinterpretation of God's command, and that his punishment was so severe on the principle of *noblesse oblige*, that the greater the man, the greater his responsibility, and that, in the case of a man as great as Moses, what would in lesser men be considered a trivial failing, weighs heavily.

Related to this is yet another possibility, suggested by a passage in the first chapter of Deuteronomy. There, after recalling the incident of the spies and the evil report they brought back about the Promised Land, Moses says: 'God was angry with me on your account, and said, You shall not enter it' (v. 37). In this passage, therefore, Moses' death on the wrong side of the Jordan is not attributed to the Merivah episode at all, but to that of the spies; and the implication seems to be that, although Moses could not be held *directly* responsible for the evil report of the majority, he was nevertheless *indirectly* responsible, since he had failed to instil into the people a sufficient faith in God and in the future God had in mind for them. A leader, in other words, must take some responsibility for the morale, and the conduct, of those entrusted to his charge.

Since this interpretation raises doubt, not only about the exact nature of Moses' sin, but even about the occasion on which it was committed, we may perhaps be bolder still and ask ourselves: is there really any need to assume that Moses *did* commit a sin grave enough to justify his exclusion from the Promised Land? It is true, as I said at the beginning, that the Bible asks the question and, in various, somewhat unconvincing ways, tries to answer it. But then those who wrote the Bible were human beings. Conceivably, therefore, they might have been mistaken. Let us suppose that they were. Then we might say something which at first sight may seen banal, namely that the reason why Moses died when he did was an extremely simple one: *he was old!* For even if the biblical assertion that he was 120 is an exaggeration, it presumably reflects a genuine tradition that he lived to a ripe old age. And that old people die – that human beings are not immortal – is a fact of life which requires no moralistic explanation!

Moses was not perfect. He committed, no doubt, many sins. But he did not die because of them. He died because he was mortal and because he was old. And because we too are mortal, therefore, like Moses, we shall not enter the Promised Land. We shall only behold it from afar. But the vision of it, if we hold on to it, can give meaning and purpose to our lives. We know that the time will come, and we know that we can contribute something towards its coming. And that is enough.

❖   ❖   ❖

Jews and Non-Jews
Shabbat Balak, 18 July 1992

Mah nishtannah, why is today's *parashah* different from all other *parashiyyot?* Because it is the only one named after a non-Jew, and even an anti-Jew, since King Balak was the leader of a Moabite and Midianite military coalition against Israel.

Furthermore, the hero of the Parashah was another non-Jew, the Aramean prophet Balaam, hired by Balak to curse the Israelites so as to demoralise them before attacking them. Whether Balaam should *also* be regarded as an enemy of the Jews, is another question, since the evidence is conflicting.

Even so, just because of this ambivalence in the Balaam story, its interpretation in Jewish tradition provides a good test-case of our relationship as Jews with our non-Jewish fellow human beings: the way we see them and the way they see us. So let that be our subject and let us begin with the *negative* evidence.

At the beginning of the story, we must assume, Balaam knows nothing about the Israelites. He has probably never met one. But as a professional soothsayer, available for hire, he is willing enough, for a price, to curse them. It is true that he hesitates, but apparently out of fear of the God of Israel rather than any love for His people. Even when the king offers to reward him with honours and riches (22:17f), Balaam still hesitates; but the prospect of gaining both a peerage and a fortune is enticing; so he sets off on the journey to the vantage point on the Moabite hills where the curse is to be uttered. Even then he hesitates, and his hesitation is marvellously symbolised by the story of the recalcitrant donkey. Nevertheless, when Balaam finally opens his mouth, it is with the intention of cursing the Israelites. That he blesses them instead is something that happens *in spite* of himself.

Therefore, if a man is to be judged by his *intentions*, Balaam is a nasty character. At best, he is unprincipled. Not surprisingly, therefore, he receives a bad press – much of the time – in subsequent Jewish tradition. In Rabbinic literature he is often referred to as בלעם הרשע, 'Balaam the wicked'. In The Ethics of the Fathers, we are told that 'an evil eye, a haughty mind and a proud soul are hallmarks of the disciples of Balaam the wicked' (5:19).

Similarly, a Midrash tells us that, while the prophets of Israel were compassionate towards their own as well as other peoples, Balaam was cruel and sought to uproot an entire nation for no reason at all (Num.R. 20:1).

Balaam became a stereotype of evil in general and of anti-Semitism in particular which has influenced Jewish attitudes to non-Jews ever since, and all too often with good cause. We *have* experienced a great deal of hostility from the non-Jewish peoples among whom we have lived.

But that is only one side of the story. Balaam did, after all, hesitate. The story of the donkey is only a literary device externalising an *internal* hesitation, and Balaam's fear of the God of Israel was at the same time the voice of his conscience. Above all, he did, in the event, *bless* the Israelites, and in words put into his mouth by the God of Israel.

Therefore, alongside the bad press, Balaam also received a *good* press. In the Talmud he heads a list of seven prophets sent by God to the Gentile world (B.B. 15b). An ancient Midrash says that in some respects he was a greater prophet than Moses (Sifre Deut., end). The whole Parashah of Balak, containing his prophecies, became so popular that at one time it was seriously proposed that it should be recited every day, along with the Shema, and it was only because it would have unduly prolonged the service that the suggestion was rejected (Ber. 12b). Nevertheless, the key verse of Balaam's prophecy, beginning מה טבו אהליך יעקב, 'How lovely are your tents, O Jacob', became part of the Jewish liturgy, as a prayer to be recited on entering the synagogue. And to cap it all, even King Balak, who never wavered in his hostility as Balaam did, is honoured in our tradition, not only by having a *parashah* named after him but because, according to the Talmud (Sotah 47a), he was an ancestor of Ruth, herself a Moabitess, and she was a great-grandmother of King David, the ancestor and prototype, according to Jewish legend, of the Messiah himself!

So there is a duality in our tradition about Balaam. He is good, and he is bad. He is one of the best, and he is one of the worst. And the duality reflects our experience of the non-Jewish peoples among whom we have lived in the course of our history. There are good and bad among them, and as long as we remember both sides of the story, we have a realistic view.

But sometimes we forget. Sometimes we see only good on our side of the divide and only bad on the other. Of course the truth is that, as there is good and bad among others, so there is good and bad among us, too, and indeed within each of us. As a matter of fact, there is a modern Midrash which runs completely counter to one of the traditions I have quoted. It is by Joseph Jacob of Pollonoye, one of the great masters of Chasidism and a disciple of the Baal Shem Tov. What, he asks, is the difference between true and false prophets? And he answers: true prophets more often than not *rebuke* the people; false prophets flatter them with sweet words; they tell them that everything in the garden is lovely, and there is no need to change. And on that basis he concludes that Balaam was a false prophet, who tried to lull the Jewish people into a false sense of security (IT, Vol. 5, p. 156).

At any rate there is a terrible spiritual danger in this tendency, shamelessly exploited by our demagogues, to see only good in ourselves and only bad in others. Anti-Semitism is a fact, and we must be constantly vigilant against it. But not all non-Jews are anti-Semites. Some are philo-Semites. Perhaps Balaam was a mixture of the two. More probably, he was neither. At least at the beginning of the story, as I have suggested, he knew nothing about the Israelites; he was open-minded and could be influenced either way.

So, too, in our time, most non-Jews know little or nothing about us, and, though they may nevertheless be a little prejudiced one way or the other, are willing, within limits, to judge us, both individually and collectively, by what they see and hear of us.

What then was it that changed Balaam's attitude? What was it that so impressed him about the Israelites that, instead of cursing them, he was moved to praise them? Perhaps the answer to that question may tell us something about the way *we* should conduct ourselves. There are three clues in his oracles.

His first reaction, when he looked down on the Israelite encampment was to exclaim, הן־עם לבדד ישכן, 'Behold, it is a people dwelling alone' (Num. 23:9). He noticed that they were *different* from other peoples. So, too, we shall never gain the respect of our non-Jewish fellow citizens if we pretend that we are the same as everybody else, if we are not true to our own convictions and traditions.

But then, in his second oracle, Balaam goes a stage further and says: לא הביט און ביעקב, 'No-one has beheld iniquity in Jacob' (23:21). He becomes aware that the Israelites are not only different but *nobly* different; there is a certain dignity and decency about their way of life. So, too, we need to remember that there is no virtue in being different merely for the sake of being different. That is the opposite of assimilationism, and just as stupid. Our aim must be that whatever distinguishes us from others should be *to our credit.* We are not by nature better or worse than anybody else. But we have a tradition called Judaism which has taught the world much of what it knows about right conduct and which, if we take it seriously, can bring out the best in us.

Nevertheless, although Judaism is our heritage, it doesn't come to us *automatically.* We have to make an *effort* to learn it, and to transmit it from generation to generation. And it doesn't transmit itself in a vacuum. Which brings us to the third of Balaam's oracles, and especially its punch-line, מה טבו אהליך יעקב משכנותיך ישראל, 'How lovely are your tents, O Jacob, your dwelling places, O Israel' (24:5).

The Rabbis took this as a reference to synagogues and schools (San. 105b), which is why it became a prayer recited on entering the synagogue. It is of course an entirely anachronistic interpretation, since synagogues didn't exist in Balaam's time or for about another thousand years afterwards. Balaam obviously meant the *encampments* of the Israelites as he saw them from the Moabite hills; in other words, their *homes.*

However, even though the reference to synagogues is an anachronism, there *is* a close connection between Jewish homes and synagogues. Each derives much of its strength from the other, and both are channels through which Judaism is transmitted from generation to generation.

And so there is a threefold message in the story of Balaam for all of us. If we wish to earn the respect of our fellow men and women, then, first, we must be true to ourselves, to our own convictions and traditions, and therefore have the courage to be different; secondly, we must make sure that the difference is to our credit, that our Judaism brings out the best in us; and thirdly, we must so conduct our homes and so support our synagogues that our Judaism is effectively transmitted from generation to generation.

❖   ❖   ❖

The Signposts of Repentance
Shabbat Ki Tavo, 8 September 1979

Since the month of Elul is traditionally a time of preparation for the penitential season, let us consider the meaning of repentance by looking at a startling passage. It is a Midrash, or Bible interpretation, which occurs three times in Rabbinic Literature: in the Yerushalmi, in the Pesikta and in the Yalkut.

Yerushalmi is the popular name of the Palestinian Talmud, even though it wasn't really compiled in Jerusalem, but in places like Tiberias, in the fourth century. Like the bigger and better known Babylonian Talmud, it is chiefly concerned with law, but often digresses into theology and all sorts of other subjects.

One of its tractates is called Makkot, which means 'corporal punishment', but deals with a variety of crimes less serious than murder, including manslaughter. Now, primitive societies didn't distinguish between murder and manslaughter. If you had killed somebody, whether or not you intended to do so, then the nearest kinsman of your victim had the right to avenge his death by killing you in return. But Judaism, even as early as in biblical times, was too humane to go along with that. Therefore it provided cities of refuge to which the unintentional homicide could escape, safe from the avenger. But by the time of the Rabbis, these cities of refuge had long ceased to exist, and therefore they could only speculate how the system worked.

How, for instance, could the manslayer be sure of getting to the city of refuge in time, ahead of the avenger? After all, he would be in a pretty agitated state of mind and might lose his way. The answer, say the Rabbis, is that there were signposts all along the route.

But the signposts to the cities of refuge were erected by divine command. God, so to speak, showed the manslayer the way. And if you knew the Bible inside out, as the Rabbis did, this notion would immediately connect in your mind with a verse in the 25th Psalm which reads: 'Good and just is the Eternal One; therefore God shows sinners the way' (v. 8). Accordingly, what follows in the Yerushalmi is an interpretation of that verse (J. Makkot 2:6).

The Pesikta d'Rav Kahana gets to the same point by a different route. It is a homiletical Midrash, that is, a collection of Bible interpretations which were commonly used in preaching, arranged in sections ('pesikta' means 'section'), one for every sabbath of the year and one or more for every festival, and was compiled in Palestine in the fifth century. One of the sections, Number 24, is devoted to Shabbat Shuvah, the Sabbath of Repentance. Therefore it comments on some of the key passages in the Bible relevant to the theme of repentance, and one of these is the verse from the 25th Psalm: 'Good and just is the Eternal One; therefore God shows sinners the way' (Pesikta d'Rav Kahana 24:7).

The Yalkut Shim'oni is an exegetical Midrash. That is to say, it is a verse-by-verse interpretation of the Bible, from Genesis to Ecclesiastes. It was compiled in Frankfurt, Germany, in the thirteenth century, but is a collection of Bible interpretations – *yalkut* means 'collection' – from much earlier sources. And when it gets to the 25th Psalm it cites the same interpretation as the Yerushalmi and the Pesikta (Yalkut to Psalm 25:8). Therefore all three get to the same point by quite different routes: the Yerushalmi *via* the law of manslaughter, the Pesikta *via* a sermon for the Sabbath of Repentance, the Yalkut *via* the verse-by-verse interpretation of Psalm 25.

Now, however, let us look at the interpretation itself. The Psalm verse begins: 'טוב וישר ה 'Good and just is the Eternal One'. On this phrase our Midrash comments: 'God is just because God is good, and God is good because God is just'. Let us pause to consider what that means. Because God is a Moral Being, therefore God must be just. But justice by itself would seem to demand that whoever has committed a sin must pay in full the appropriate penalty. For instance, if you have killed somebody, then you must forfeit your own life. But in a deeper sense, that isn't really just, since you may have acted unintentionally. And because God is just in this deeper sense, therefore God is also good, that is to say, compassionate. In other words, justice and mercy, which so often conflict on the human level, co-exist in God's ways in perfect harmony.

Then all three sources continue as follows. 'Wisdom was asked: "What is the sinner's punishment?" And Wisdom answered, quoting from the book of Proverbs (13:21): "Misfortune pursues sinners".' Now 'Wisdom' – in Hebrew *chochmah* – is a kind of common-sense philosophy which flourished among Jews towards the end of the pre-Christian era, especially under Greek influence, and which, though not anti-religious, existed more or less independently of the official religion. It is represented in the Bible by books such as Proverbs and Ecclesiastes and in the Apocrypha by books such as Ben Sira or Ecclesiasticus. Its spirit is therefore what we would call 'secular'. From that point of view, the important thing about sin is that it gets you into trouble – with the authorities, or with the person you have offended, or perhaps with the forces of nature. It is not in your best interest; it is not expedient; 'crime doesn't pay'. Of course we all know that it doesn't always work that way. Nevertheless, as a general rule and in the long run, I suppose it would be true to say that evil deeds tend to produce unpleasant consequences for the doer as well as the done-by, and that sin is therefore an offence against yourself. At any rate, that is one point of view.

But our Midrash continues: 'Then Prophecy was asked: "What is the sinner's punishment?" And Prophecy answered, in the words of Ezekiel (18:4): "The soul that sins shall die".' The point here is that sin is not merely an offence against yourself, or even against society:

it is an offence against God, who has taught you the correct way to
behave, and given you the ability to do so. But any offence against
God is a kind of treason, unpardonable and deserving of the ultimate
penalty, death. That is the logic of a certain kind of theology; but it
is not the view ultimately taken by Judaism.

At this point the Pesikta and the Yalkut, though not the Yerushalmi,
introduce another and even more daring element into the argument.
'Then the Torah itself was asked, "What is the sinner's punishment?"
And the Torah, referring to the book of Leviticus (5:6), answered:
"Let them bring a guilt offering, and they will be forgiven".' That is to
say, strictly speaking the sinner deserves death. But since no human
being is wholly righteous, and since therefore the conclusion of that
logic would be the destruction of all humanity, God has therefore
provided a means of escape from that dilemma in the form of the sacrificial cult: God will accept the guilt-offering instead.

Of course, by the time of the Pesikta and the Yalkut the Temple
had long ceased to exist, and therefore the answer of the Torah was
no longer adequate either. So we have had three opinions, all of
which are, in one sense or another, rejected, and in an ascending
order of authority: first from the Hagiographa, then from the
Prophets, and finally from the Torah itself. That is what is so daring
about this Midrash.

What, however, is the true answer? Christianity accepts the logic
underlying the sacrificial cult, that, since sin is an offence against
God, therefore its expiation requires a sacrifice. But whereas Judaism
had taught that God, being merciful, was content with a mere token
offering, in the form of an animal sacrifice, Christianity demanded
nothing less than the self-sacrifice of a superhuman, indeed divine,
being. Only this was of sufficient magnitude to atone for the immen-
sity of human sinfulness.

But such was never a Jewish view. Instead, our Midrash, according to all three sources, concludes as follows. 'Finally, the Holy
One, ever to be blessed, was asked: "What is the sinner's punishment?" And God replied quite simply: יעשה תשובה ויתכפר לו, "Let him
repent, and he will be forgiven", as it is written in the 25th Psalm,
על כן יורה חטאים בדרך, "Therefore God shows sinners the way".'

To understand this fully, we must remember that the word 'therefore' follows immediately on from the statement, טוב וישר ה', 'Good
and just is the Eternal One'. God is not only just; God is also good,
which is taken to mean kind, generous and merciful. Therefore God
does not exact the full penalty, does not demand the death of the sinner. God doesn't even insist on a token offering, such as was provided for in the sacrificial cult. All God requires is *t'shuvah*, which,

though usually translated 'repentance', really means 'return'. In other words, we merely have to make an effort to return to the right path. And if it be objected that our effort may be insufficient, the answer is that, in response to such an effort, however feeble, God provides the help we need. 'God shows sinners the way'. Just as God gave instructions for the erection of signposts to enable the manslayer to find his way to the city of refuge, so God has given all human beings signposts enabling them to find their way back to God. And just as it was a great step forward when Judaism distinguished between wilful and accidental homicide, so it was a great step forward when it transferred its emphasis from the God of Justice to the God of Mercy, and from outward acts of atonement to that inner re-direction of mind and will which we call *t'shuvah*.

As the penitential season approaches, it is up to us to make that initial effort, and then to look out for the signposts which may guide us further along the way. Then our initial effort will be sustained by a power greater than our own, and gain in momentum. For the essence of the Jewish conception of repentance, expressed so dramatically in our Midrash, is that God is not only or even primarily the Power that seeks to punish; God is, rather, the Power that seeks to guide, to help, to heal and to redeem.

❖   ❖   ❖

The Stranger Who Lives Among You
Shabbat Ki Tavo, 19 September 1992

Our Torah portion describes in graphic detail one of the prettiest ceremonies of ancient Israel: the bringing of the firstfruits to the Temple in Jerusalem as an act of thanksgiving for the land and its produce. It is described in even greater detail in the Mishnah, which devotes a whole tractate to it.

So pretty is the ceremony that it seems a pity that it is no longer practised, except for some modern, secular versions in the State of Israel. But the Rabbis took the view that it applied only to the land of Israel, and only as long as the Temple existed, and so it came to an end nearly two thousand years ago. Already the Mishnah, therefore, relied on orally transmitted recollections of how it used to be done.

What relevance, then, does it have for us? There are, I think, two points worth making about that: the one obvious, the other not so obvious.

The obvious point is that, although, by tradition, the ceremony itself is no longer observed, the *spirit* of it can be, and should be. For what is that spirit? It is grateful appreciation of the bounty of the land. But the bounty of nature is not confined to the land of Israel; it is universal; and it is therefore right that we should give thanks for it wherever we live, as we do especially on our harvest festivals. And our gratitude should give rise to a sense of responsibility for the earth as a whole and especially towards those of its inhabitants who do not share our good fortune.

That point is emphasised already in our Torah portion when it says, 'You shall rejoice in all the bounty which the Eternal One, your God, has given you – you, and the Levite, והגר אשר בקרבך, and the stranger who lives among you' (Deut. 26:11). It is reinforced by the general principle laid down by the Rabbis that the way to compensate for our inability to take offerings to the Temple is through צדקה, *giving* to those in need.

That, then, is the obvious point. The not-so-obvious one relates to the same word *ger* which in biblical times meant 'stranger' but which the Rabbis used in the sense of 'proselyte'. Once you take it in that sense, the question arises as to whether proselytes were included in the ceremony of the firstfruits, and the answer is yes because the Bible says so.

But then a further question arises: did they perform the whole of the ritual in exactly the same way as born Jews? Of course, you might think. Why should there be any doubt about it? Because the bringer of the firstfruits was required to make a formal declaration, which began: 'I declare this day before the Eternal One, your God, that I have come into the land אשר נשבע ה' לאבותינו לתת לנו, which God promised our ancestors to give us' (Deut. 26:3). And how could a proselyte say that?

From a literalistic point of view he couldn't, and that is the view taken by the Mishnah, which states categorically: הגר מביא ואינו קורא, 'A proselyte brings the firstfruits but does not recite the declaration' (Bik. 1:4). But that is not the end of the story.

You have to know that an opinion stated anonymously in the Mishnah is generally taken to represent the opinion of Rabbi Meir, who lived in the second half of the second century, and is generally taken as authoritative. But in this case we have a contrary opinion in a Baraita, literally an 'external teaching', that is to say, a tradition from the same period as the Mishnah but for some reason not included in it. This Baraita, which occurs in the so-called Yerushalmi or Palestinian Talmud, gives the opinion of Rabbi Judah ben Ilai, a contemporary of Rabbi Meir, who is quoted as saying הגר עצמו מביא וקורא,

'A proselyte himself both brings the firstfruits and recites the declaration' (Bik. 1:4).

So here we have a flat contradiction between two contemporary authorities of the second century, both of the greatest eminence. How does one resolve such a conflict? The answer would normally be: with difficulty. But in this case the Yerushalmi makes it easy for us by citing a third authority, the great Rabbi Joshua ben Levi, who lived two generations later and said: הלכה כרבי יהודה, 'the law is in accordance with Rabbi Judah' (Bik., end of chapter 1).

So that settles the issue: a proselyte does recite the declaration! But how can that be? How can he refer to the land 'which God promised our ancestors to give us'? Naturally, the Yerushalmi discusses this question and comes up with a very interesting answer. In the book of Genesis, Abraham's name is explained by a play on words, when God says to him, כי אב גוים נתתיך, 'for I have made you the ancestor of a multitude of nations' (17:5). And on that basis, says the Yerushalmi in justifying Rabbi Judah's view, proselytes too may claim Abraham as their ancestor.

The whole question arose again a thousand years later when a learned and conscientious proselyte of the name of Obadiah wrote a letter to Moses Maimonides in Cairo, asking him, not about the ceremony of the firstfruits, which was not a live issue, but whether in his prayers *generally* he should use expressions such as 'the God of our ancestors, who brought us out of Egypt', and the like, or whether he should modify them in some way.

In his reply, which is one of the gems of medieval Jewish literature, Maimonides is unequivocal: his inquirer, Obadiah, should say all these things, and not change a single word. He quotes the Genesis verse in which God says of Abraham, 'I know him, that he will instruct his children *and his household* after him to keep the way of God' (Gen. 18:19). Then he continues: 'Therefore, every one to the end of all generations who becomes a proselyte and declares the unity of God ... is a disciple of Abraham ... and all are members of his household ... There is no difference at all between us and you in any matter'.

Furthermore, Maimonides goes on to say, 'Do not esteem your pedigree lightly. For if we, who are born Jews, trace our ancestry to Abraham, Isaac and Jacob, your pedigree goes back to the One who created the world, for so it says explicitly in Isaiah (44:5): "One will say, I am God's, and another will call himself by the name of Jacob"'. (Maimonides takes the Isaiah verse to refer to two categories, proselytes and born Jews, and infers from it that of the two, it is the proselytes who have the higher pedigree).

He then discusses the Mishnah passage about the bringing of the firstfruits, which, as we have seen, represents the opinion of Rabbi Meir, and proves from the Yerushalmi passage that it is to be rejected in favour of the more universalistic view of Rabbi Judah that proselytes *do* recite the declaration, and he concludes: 'Thus it has been demonstrated that you must say, "which God promised our ancestors to give us", since Abraham is your ancestor as well as ours. And the same applies to all the other benedictions and prayers: do not change any of them at all'.

And so what seems at first a merely technical question about the position of proselytes with respect to an ancient and long discontinued ritual, broadens out, especially in Maimonides' treatment, into a question about the very nature of the Jewish community. Are we a closed society or an open society? The ancient Rabbis were very clear about that. 'The gates are open at all times', they said, 'and whoever wishes to enter may enter' (Exod.R. 19:4).

For historical reasons, and especially the hostility of medieval Christendom, that generously welcoming attitude was not always maintained. The gates remained open, but more in theory than in practice. In modern Orthodox Judaism they are heavily guarded, and only the most persistent get through them. And even Reform Judaism in this country used to pride itself on the stringency of its 'immigration policy'. For many years its most popular self-definition was a pamphlet by Rabbi André Ungar entitled *Judaism for our Time*. It was first published in 1958 and republished in 1968 and 1973. In it the author wrote: 'In general, our attitude to would-be proselytes to Judaism is one of discouragement' (p. 22). That attitude contrasted sharply with ours. In the very same year of 1958 in which the Reform movement published André Ungar's pamphlet, the Liberal movement published a booklet of mine, on *The Practices of Liberal Judaism*, in which I wrote: 'The general policy of Liberal Judaism is to welcome proselytes' (p. 53). In more recent times, though, the Reform movement has come round to our view, and in its most recent book of self-definition, *Faith and Practice*, published in 1991, the author, Rabbi Jonathan Romain, writes, 'The Reform policy is to return to the more welcoming attitude of the *Talmud*' (p. 177).

Our position is clear. Jewish society is a truly open society. We will not, of course, use any kind of pressure or persuasion to induce others to join us. That would be reprehensible. But those who *choose* to join us are welcome. They are honoured, and even *especially* honoured, members of our household.

❖   ❖   ❖

Good God?

Shabbat Ha'azinu, 10 October 1992

הצור תמים פעלו, כי כל־דרכיו משפט, אל אמונה ואין עול צדיק וישר הוא, 'The work of the Rock is perfect; for all God's ways are justice; a God of faithfulness and without iniquity, just and right is God' (Deut. 32:4). In this verse we recognise the traditional conception of God as being all-powerful, all-wise and all-good.

In recent years that view has been challenged in at least one respect. Some theologians have questioned whether, after the Holocaust, it is still possible to believe that God is all-powerful, for in that case, they say, God should surely have intervened to stop it. Therefore they have put forward the extraordinary idea that perhaps God is, like the universe, still in process of becoming, and therefore *not yet* all-powerful.

I have never been convinced by the argument. For we have always known that God doesn't intervene to stop human beings from abusing their free-will, even in the most monstrous way. The whole of history testifies to that, and Jews, as well as Christians and Muslims, have always affirmed God's omnipotence in spite of it. They have simply taken the view that, for whatever reason, God chooses not to exercise a power to intervene which the Creator of the universe undoubtedly possesses.

But what about the other horn of the dilemma, namely God's wisdom and goodness? Can we still cling to that? So far nobody, or practically nobody, has questioned it, presumably because a God lacking these qualities would not be worthy of worship. Nevertheless, it is an intriguing question whether these aspects of God's nature have ever been questioned in Jewish tradition. Two passages come to mind which *seem* to do just that.

The first is so well known that I will mention it only briefly. It is a story in the Talmud about two rabbis, Joshua and Eliezer, who debate a point of law. Joshua, supported by all his colleagues, takes the common-sense view, but Eliezer, in a minority of one, disagrees. After putting forward every possible rational argument – reinforced, for good measure, by a few miracles – Eliezer appeals to the highest authority, God, whereupon a *Bat Kol*, a Heavenly Voice, is heard to say to Joshua and his colleagues: 'What do you mean by arguing with Rabbi Eliezer? Surely you know that the Halachah [the authoritative ruling] is always in agreement with his views!' Then Rabbi Joshua produces his punch-line, לא בשמים היא, that the Torah 'is not in heaven' (Deut. 30:12), and thereby wins the argument. And how did

God react to that? God laughed, the Talmud tells us, and said: 'My children have defeated Me!' (BM 59b).

The question which this passage raises is of course: how is it possible for human beings to win an argument against God? How can human wisdom ever be superior to divine wisdom? But let us for the moment leave that question hanging in the air, and turn to the other, less well known passage.

It occurs in the Midrash (Num.R. 19:33) and makes the astonishing point that on three occasions God was taught a lesson by Moses. The first occurred when God was about to punish the Israelites for the sin of worshipping the Golden Calf. But Moses, like a brilliant defence lawyer, gets them off, so to speak, on a technicality. He points out that the Ten Commandments begin אנכי ה' אלהיך, 'I am the Eternal One, your God', in the singular, not אלהיכם, 'your God' in the plural. Therefore the Israelites could reasonably argue that the prohibition, 'you shall have no other gods before Me', applied only to Moses, not to them. God concedes the point, saying למדתני, 'you have taught Me something'.

The second instance relates to the difficult phrase, also in the Second Commandment, פוקד עון אבות על בנים, that God 'visits the iniquity of the parents on their children'. Moses objects: 'Surely many wicked people have had righteous children!'. Again God concedes the point and says למדתני, 'you have taught me something'. Indeed, God goes on to say: 'By your life, I will annul My words and uphold your words', and proceeds to formulate the general principle, which is to be found in the twenty-fourth chapter of Deuteronomy, that 'parents shall not be put to death for their children, and children shall not be put to death for their parents' (v. 16).

The third instance relates to another discrepancy. In the second chapter of Deuteronomy Moses recalls how, after Sinai, God had commanded the Israelites to go and fight against Sihon, king of the Amorites (v. 24), but how, in the event, he, Moses, had in the first instance sent messengers with דברי שלום, 'words of peace' (v. 26). Once again, God decides that Moses is right, and therefore lays it down as a general principle that, as it says in the twentieth chapter of Deuteronomy, 'When you approach a city in order to fight against it, וקראת אליה שלום, you shall first offer it peace' (v. 10), or, as we might say, you shall always seek a political solution to any conflict before resorting to a military one.

Now the question is, how shall we understand this extraordinary Midrash? Did the Rabbis who constructed it really believe that Moses, on some occasions, knew better than God? And if so, how shocking! But you have to understand the Rabbinic mind. The Rabbis were not poker-faced literalists. To them the interpretation of Scripture was, among other things, an intellectual game, and one which they played with a sense of fun and humour. And if you ask, how could they joke about such matters as God's wisdom and goodness, the answer is: precisely because they were so secure in their conviction that God is all-wise and all-good, and so sure, too, that those to whom they addressed themselves shared that conviction and would therefore recognise a tongue-in-cheek interpretation for what it is.

But though the Midrash is therefore not to be taken in dead-pan earnest, the discrepancies in Scripture to which it points are real enough. Therefore what the Rabbis, in this passage and a few others like it, stumbled upon, though they did not perhaps fully appreciate its significance, or feel free to spell it out, is something we take for granted: that the Bible is the record of a *developing* religion in which there are various strata. It isn't that God says one thing and Moses another. It is that the Bible preserves different stages in the efforts of our Israelite ancestors to understand the unchanging truth about the nature and will of the one-and-only God.

And now that we have established that, let us go back to the talmudic story. On the face of it, God says through the *bat kol*, that Rabbi Eliezer is right but concedes defeat when Rabbi Joshua produces his knock-out argument that the Torah is not in heaven. What are we to make of that? The answer, surely, is perfectly clear. What the *bat kol* says is not what God seriously means. It is, rather, a test! The purpose of the test is to establish whether the Rabbis have grasped the fact that the age of revelation is over and that henceforth the way forward for them is not to look for supernatural oracles but to apply their God-given intelligence to the interpretation of the texts and traditions already available to them and, when all else fails, to decide disputed issues by democratic majority vote. Have the Rabbis attained that degree of maturity? God hopes they have, and by challenging the *bat kol* they prove it. They pass the test. That is why God *laughs* and says, with tongue-in-cheek delight, 'My children have defeated Me'.

Finally, let us return to the theme with which we began. There is nothing in the passages we have looked at, or others like them, properly understood, to suggest that our ancestors ever seriously doubted that God is all-powerful, all-wise and all-good. Nor, I submit, do *we* have any compelling reason to do so. For nothing fundamental has changed. Evil, even on a horrendous scale, has always been a feature of human life on this planet, and our ancestors affirmed their belief in God's perfection, not in ignorance, but in full knowledge of it.

And sometimes I wonder whether our quick readiness to question it is not a projection onto God of our own shortcomings.

Admittedly, there are evils, such as natural disasters and the fact that animals prey on one another, for which we humans are not responsible. They constitute a huge problem, and nobody pretends to have a satisfactory explanation of it. Nevertheless we should consider how wonderful life on earth could be if we hadn't messed it up! There is, after all, no need for crime or war or famine or poverty or unemployment or global warming or environmental pollution; these things are our doing, not God's. There is no need to waste a vast proportion of our resources on the production of armaments. The wealth which the earth contains, responsibly harvested and fairly distributed, is amply sufficient to enable the entire human population to enjoy a standard of living which most of them can't even dream of. Shall we then blame God for our deficiencies?

There is a verse which is very relevant here. It follows on from the one I quoted earlier: 'The work of the Rock is perfect; for all God's ways are justice; a God of faithfulness and without iniquity, just and right is God'. For then it continues: שחת לו לא בניו מומם, דור עקש ופתלתל, 'Is corruption God's? No; God's children's is the blemish; a generation crooked and perverse' (Deut. 32:4f).

God is not lacking in power, wisdom or goodness. It is we who are lacking in readiness to do God's will. It is *our* goodness that needs to be questioned, not God's. We may still sing: הודו לה' כי טוב, 'Let us give thanks, for God is good' (Psalm 118:1).

❖   ❖   ❖

Sword or Book
Shabbat R'eh, 25 April 1984

Choose! That is what Moses says to the people. Choose between obedience and disobedience, between the God of Israel and the Baalim, between Hebraism and Paganism, between good and evil, between right and wrong, between blessing and curse, between the green pastures of Mount Gerizim and the bleak barrenness of Mount Ebal, between life and death. In other words: do God's will, and all will be well; don't, and there'll be disaster.

There *is* a law of retribution, but it doesn't mean that individuals necessarily get what they deserve – that the good are always rewarded and the bad always punished – but that every one of us, by the choices we make, helps to determine what will ultimately happen to the nation; and in view of the interdependence of the nations of which we are so much more conscious than our ancestors were, we must add: what will ultimately happen to humanity as a whole.

The prophet Isaiah made the same point when he said: 'If you are willing and obedient, you shall eat the good of the land; but if you refuse and rebel, you shall be devoured by the sword' (1:19f). And on that verse we have an interesting Rabbinic comment, or rather two.

The first, by Rabbi Akiva's pupil Shim'on ben Yochai, concentrates on the phrase, 'you shall eat the good of the land', and says: 'A loaf and a rod came down from heaven wrapped together' whereupon, the passage continues, God said to the Israelites: 'If you will observe the Torah, here is bread for you to eat; and if not, here is a rod to beat you with' (Sifre Deut. 40; ed. Finkelstein, p. 81f).

The other comment, by Rabbi Eleazar of Modiin, fastens on Isaiah's phrase, 'you shall be devoured by the sword', and says: 'A book and a sword came down from heaven wrapped together, and God said to the people: If you observe the Torah which is written in this book, you will be saved from the sword; if not, it will finish up by devouring you' (*ibid.*, Lev.R. 35:6, Deut.R. 4:2).

What do we know about this Rabbi Eleazar? Not a great deal. But we do know that he was a contemporary of Rabbi Akiva and lived through the Bar-Kochba Revolt, the war against the Romans which that would-be Messiah launched so recklessly, and with such catastrophic consequences for the Jewish people. Indeed, the Talmud tells a story about him in that connection. During the long siege of Betar, which was Bar-Kochba's last stronghold, Rabbi Eleazar wore sackcloth, and fasted, and prayed daily that God might avert the impending disaster. It seems, therefore, that he was not very enthusiastic about the war or confident about its outcome. Perhaps, like Rabbi Yochanan ben Zakkai in the previous war against Rome sixty years earlier, he had been all along an advocate of non-violence. Certainly, that would not be surprising in view of his teaching about the choice between the book and the sword. If so, it would not necessarily follow that he thought that at this late stage, during the siege of Betar, the Jews should simply surrender to the Romans. But an ill-wisher, so the story continues, gave Bar-Kochba a hint to that effect, whereupon he, Bar-Kochba, flew into a rage, ordered Rabbi Eleazar to be brought before him, and kicked him to death.

It is obvious who is the hero of this story, and who the villain, from the point of view of the Rabbis who told it. But to remove any doubt, the story ends with the information that immediately a *bat kol* (Heavenly Voice) was heard to say, quoting from the prophet

Zechariah, 'Woe to my worthless shepherd, who deserts the flock! May the sword smite his arm and his right eye!' (11:17). And immediately after that, the story ends, Betar was captured and Bar Kochba slain (J. Taan. 4, 68d, Lam.R. 2, 2, 4).

But back to Rabbi Eleazar's image of the sword and the book. Does that ring a bell in your mind, especially the sword? Well, it might remind you of the strange story at the end of the third chapter of Genesis, of how God drove Adam and Eve out of the Garden of Eden and placed at its entrance 'the flaming light of a revolving sword, to guard the way to the tree of life' (v. 24). Whatever the precise meaning of that story may be, you have there the same juxtaposition, on the one hand the sword, on the other hand *etz chayyim*, the 'tree of life', which Jewish tradition identifies with the Torah on the basis of the Proverbs text, 'It is a tree of life to those who hold it fast, and those who cling to it are rendered happy. Its ways are ways of pleasantness, and all its paths are peace' (3:18, 17). And indeed, in one version of Rabbi Eleazar's parable it is given as an interpretation of the Genesis passage rather than the Isaiah one.

Another bell which the image of the sword might have rung in your mind is the sword of Damocles. He was a servant of Dionysius, king of Syracuse around 400 BCE, and the legend is that when the king heard that Damocles was speaking too glibly about his – the king's – good fortune, he invited him to a banquet and made him sit beneath a naked sword that was suspended from the ceiling by a single thread. It was the king's way of demonstrating how precarious is human life, especially for a king.

But notice the fundamental difference between the Greek legend and the Rabbinic Midrash. The Midrash doesn't say that the future is unpredictable, that fate is an unfathomable mystery, that anything can happen at any time. On the contrary, it says that history is governed by a moral law of cause and effect which is perfectly understandable, and that by recognising it, and acting accordingly, we can influence the future favourably. The sword doesn't hang by a single thread. It isn't liable to come crashing down on us at any minute, regardless of what we do. We can grasp the Torah, and build on it an enduring civilisation. The choice is ours.

❖   ❖   ❖

Part Two

❖   ❖   ❖

SEASONS OF THE JEWISH YEAR

Season of Freedom

The Fifth Cup
Pesach, 7 April 1974

Of the many fascinating customs of the Seder, perhaps the most intriguing is the Cup of Elijah; that is, to set on the Seder table, in a prominent position, a particularly beautiful silver goblet, and to fill it to the brim with wine, but not to drink from it.

The earliest reference to this custom is in a commentary on the Shulchan Aruch by Jacob Reischer, who was born in Prague about 1670 and died at Metz in 1733. Reischer says that 'in these regions', meaning Central Europe, it is customary to pour out a cup for Elijah in allusion to a statement in the Talmud (RH 11b) that 'in the month of Nisan the Israelites *were* redeemed, and in the month of Nisan they *will be* redeemed' (to Orach Chayyim 480, note 6). The extra cup is therefore a symbol of the hope for the redemption of the future, as is indeed implied by its association with Elijah, who, in Jewish folklore, is the harbinger of the Messiah.

A slightly different interpretation was given by Elijah's namesake, the Vilna Gaon, who died in 1797. According to him, the extra cup is poured out, but not drunk, on account of an ancient dispute as to the number of cups that should be drunk during the Seder, whether it is four or five, and it is called the Cup of Elijah because, according to Rabbinic tradition, all unresolved questions of Jewish Law will ultimately be resolved by Elijah (E.D. Goldschmidt, *Die Pessach-Haggada*, p. 25, footnote).

If the Vilna Gaon is right, we must go back to the origins of the dispute in question. The Mishnah says that one who celebrates the Seder should not drink less than four cups of wine (Pes. 10:1). This would suggest that it is permissible to drink more, but that there is no need to do so. There was, however, one rabbi in second-century Palestine who believed that one *should* drink a fifth cup. His name was Tarfon, and we must ask ourselves what his reason might have been.

In the Ethics of the Fathers Tarfon is quoted as the author of two famous statements. The first is: 'The day is short and the task is great and the labourers are idle and the reward is great and the Master of the House is urgent.' The second is: 'It is not required of you to complete the work, but neither are you free to desist from it' (Avot 2:15f). Both these sayings reveal Rabbi Tarfon as an *activist*. He was not one of those who sit back and say 'God will provide'. He believed that human beings must take the initiative, that they must give God a helping hand in bringing nearer the time of redemption. That is clue number one.

The second clue is that Tarfon was a very close friend of Rabbi Akiva who, in turn, was the leading supporter of the Bar-Kochba Rebellion. Moreover, both of them are mentioned in the famous story in the Haggadah about the five rabbis who celebrated the Seder at B'ne B'rak and discussed the Exodus from Egypt all through the night, until a disciple had to remind them that it was time to recite the morning Shema. Now it has been conjectured that these five rabbis were not really debating only the Exodus from Egypt but rather a new deliverance, this time from Rome; that they were in fact planning the Bar-Kochba Rebellion; and that this is what took them so long.

A third clue is to be found in the very passage in the Talmud which mentions the Fifth Cup, for it tells us that Rabbi Tarfon wanted it to be drunk in connection with the recitation of the so-called 'Great Hallel', that is Psalm 136, which the Rabbis regarded as a messianic psalm.

Yet another clue may be found in one of the explanations of the Four Cups, which occurs for the first time in the Palestinian Talmud (Pes. 10:1), namely that they refer to the four 'redemptions' mentioned in the sixth chapter of Exodus, 'I will *release* you from your labours in Egypt, and I will *deliver* you from your enslavement there, and I will *redeem* you with an outstretched arm and with mighty acts of judgment, and I will *adopt* you as My people' (vv. 6f). But if the four verbs in that passage correspond to the four cups, it must surely have been noticed by the Rabbis that there is a fifth verb in the next verse, which says, 'And I will *bring* you into the land which I solemnly promised to give to Abraham, Isaac and Jacob.' Perhaps, therefore, Rabbi Tarfon favoured a fifth cup as a symbol of the final act of the drama of redemption: the entry into the Promised Land.

There is also another possibility. According to an ancient Midrash (Gen.R. 88:5), the Four Cups allude to the four world empires that oppressed Israel: Babylon, Persia, Greece and Rome. If so, what could be the significance of the Fifth Cup? Surely it must refer to

Gog and Magog, the final enemy who, according to Jewish mythology, must be vanquished before the Messianic Age can begin. And just that was suggested by a German scholar of the twelfth century, Rabbi Joel ha-Levi (Menachem M. Kasher, *Haggadah Sh'lemah*, p. 95).

From all these clues we may safely assume that Rabbi Tarfon advocated a fifth cup as a symbol of the final redemption which he regarded as imminent. But the majority of his colleagues didn't agree with him, and the disagreement was left unresolved. Because of the doubt, the Fifth Cup became associated with Elijah, who would ultimately settle the issue. And for the same reason it was considered optional. Maimonides, for instance, wrote in his Mishneh Torah: 'He should pour out a fifth cup and recite over it the Great Hallel, but this is not obligatory in the same way as the Four Cups' (*Hilchot Chametz u-Matzah* 8:11). Later still it was laid down that after the fourth cup no more wine should be consumed at all, which is what we find in the Shulchan Aruch (O.Ch. 481:1). And finally the compromise as we know it was reached: to pour out a fifth cup, but not to drink from it.

So much for the historical background of the custom. But it has more than historical interest, for the underlying issue is whether the time of redemption has come. What then is redemption? About that there are two views, and to identify them we must conduct another little excursion into history.

The Mishnah lays down a general rule for the recounting of the Exodus at the Seder. The rule is: מתחיל בגנות ומסיים בשבח, that one should begin with shame and end with praise (Pes. 10:4). But what is the 'shame' referred to? About this we find in the Talmud (Pes. 116a) two opinions. The first is attributed to the third-century Babylonian scholar Samuel. Samuel was a wealthy man, the leading authority on civil law, and no doubt prominently involved in governmental affairs. He was the author of a famous statement to the effect that the only difference between the present world and the Messianic Age is שעבוד מלכויות, that in the Messianic Age Israel will no longer be subjugated by foreign powers (Ber. 34b). Not surprisingly, therefore, Samuel saw the 'shame' referred to in the Mishnah also in political terms. The shame consisted in the slavery. Therefore, according to him, the Haggadah should begin: עבדים היינו לפרעה במצרים, 'We were Pharaoh's slaves in Egypt ...'

The other view was held by Samuel's great contemporary and rival, Rav. Rav was a specialist in ritual law, particularly in liturgy, and the reputed author of several prayers which we recite to this day, including the *Aleinu*, or at any rate the second part of it which begins: 'Trusting in You, Eternal God, we hope soon to behold the glory of Your might, when false gods will cease to take Your place in the hearts of men, and the world will be perfected under Your unchallenged rule.' According to Rav, therefore, it is not enough that the oppressive government should be overthrown: the rule of God must be established in the human heart. Redemption is not only external, it is also internal. It is not a political process alone, but a spiritual process. 'Stone walls do not a prison make nor iron bars a cage.' Rav understood the 'shame' of the Mishnah, too, in spiritual terms. Consequently, in his opinion the Haggadah should begin: מתחלה עובדי עבודה זרה היו אבותינו, 'Originally our ancestors were idol worshippers, but now we have been drawn to the worship of the true God ...'

Two apparently conflicting views of the nature of redemption: political and spiritual, external and internal! But here, as with the Fifth Cup, a compromise was reached: *both* passages were to be recited, for redemption, Jewish tradition seems to say, has both these aspects; neither can succeed without the other; we must be redeemed both from the outward slavery of oppression and from the inner slavery of the Evil Inclination; only when both are achieved is the process complete.

Judaism often speaks about redemption, and never more passionately than at Pesach. But the redemption of which it speaks is not an accomplished fact. The Feast of Pesach looks back into history, of course. It says to us: 'Remember this day on which you came out of Egypt' (Exod. 13:2). But the Exodus from Egypt is regarded only as a prototype of a much greater redemption which, when it occurs, will throw the Exodus into the shade. 'Remember not the former things, nor consider the things of old; for behold, I will do a new thing' (Isa. 43:18f). Pesach recalls the past, but only in order to direct our minds to the future, to the time of the ultimate redemption, both in Samuel's sense, of deliverance from external oppression, and in Rav's sense, of liberation from the evil within.

But that time is not yet. The longing for it is expressed in the refrain of an ancient Seder song: במהרה בימינו בקרוב, 'Speedily, soon, in our days.' But a hope is not a fact, and we are not allowed to pretend that it is. In the words of Ignaz Maybaum, 'Jewish messianism is this ardent prayer, "'Soon, in our days", but remains undeceived in the face of historic episodes with the semblance of eternity. Here, Jews say again and again: "Not yet."' (*Jewish Existence*, p. 158)

This 'not yet' is what the Cup of Elijah symbolises. It stands there, on the Seder table, as a symbol of our longing for the Messianic Age. But we do not drink from it because we know that the hour has not yet struck. The great dogma of Christianity is that the Messiah has already come. The great dogma of Judaism is that the Messiah has not yet come. That is the message of the Fifth Cup.

❖   ❖   ❖

The Mystery of the *Afikoman*
Pesach, 18 April 1979

The Passover Haggadah is an inexhaustible source of sermon subjects. This morning let us investigate the *afikoman.* And since nearly everything in the Seder goes in fours – Four Sons, Four Questions, Four Cups – let me say four things about it, all of which begin with the letter M.

The first is that it is a *mystery.* It is a mystery because throughout the whole of our vast literature the word occurs only once – and, of course, in passages dependent on that one. That one passage is in the Mishnah, which is our second 'M'. The Mishnah is a compendium of oral traditions supplementing the written laws of the Bible. It was compiled in Palestine round about the year 200 of the Common Era, that is, about five generations after the destruction of the Temple. One of its sixty-three tractates deals with the festival of Passover; the last chapter of that tractate gives a detailed, step-by-step description – the oldest we possess – of the Seder; and almost the last sentence of that chapter reads: אין מפטירין אחר הפסח אפיקומן, which means something like: 'After eating the paschal lamb we do not conclude with *afikoman*' – except that the word for 'with' is missing.

The reference to the paschal lamb shows that the passage dates from before the destruction of the Temple, for after that the lamb was no longer eaten. Is it possible then that the compiler of the Mishnah merely repeated an old tradition as he remembered it, and that even he no longer knew exactly what it meant, because so much time had elapsed? And might this account for the omission of the word 'with'? However that may be, we do know that only a generation later the word *afikoman* was a source of genuine puzzlement. For the Talmud asks: מאי אפיקומן, 'What is *afikoman?*' (Pes. 119b) and proceeds to give two opinions in the names of the two leading scholars of Babylonian Jewry in the first half of the third century: Rav and Samuel. According to Rav, the Mishnah means that we may not go מחבורה לחבורה, from one company celebrating the Seder to another. According to Samuel it means that we may not eat additional items of food such as mushrooms and pigeons, or, as others add, dates, parched corn and nuts.

Unfortunately the Talmud does not explain how these interpretations were derived from the word *afikoman*. The first to attempt such an explanation was the twelfth-century French-Jewish commentator and grandson of Rashi, Samuel ben Meir. He suggested that the word *afikoman* might come from the Aramaic *appiku minnaichu*, 'Remove from yourselves'. Accordingly, what the Mishnah forbids us to do at the end of the Seder is to say to the celebrants: 'Remove the dishes, and let us go and eat in another place' (that would explain the view of Rav) or else: 'Remove the dishes, and let them bring in the dessert' (which would explain the view of Samuel).

But ingenious though that interpretation is, it has not been accepted by modern scholars. For they are agreed about one thing at least: that the word *afikoman* is neither Hebrew nor Aramaic but Greek. What they are *not* agreed about is what it means. As to that, there are two main theories. According to one, the word means 'dessert'. That would accord with the opinion of Samuel. According to the other, it means 'revelry'. That would accord with the opinion of Rav if the purpose of going 'from company to company' was to engage in some kind of entertainment.

However, the trouble with both of these theories is that they fail to explain one crucial fact: that the word *afikoman* came to be applied to a piece of Matzah – there is the third of the four 'M's – the one that is broken off, hidden away, and searched for by the children at the end of the meal. Furthermore, it is then *eaten*. In other words, whereas according to the Mishnah, the *afikoman* is something which is *forbidden*, according to the tradition, as it developed, it is actually *enjoined*. On the 'revelry' theory that makes no sense at all. On the 'dessert' theory it can perhaps be explained, as it usually is, by saying that, since it was forbidden to eat a dessert in the ordinary sense, it became customary to eat one final piece of Matzah *in lieu* of a dessert. But it is far from convincing.

Let us suppose, however, that the rule of the Mishnah was not correctly transmitted. That is certainly possible, for we have already seen that there is, in any case, a preposition missing. Let us suppose then, that the original version was: אין מפטירין אחר הפסח אלא אפיקומן, 'After the paschal lamb we do not conclude by eating *anything except afikoman*'. Then the word would have referred all along to what we know it was later taken to mean: a piece of Matzah; and the point would have been that the only thing that may be eaten after the paschal lamb is unleavened bread, because only that was of comparable importance, and therefore only its taste was to linger in the mouth of the celebrant. Indeed, after the destruction of the Temple the unleavened bread became the *principal* food of the Seder.

The only question that remains is: why should this particular piece of Matzah, which is eaten at the end of the Seder, be called *afikoman*? This is where we have to turn to a third theory, not as widely known as the other two. It was first put forward in 1925 by an Austrian Jewish scholar of the name of Robert Eisler – and promptly dismissed by other scholars because they considered him too crazy to be taken seriously. It was resurrected and restated only in 1966, when Professor David Daube gave a lecture on the subject in the crypt of St Paul's Cathedral. The essence of the theory is that the word *afikoman* is the Greek *ephikomenos*, which means 'he that cometh'. On linguistic grounds alone, says Dr Daube, who is a considerable Greek scholar, that is the most natural interpretation. And who is 'he that cometh?' Why, of course the Messiah, providing us with our fourth 'M'.

Why, though, should a broken piece of Matzah symbolise the Messiah? Well, we know that Pesach is a messianic festival. As it commemorates the redemption of our ancestors in the past, so it also looks forward to the still greater redemption yet to come at the end of days. That much is quite clear from the Rabbinic sources, and it gave rise to various rituals expressing the hope for the coming of the messianic age, among them the Fifth Cup or the Cup of Elijah, the proclamation, 'Next year in Jerusalem', and several more.

But why should one of these have become associated with the Matzah in particular? The reason is not far to seek. For bread is a symbol of plenty, and the Messianic Age is a time of plenty. The 136th Psalm, known as 'The Great Hallel', which is recited at the conclusion of the Seder, was probably considered a messianic psalm because it includes the phrase, נותן לחם לכל־בשר, that God 'will give bread to all flesh' (v. 25). The phrase was sometimes fancifully interpreted as referring to the messianic age, when bread will miraculously come up, ready-baked, out of the ground (cf. Psalm 104:14). And expressions such as לחמו של עולם הבא, 'the bread of the world to come' (Gen.R. 82:8) are not unknown in Rabbinic literature.

Let us then assume that during the last decades before the destruction of the Temple, when Roman rule was most bitterly resented and messianic expectation ran particularly high, there grew up among some Palestinian Jews the custom of concluding the Seder by eating a piece of Matzah as a symbol of the expected Messiah. It would have been done at the end of the Seder because it is at this point that the whole celebration reaches its climax and looks to the future.

Of course, such a messianic ritual could not have been openly proclaimed. That would have been too dangerous. It would have invited instant Roman reprisal. Therefore it was given an obscure Greek name, *afikoman*, and only a few, reliable people were initiated into the secret of its true meaning. That may explain, too, why in the story of the Four Children only the *chacham*, the wise one, is to be told all the laws and customs of the Seder, and presumably their meanings, including that of the *afikoman*, the most mysterious of them all. But if it was an esoteric ritual, then it could well be that the upheavals of the Roman War and the Bar Kochba Rebellion caused its meaning to be forgotten, so that already the compiler of the Mishnah recorded it incorrectly, and the next generation of Rabbis could only guess what it meant.

Here then is one possible and plausible explanation of the *afikoman*, and it brings all our four 'M's together, for the Mystery of the Mishnah is explained by the Messianic Matzah.

❖   ❖   ❖

The Paradox of Law and Freedom
Pesach, 25 April 1981

For as from out the house of bondage went
    The host of Israel, in their midst they bore
The heritage of law and freedom, blent
    In holy unity for evermore.

And still from rising unto setting sun
    Shall this our heritage and watchword be:
'The Lord our God, the Lord our God is One,
    And law alone it is that makes us free!'

These words come from a poem by Alice Lucas, sister of Claude Montefiore, and they state a paradox. For we tend to think of law and freedom as opposites – the more law, the less freedom; the more freedom, the less law. Yet the poem asserts not only that they can be 'blent in holy unity' but even that 'law alone ... makes us free'.

The paradox is rooted in the Bible, and more precisely in the story of the Exodus, where more than once Moses says to Pharaoh in God's name: שלח עמי ויעבדוני, 'Let My people go that they may serve Me' (Exod. 7:16, 26; 9:1, 13). Actually, the Hebrew is more startling than the usual translation conveys, for *ya-avduni* comes from the same root as *eved*, 'slave'. The meaning therefore is: let the Israelites cease to be Pharaoh's slaves and become God's slaves instead. Yet this exchange of one slavery for another is the great *liberation* which Pesach celebrates!

The same point is made, more explicitly, in the twenty-fifth chapter of Leviticus, in the context of a provision for the emancipation of Hebrew slaves in the Jubilee, the reason for which is said to be: כי לי בני ישראל עבדים, עבדי הם 'For to Me [God] the children of Israel are servants; they are *My* servants' (Lev. 25:55). On that verse the Talmud comments: עבדי הם, ולא עבדים לעבדים 'They are *My* servants, and not servants to servants' (B.M. 10a). The sense is that to be in bondage to fellow human beings, like Pharaoh, who themselves owe obedience to God, is degrading; but to be in bondage to God is liberating.

We find the same idea in Philo, the Jewish philosopher of first-century Alexandria, who wrote, 'That man alone is free who has God for his leader' (TJQ, 311.41). But it receives particular emphasis in Rabbinic literature, and especially in the Ethics of the Fathers. There we read, for instance: 'Those who take upon themselves the yoke of the Torah, from them shall be taken away the yoke of political oppression and economic hardship; and those who throw off the yoke of the Torah, upon them shall be laid the yoke of political oppression and economic hardship' (3:8).

Better known is a saying, in a chapter appended to the same tractate, by the third-century rabbi, Joshua ben Levi. It is a comment on a verse in the thirty-second chapter of Exodus which refers to the second pair of stone tablets inscribed with the Ten Commandments, the ones Moses received on Mount Sinai after he had broken the first pair, and says: 'The tablets were the work of God, and the writing was the writing of God, *charut al ha-luchot,* engraved upon the tablets' (v. 16). The comment makes one of the famous puns of Rabbinic Literature: 'Read not *charut,* engraved, but *cherut,* freedom, for no-one is free but those who occupy themselves with the study of Torah' (Avot 6:2). That comment, in turn, was expounded by Rabbi Israel Lipschutz of the eighteenth and nineteenth centuries, in his Mishnah commentary, *Tif'eret Yisrael,* as follows: 'For only those who occupy themselves with the study of Torah are not enslaved to materialism, and this is what freedom is: that one's soul is not the slave of bodily desires' (*Tif'eret Yisrael* to Avot 6:2).

The point that emerges, then, is that there are two kinds of liberation: externally, from political oppression, and internally, from bondage to bodily appetites or, more generally, unworthy goals. And which of these does the Exodus from Egypt exemplify? The answer is: *both,* but it is the inner liberation which is our theme this morning.

It is a theme much stressed in the Kabbalah, the tradition of Jewish mysticism, and it is well summed up by Professor Gershom

Scholem: 'The exodus from Egypt, the fundamental event of our history, cannot, according to the mystic, have come to pass once only and in one place; it must correspond to an event which takes place in ourselves, an exodus from an inner Egypt in which we are all slaves' (*Major Trends in Jewish Mysticism, first lecture,* p. 10).

This recognition, that political freedom is not enough, that we also need an inner freedom which is perhaps even harder to attain, and which results from self-submission to God's will, is not, of course, confined to Judaism. There is, for instance, a Christian prayer which refers to God as 'the author of peace and lover of concord, in knowledge of whom standeth our eternal life, *whose service is perfect freedom*'.

So there is a whole chorus of voices proclaiming the same paradox, that freedom is not unrestraint. Without laws, we are liable to become ensnared and enslaved by passions and fashions which, far from enlarging, actually restrict our freedom. If your life is dominated by an irresistible urge to gain more power, more pleasure or more wealth, or if your mind is riddled with prejudice and hatred, you are not truly free. We are so made that we function to the fullest extent of our capabilities only when our life is governed by a set of rules, and only if they are the right rules. Idolatry has a narrowing, diminishing, stultifying effect on those who are seduced by it. Only true religion liberates. Alice Lucas was right. In Judaism, law and freedom are not opposite. They go together, 'blent in holy unity', for 'law alone it is that makes us free'.

❖   ❖   ❖

Rebellion and Redemption
Pesach, 29 March 1983

One of the most intriguing stories of the Haggadah is the one about the all-night Seder: 'It once happened that Rabbi Eliezer, Rabbi Joshua, Rabbi Eleazar ben Azariah, Rabbi Akiva and Rabbi Tarfon were sitting round the Seder table at Bene Berak, and went on discussing the Exodus from Egypt all through the night, until their disciples came and told them: Masters, it is time to recite the morning Shema!'

The most intriguing fact about this story is that it is to be found nowhere else except in the Haggadah: not in the Mishnah or the Talmud or the Midrash or any of the numerous works of the vast Rabbinic Literature which normally delights in telling just that kind of a story. It is first found in Seder Ram Amram, the oldest Jewish prayer book, which dates from the ninth century and includes, for the first time, a complete Haggadah text. Where then did Rav Amram get it from? He would hardly have invented it, so it must have been an oral tradition, transmitted by word of mouth for seven hundred years! Why? Why was it not written down?

Intriguing, too, is the *locale* of the story. B'ne B'rak was a town about five miles east of Jaffa, already mentioned in the Bible (Joshua 19:45). It was also the home of Rabbi Akiva, and it is to be assumed that it was in his house that the all-night Seder took place. It was a house on which the Romans kept a close watch. An ancient Rabbinic source tells us that on one occasion they recited the Shema silently there because there was a *quaestor* – a sort of Roman Gestapo or KGB man – standing outside the door (Tosefta Ber. 2:13).

And why were the Romans so interested in Akiva's house? Presumably because he was a supporter of Bar-Kochba. In fact, it was due to Akiva that he became so known in history. His real name was Bar-Kosba, and his opponents called him Bar-Koseva to imply that he was a liar, a false Messiah; but Akiva called him Bar-Kochba, 'Son of a Star', in allusion to a verse in the book of Numbers which says that 'a star shall come forth out of Jacob' (24:17; J. Taan. 68d). That is to say, he hailed him as the Messiah.

Is it then possible that the five Rabbis of the Haggadah were not, after all, discussing the ancient deliverance from Egyptian bondage but a new deliverance, which had not yet taken place, from Roman rule? In other words, that they were planning the Bar-Kochba Rebellion? Well, perhaps not exactly 'planning', for we know that at least one of the five, Rabbi Joshua, was strongly opposed to any such action. He once said it would be suicidal, like a rooster putting its beak into the mouth of a lion (Gen.R. 64:10). But though the five Rabbis would not have been in agreement about the rebellion, they might very well have been debating the pros and cons of it.

Certainly Seder night would have been an almost irresistible occasion for doing so. For Pesach is the festival of redemption in a double sense: it recalls the deliverance from Egypt, but it also looks forward to the still greater deliverance of פסח לעתיד לבא, the Passover of the future. Several features of its observance have such messianic overtones, among them the four cups of wine.

Why four? The tradition offers various explanations, but one of the oldest says that the four cups allude to the four world empires which must pass away before the messianic age can come (J. Pes. 10:1, Gen.R. 88:5). And which are these empires? Babylon, Persia, Greece and Rome (Louis Ginzberg, *The Legends of the Jews*, Vol. V, p.

223, note 82). Therefore in Roman times the celebration of Pesach, and especially the drinking of the four cups, inevitably focused attention on the hope for the downfall of the Roman empire; and if the Seder of our story took place, say, in the year 132 CE, then it is almost unimaginable that the impending Bar-Kochba Rebellion would *not* have been hotly debated all through the night, particularly in the home of Rabbi Akiva in B'ne B'rak.

If that is what happened, would it explain why the story was transmitted orally and not written down until the ninth century? Yes, it would: partly because, as long as the Romans were in control of Palestine it would have been unsafe to give too much publicity to such stories of plots against the Empire, and partly for another reason which has only become clear to me recently, thanks to the publication of a remarkable book called *The Bar Kokhba Syndrome* by Yehoshafat Harkabi, former head of Israel's Military Intelligence and now Professor of International Relations and Middle Eastern Studies at the Hebrew University of Jerusalem.

What Harkabi points out is that Jewish literature is *generally* silent about the Bar-Kochba Rebellion. Our knowledge of it derives chiefly from Latin sources, and the few references to it in Rabbinic writings are in the main censorious. That is to say, our Jewish tradition, prior to modern times, did not glorify the episode; it tended, rather to deprecate it, and to regard Bar-Kochba as a sinner. It portrays him as having been quick-tempered and arrogant and almost atheistic in his self-aggrandisement and contempt for divine help (pp. 40, 41, 43) and above all as having brought a colossal calamity upon Israel.

According to Harkabi, the Rebellion led to 'the most severe national politico-military disaster in Jewish history, greater than that of the two Temple destructions' (27). He quotes the Roman historian Dio Cassius to the effect that '... 985 villages were laid in ruin. In the raids and battles, 580,000 were killed, and who can count the numbers of those who perished in famine, plague and fire? So Judea became a complete desolation' (45). He also quotes this horrendous account from rabbinic sources, that 'for seven years the people of the world harvested their vineyards without manure as fertilizer but with Jewish blood' and that the Romans 'killed until the blood flowed out of the doorways ... and the horses waded in blood up to the nostrils' (47).

Although that is obviously exaggerated, Harkabi himself estimated that up to ninety percent of the population of Judea may have been wiped out; in other words, the disaster was nearly total (46). Only the Jews of Galilee, because they did not take part in the rebellion, escaped unharmed, and it was there at places like Usha and

Tiberias that Jewish life and learning continued, and Judaism was perpetuated. Again he writes, 'It was an unparalleled disaster, for the situation of the Jews worsened immeasurably thereafter. If the Bar-Kokhba Rebellion came into being because of the Romans' persecutions, these persecutions grew more intense afterward as a result of the uprising. The rebellion aggravated what it sought to alleviate' (63).

No wonder, then, that Judaism tended to suppress the memory of the Bar Kochba Rebellion and that the story of the all-night Seder found no place in Jewish literature until centuries after the Roman period, when it could be innocently tagged on to the passage beginning *Avadim hayinu*, 'We were slaves to Pharaoh in Egypt ...', which ends, 'And whoever lingers over the telling of the story of the Exodus deserves to be praised', so that it seemed merely to illustrate that principle.

As a matter of fact, Judaism made very little of other military episodes, too. What does the Talmud tell us about the Maccabean Rebellion? Only the tale of the miracle of the oil. What does it tell us about the Great Revolt of the first century, ending in the fall of Masada in the year 73? Very little. We know about it only from Josephus. The fact is that normative, classical Judaism had little time for warlike adventures. Which is not to say that it took an altogether pacifist line. It knew that there are times when one must defend oneself, and when one must resist tyranny. But it never believed that anything very positive was gained by war. It never praised the Zealots, for instance. On the contrary, from its point of view the real hero of the Roman War was Yochanan ben Zakkai, who escaped from Jerusalem in a coffin and founded the academy of Yavneh. For it was Yavneh that preserved Judaism, not the War – which nearly destroyed it.

But above all our tradition took a poor view of Bar-Kochba, because he caused so huge a calamity by his rebellion, and because it was entirely unrealistic to suppose that, in the circumstances of the time, it could succeed. It was not only a miscalculation but a case of irresponsible recklessness. And that is what Harkabi means by 'The Bar Kokhba Syndrome'.

Only in modern times has Bar-Kochba become a hero instead of a villain, and that chiefly in Zionist and especially in Revisionist circles. For instance, Jabotinsky wrote a hymn which became the anthem of the Herut Party, proudly invoking Bethar, where Bar-Kochba made his last stand against the Romans, as well as Masada (105). And when I was a teenager in Germany I belonged to a Zionist sports club called Bar-Kochba, without realising at the time what a turning upside down of traditional Jewish values was involved in the choice of that name.

But back to the Haggadah and Pesach. It is indeed *zeman cherutenu,* the season of our freedom, of our liberation; and liberation is, on one level, a political process, and one which may sometimes require the use of force, calling for the soldierly virtues of courage, bravery and heroism. But liberation is never *only* a political process. Political liberation – the overthrow of an oppressor or the attainment of national independence – is sometimes necessary, but it is never sufficient. The all-important question is what you do with your freedom when you have got it, and that is a matter of morality.

A medieval commentary makes that point when it expounds the other ancient explanation of the four cups of the Seder, namely that they refer to the four verbs in the sixth chapter of Exodus about the liberation from Egypt. 'I will *lead* you out', it says, means that our ancestors were released from slavery; 'I will *deliver* you', that they were freed from Egyptian rule; 'I will *redeem* you', that the Egyptians were defeated; 'I will *take* you as My people' that God chose us and gave us the Torah; and this, the Midrash concludes, was the greatest act of redemption, for it affected the *soul* of our people, whereas the other three affected only their bodies (*Sefer ha-Michtam,* q. Menachem Kasher, *Haggadah Sh'lemah,* 90b-91a).

Professor Harkabi makes a further point when he writes, 'In our time, the interdependence of the nations ... produces a situation where one people like the Jews cannot be redeemed in an unredeemed world ... So any final Redemption must be indivisible, comprehensive, and simultaneous ... The redemption of the people Israel is predicated on the redemption of all nations of the world' (149-151).

Finally he remarks: 'We can and must seek ways that lead toward improved forms of social and political life, but redemption is an extra-historical event and the human attempt to make it part of history is doomed to failure' (155).

That is why the rebellion debated during that all-night Seder at B'ne B'rak, if that is what happened there, could not have brought redemption even if it could have succeeded, and many of the sages knew it. One of them said to Rabbi Akiva: 'Grass will grow in your cheeks, and still the son of David will not have come' (J. Taan. 68d).

But the hope persists, and the festival of Pesach renews it powerfully within us. It is ליל שמורים, a night of vigil (Exod. 12:42), when, as an eighteenth-century rabbi expounds the phrase, God and Israel together keep watch and wait for the time of the final redemption (Zevi Elimelech of Dynow, q. in IT, III, p. 104). במהרה בימינו, May it come speedily, in our days.

❖   ❖   ❖

Time
Pesach, 21 April 1984

I have been thinking about time. It isn't a subject I often think about. I don't really have time to think about it, most of the time. But when you do start thinking about it, what a complicated subject it turns out to be! Even if we had all the time in the world, we would never get to the bottom of it. But let me share with you just one or two thoughts about it which have been running through my mind.

I suppose there are basically two kinds of time, though each has innumerable ramifications. One kind is, so to speak, built into the universe. It is 'given' by the sequences of nature: the succession of night and day; the phases of the moon; the alternation of the seasons; the life-cycle from birth to death, and, at an infinitely slower pace, the process of evolution. These things are independent of us. They would go on just the same if we were not around.

But then there is another kind of time which we humans impose on ourselves. To some extent this, too, is governed by what happens in nature. Day and night are determined by the rotation of the earth, anniversaries by its movement round the sun, coming-of-age ceremonies by the life-cycle. But beyond that, it is arbitrary. It is we humans who decide that the day shall be divided into twenty-four hours, that every seventh day shall be a day of rest, that the festivals shall be celebrated on certain fixed dates, that the age of majority shall be what it is, and so forth. And if any proof were needed that these things are human-made, it would be furnished by the fact that they vary from culture to culture.

Let us then speak of natural time and cultural time. They link up at certain points, but are otherwise independent of each other. There is indeed a tendency to root what are really only cultural conventions in the natural order, so as to give them cosmic significance and thus greater authority; and a perfect example of that in our Jewish tradition is the Sabbath. Why do we observe it on the day we do? The Exodus version of the Ten Commandments tells us: because 'in six days God made heaven and earth, the sea, and all that in them is, and rested on the seventh day; wherefore God blessed the sabbath day, and hallowed it'. It is a charming poetic fancy but no more. In nature Saturday is no different from any other day of the week.

Now if the Sabbath is a humanly-fixed though divinely-inspired institution, surely the same applies to the Festivals. Indeed, our tradition admits as much. Take, for instance, the phrase: מועדי ה' אשר תקראו אותם מקראי קדש, 'the appointed seasons of the Eternal One, which you shall proclaim to be holy convocations' (Lev. 23:2). A comment on this in the Talmud suggests that the word *otam*, 'them', should be read *attem*, 'you', which would make the personal pronoun more emphatic, so that the phrase would mean, 'which you *yourselves* shall proclaim' (RH 24a). And the Midrash makes the same point. 'When the ministering angels', it says, 'assemble and ask God "When is Rosh Hashanah, and when is Yom Kippur?" God says to them, "Why do you ask Me? Let us go down together, I and you, to the בית דין של מטה, the terrestrial court"' (Deut. R. 2:14). In other words, authority for the fixation of the Jewish festivals has been delegated by God to the Sanhedrin in Jerusalem. That is a recurring *motif* in our literature, and it is a fanciful way of saying that the sacred calendar is human-made.

It is quite clear, therefore, that cultural time is a pattern we humans superimpose on natural time. For us Jews this time is Pesach. For our Christian neighbours it is Easter. For other communities, I daresay, it has still other meanings. It is all a matter of convention. But to say that is not to belittle it. On the contrary, the time pattern we impose on our lives is a way of filling them with significance.

More specifically, our Jewish calendar does this on three levels. First, as creatures of nature; and it is here that the two time systems link up. Pesach was a shepherds' festival, celebrating the skipping of the new-born lambs, and a farmers' festival, celebrating the first ripening of the barley, before, amalgamated, it became a commemoration of the Exodus; and the old seasonal character of the festival still persists. It lingers on in the green herbs, and in the haunting words of the Song of Songs, 'For lo! the winter is past, the rain is over and gone, the flowers appear on the earth, the time of singing has come, and the song of the dove is heard in our land' (2:11f).

Our calendar is therefore, among other things, a celebration of nature; and that is not unimportant. We are part of nature, and should feel at home in it, appreciate it, and give thanks for it; and there is something stunted about a way of life which neglects that dimension.

The great Hebrew poet Chaim Nachman Bialik felt that way about the life of the East European Yeshivah which he had left behind. In his mammoth poem *Ha-Matmid*, 'The Perpetual Student', he describes it as a sort of prison, where the young boy misses out on that whole aspect of life, barely visible through the narrow window. Here is an extract from the poem, superbly translated by Maurice Samuel:

> Six years, six whole years, that are gone like shadows,
> Six chosen years of youth, for ever gone,
> As if they had not been, as if their flight
> Had passed above all things except this prison,

Had touched all things except the lonely boy,
As if, beyond these walls, the world has ceased,
And all the breathless changes of the world,
The cerements of winter, spring's rebirth -
As if the splendour of the sun, extinguished,
No longer sought a path athwart the branches
Of the old oak creaking at the window pane;
As if night's tenderness and day's delight
Had been forgotten things, and spring had lost
Her immemorial magic everywhere ...

The second dimension of human life which the religious calendar endows with significance and sanctifies is the pilgrimage of the individual from birth through childhood, adulthood, old age, death and perhaps beyond. The third dimension is the life of the community as it travels through the ages of history.

Pesach is the most historical of all our festivals. By every means which Jewish ingenuity has managed to devise – by word and song, by sound and sight and taste – it impresses on us the meaning of history seen as *Heilsgeschichte*, as redemptive history, as a process that leads purposefully towards a culmination when all that is now imperfect will become perfect, 'from bondage to freedom, from sadness to joy, from mourning to celebration, from darkness to light, from servitude to redemption' (ULPS Haggadah, p. 26). 'In every generation we should regard ourselves as if we personally had come out of Egypt' (ibid., p. 22). Thus Judaism, especially at Pesach, spares no effort to make us feel in our very bones the thrust of the forward movement of history towards its messianic goal.

❖   ❖   ❖

Chad Gadya
Pesach, 8 April 1988

The *Chad Gadya* is undoubtedly the most popular of all the Seder songs; it appears in all Ashkenazi Haggadot, and, wonder of wonders, most Jewish families sing it to the same tune, give or take a few notes. But where does it come from, and what does it signify?

The earliest Haggadah that contains it was printed in Prague in 1590. Therefore most of the books, including the *Encyclopaedia Judaica*, tell us that it dates from the sixteenth century. However, it may be quite a bit older than that. In fact, it *must* be if the Polish-born

Israeli scholar Rabbi Menachem Kasher, who died recently in his nineties, is right. In his *Haggadah Sh'lemah* ('The Complete Haggadah') he refers to a manuscript prayer book of the year 1406 which mentions the *Chad Gadya* and says that it was found on a parchment in the academy of the *Rokeach*, which is a pseudonym meaning 'peddler of spices', taken from the title of the principal work of Eleazar ben Judah, who was a member of the famous Kalonymos family and one of the so-called *Chasidey Ashkenaz*, the saints of medieval German Jewry. This Rokeach lived at Worms, where, incidentally, he witnessed the Crusaders burst into his house, killing his wife, his daughter and his son, and was severely injured himself. He died about 1230, and therefore, if the parchment found in his academy goes back to his lifetime, the origin of the *Chad Gadya* can be pushed back to the thirteenth century.

Even if that is correct, it doesn't follow that it was an original Jewish creation. For the fact is that similar ditties are to be found in many cultural traditions around the world. The *Jewish Encyclopaedia* mentions, for instance, an old German folk-song beginning *Der Herr der schickt den Jokel aus* and a French nursery-rhyme, *La Petite Fourmi qui Allait à Jérusalem*, and it seems that whole volumes have been written by folklore experts pointing out parallels in many literatures.

Nevertheless, the *Chad Gadya* as we have it is, if not a Jewish creation, a Jewish adaptation. For to the general theme of the *Chad Gadya* – that there is a moral chain of cause and effect, that those who destroy will themselves be destroyed, that in the end justice will prevail and God will triumph – there are some striking parallels in ancient Jewish sources. In the Ethics of the Fathers, for instance, we are told that on one occasion, when Hillel saw a skull floating on the face of the water, he remarked: 'Because you drowned others, you were drowned; and in the end those who drowned you will be drowned in their turn' (2:7).

Even more pertinently, the oldest Midrash on the book of Genesis contains a legend about Abraham arguing with Nimrod. Nimrod proposes, 'Let us worship fire', but Abraham retorts, 'Let us rather worship water, which extinguishes fire'. Nimrod: 'Very well, then, let us worship water'. Abraham: 'Let us rather worship the winds which drive the clouds'. Nimrod: 'Very well, then, let us worship the winds'. Abraham: 'No, let us rather worship human beings, who withstand the wind'. At which point Nimrod, as well he might, loses his temper (Gen.R. 38:13).

Then there is a passage in the Talmud which goes like this: 'Ten strong things have been created in the world. The rock is strong, but the iron cleaves it. The iron is strong, but the fire melts it. The fire is strong, but the water extinguishes it. The water is strong, but the clouds carry it. The clouds are strong, but the wind scatters them. The wind is strong, but the body breathes it. The body is strong, but fear breaks it. Fear is strong, but wine banishes it. Wine is strong, but sleep works it off. Death is stronger than all these, and charity [the Hebrew word for 'charity' also means 'righteousness') delivers from death, as it says in the book of Proverbs, וצדקה תציל ממות (10:2)' (B.B. 10a).

Whether or not the *Chad Gadya* was based on pre-existing non-Jewish models, the Jewish formulation of it must surely have been influenced by these ancient Jewish prototypes, or at least carried resonances of them in the minds of those who sang it. Furthermore, once it became an accepted part of Jewish tradition, it was interpreted in typically Jewish fashion as an allegory, not only about the cosmic law of cause and effect, but also, more specifically, about the historical experiences and future hopes of the Jewish people. For example, according to the most common interpretation, the father of the story is God, the two *zuzim* are Moses and Aaron, the kid is the Jewish people, the cat Assyria, the dog Babylon, the stick Persia, the fire Greece, the water Rome, the ox represents the Saracens, the butcher the Crusaders, and the Angel of Death the Turkish Empire which then ruled Palestine.

Now it may well be that all this is taking the *Chad Gadya* much too seriously. It is, after all, only a nursery rhyme, intended to keep the children entertained and therefore awake until midnight. And yet it is undoubtedly in the spirit of the Seder to read such symbolic meanings into things which in themselves are ordinary or trivial. If the Matzah and the Maror and the Charoset can be made to bear historical and moral lessons, then why not a nursery rhyme? And not only that, but the particular interpretation in question is thoroughly in accord with the spirit of the occasion. For Pesach is the Messianic Festival. It is *not* only a historical festival. Yes, it commemorates the Exodus from Egypt, which happened a long time ago. But it does so for a purpose: to teach us that history is not a meaningless jumble of unconnected events; that it is not 'a tale told by an idiot, full of sound and fury, signifying nothing' (*Macbeth* 5:5:16); but a purposeful process which, though it involves many setbacks and terrible suffering, moves fundamentally from imperfection to perfection or, as the Haggadah puts it, from גנות to שבח, from degradation to glory, or, as the Haggadah also puts it, 'from bondage to freedom, from sadness to joy, from mourning to celebration, from darkness to light, from servitude to redemption'. The point of the *Chad Gadya*, which is the point of the whole festival, is that God will have the last word.

❖   ❖   ❖

Liberation
Pesach, 10 April 1990

זמן שמחתנו, 'The Season of our Freedom'. If there is a single phrase
which captures the essence of this festival, that must be it. But what
exactly does it mean? Let us consider one of the major symbols of
Passover: the four cups of wine which every Jew is required to drink
at the Seder table. Of the many explanations of that custom found in
our tradition, the oldest and most familiar sees in it an allusion to a
passage in the sixth chapter of the book of Exodus, where four verbs
are used to describe the deliverance of our ancestors: 'I will *lead* you
out from under the Egyptian yoke; I will *deliver* you from their
bondage; I will *redeem* you with an outstretched arm; I will *take* you
as My people' (vv. 6f).

That explanation is found already in the Jerusalem Talmud, dating from around 400 CE But the first recorded attempt to identify
the different phases of the process of redemption which the four
verbs might be taken to represent dates from the thirteenth century
and comes from the pen of one David ben Levi who lived in the
Provençal town of Narbonne and wrote a commentary on the Talmud called *Sefer ha-Michtam* (see Psalm 16:1).

There were, he says, four distinct stages in the liberation of our ancestors, and about each one of them we should gratefully say *Dayyenu*, 'It
would have been enough'. First, והוצאתי אתכם מתחת סבלות מצרים, 'I will
lead you out from under the Egyptian yoke'. That means exactly
what it says: release from slavery, from the necessity to toil inces-
santly just to earn enough to stay alive. It refers, we might say, to economic liberation.

Secondly, והצלתי אתכם מעבודתם, 'I will deliver you from their
bondage'. That is not another way of saying the same thing, for
Scripture doesn't repeat itself. The 'bondage' referred to here, says
David ben Levi, is not the bondage of economic exploitation but the
bondage of governmental oppression. The reference here is to political liberation.

Thirdly, וגאלתי אתכם בזרוע נטויה, 'I will redeem you with an outstretched arm', an expression which is traditionally understood as a
reference to God's power, especially as manifested in the Ten Plagues.
The point then is, says our Provençal scholar, that not only did the
Israelites escape from tyranny, but the tyrant was defeated, his arrogance was punished, his power was broken, and therefore we became
free, not only individually but collectively, free to embark on a course
of what would nowadays be called national self-determination.

Fourthly, ולקחתי אתכם לי לעם, 'I will take you as My people'. Here David ben Levi comments: 'If God had brought us out of Egypt in the manner described but left us unchanged, without bringing us near to God and making us God's people, and if therefore we had remained as we were at the beginning, before we ever entered Egypt, even that would have been enough; but God went further and והגדיל לעשות עמנו, did great things for us [Psalm 126:3], in that God made us לעם סגולה, a chosen people, and gave us a perfect Torah. And this, the fourth act of redemption, was the greatest of them all, שזו לנפש והשאר לגופות, for it touched the soul whereas the others only touched the body' (Menachem Kasher, *Haggadah Sh'lemah,* p. 91a). In other words, the climax of the whole process is spiritual liberation.

So much for David ben Levi's interpretation. But now let us ask ourselves where we stand in relation to his four freedoms. Do we think we possess them? Do we value and cherish them? Of course we do – at least in so far as our own people is concerned. But when it comes to the rest of humanity, I am not so sure.

Economic liberation? We can certainly lay claim to that. We are no longer slaves. Most of us, moreover, are comfortably middle class. Most of us have never suffered serious economic hardship, have never known what it is to starve. We are indeed aware that some of our fellow Jews, even in this country, are not so fortunate. But they, we tell ourselves, are looked after by Jewish Care, and other communal charities, and we do our bit by sending them the occasional cheque in response to their appeals.

Our discomfort increases when we think of the starving masses of the Third World; but what can we do for them except shrug our shoulders? We are worried, too, about the destitute and homeless here in Britain, and vaguely conscious that their number has increased in recent years. But many of them, we tell ourselves, are lay-abouts or drop-outs or drug-addicts and have nobody to blame but themselves, and many are recent immigrants who, if they have any guts, will in time pull themselves up by their own bootstraps, as we Jews did when we first came to this country as refugees. Besides, for the really hard-up there's always social security. We adopt the convenient philosophy that, although there are no doubt many exceptions, nevertheless, by and large, the rich deserve to be rich and the poor to be poor, and therefore we may continue to enjoy our comfortable way of life without any need to question the ordering of society. We rejoice in our own economic liberation; we care little for the economic liberation of others.

As for political liberation, of course we treasure that. We believe in democracy and are only too delighted that it is making a come-

back in Eastern Europe, in Latin America, in South Africa and even
in Nepal! But our involvement in civil rights movements, except on
behalf of our fellow Jews in the Soviet Union, has been slight! In the
United States it took a plunge when it was discovered that Black
Americans didn't always reciprocate our love for them by loving the
State of Israel. And though we welcome the changes now afoot in
South Africa, I suspect that, deep down, many of us still tend to identify with the whites rather than the blacks of that country, and have
no great difficulty in believing that Margaret Thatcher knows better
than Nelson Mandela what is best for them. We care a great deal
about our own political liberation, but not so much about the political liberation of others.

As for national self-determination, that has our enthusiastic
endorsement where the Jewish people are concerned. After all that
we have suffered, we are jolly well entitled to a country of our own,
and anyone who dares to question it, or to criticise any of the policies which its elected government considers necessary for its security, is an anti-Zionist, an anti-Semite and a deadly enemy.

But while we are positively ferocious about our own, Jewish right
to self-determination, we are not so sure about such claims when
made by other peoples. Welsh, Scottish, Basque, Kurdish, Armenian
nationalism leave us cold. We care little whether Lithuania, Latvia
and Estonia gain their independence or stay in the Soviet Union as
long as they tolerate no resurgence of anti-Semitism. And Palestinian
nationalism is a fraudulent, artificial creation which has no right to
exist and certainly not to covet Israeli-held territory. We are insistent
on our own rights in the matter of national self-determination, but
dismissive of the rights of others.

Finally, spiritual liberation. Are we God's chosen people, liberated from idolatry? We certainly say so in our prayers. The *Aleinu*, in
its traditional form, asserts that God has not made us like other
nations or assigned to us 'a lot like that of all their multitude'; for, as
the Sefardi liturgy continues, 'they worship vain and worthless
things, and pray to a god who cannot save', whereas we worship the
supreme Ruler of rulers, the Holy One, ever to be blessed.

But the reality isn't quite like that. Most Jews, both in Israel and in
the Diaspora, are more or less secular. Of the rest, relatively few take
their religion seriously. Except, of course, the ultra-Orthodox. But
their Judaism is curiously compatible with a narrow Jewish nationalism. They seem to worship a Deity who cares tremendously that
Jews should perform the correct rituals and that no Gentile should,
Heaven forbid, enter the Jewish community by a non-Orthodox

route. Their God is first and foremost the God of Israel and only in
a manner of speaking the God of humanity.

So we are not as liberated as we think we are. We are still, many
of us, idol worshippers. Our idols are wealth, comfort, power, self-
interest. In our fierce determination to survive, we have largely lost
sight of the purpose of our existence, of our Jewish mission. There is
indeed the Progressive movement which continues to stress, as it has
always done, the universal side of Judaism, but its universalism is
largely a matter of rhetoric. There was a time when leaders of Progressive Judaism, like Rabbi David Einhorn, fought against slavery.
Today our protestations of universalism are little more than pious
platitudes.

There is a crying need for a fresh start. That is the message of a
remarkable book by an American Jewish scholar, Marc H. Ellis, entitled *Toward a Jewish Theology of Liberation*. The title refers to the Christian 'liberation theology' movement which has been gaining ground
for some years now, particularly in the black communities of the
United States and among Latin American bishops, the essence of
which is that, as Ellis puts it, 'it speaks for those on the underside of
history, the marginalized and the oppressed' (p. 66).

So, too, says Ellis, we Jews need to rediscover that our God is the
God of all humanity, who weeps for those who suffer and demands
of us that we should identify ourselves with them, and make their
cause our cause. As we say in the Hallel, 'God raises the poor from
the dust and the wretched from the mire' (Psalm 113:7). So, if we
wish to be God's witnesses, must we. It isn't the rhetoric of universalism that is required of us, but solidarity. That must be the key
word of a Jewish liberation theology: solidarity with the downtrod-
den and the oppressed of all races and nations. Our task, as we keep
on saying in the *Aleinu*, is לתקן עולם במלכות שדי, to perfect the world by
bringing it into accord with God's will, to correct the ills of human
society. We have licked long enough the wounds of the Holocaust,
and celebrated long enough the establishment of the State of Israel.
The time has come to break out of the prison of our self-pity, self-
congratulation and self-absorption, and resume our Jewish task of
Tikkun Olam. If we were to do that, says Marc Ellis, then we would
regain our spiritual health and vigour.

❖   ❖   ❖

The Passover of the Future
Pesach, 6 April 1993

Every year when I ask myself what is the innermost secret of this many-splendoured and multi-faceted festival I come up with the same answer: that first and foremost it is a *messianic* festival.

I say this partly because so many of its rituals have a messianic symbolism: the Four Cups, representing, it is said, the Four World Empires which must pass away before the Messiah's reign can begin; the Fifth Cup which will be drunk only when he has come; the association of that cup with his herald, the prophet Elijah; the opening of the door to let him in; and the *Afikoman* which is probably a code-word for the Messiah.

I say it also because so many of the texts of the Haggadah spell out the message explicitly. In the *Ha Lachma Anya* we say: 'This year enslaved, next year free; this year here, next year in the Land of Israel.' One of the Seder songs implores God to rebuild the Temple 'speedily, speedily, soon in our days.' Another reaches its climax when God slays the Angel of Death. And the whole Seder ends with the words, 'Next year in Jerusalem!'

But I say it chiefly because it is the conclusion to which one comes when one reflects on the deeper meaning of the festival. It commemorates a historical event, but sees that event in a particular way: as a *movement*, in the words of the Haggadah, 'from bondage to freedom, from sadness to joy, from mourning to celebration, from darkness to light, from servitude to redemption.' And it implies that in that movement lies the significance, not just of that event, but of history as a whole.

In the first instance, of *Jewish* history. For however wonderful the liberation from Egyptian slavery was, it did not endure. Our people were conquered and oppressed again and again, and it was therefore inevitable that the celebration of Pesach would turn their minds to a still greater and more lasting liberation yet to come. The key phrase, which occurs repeatedly in Rabbinic literature, is בו נגאלו ובו עתידין להגאל, 'In that month they were redeemed in the past, and in that month they will be redeemed in the future' (Mechilta, Bo, 14; RH 11a), and a distinction was made between פסח־מצרים, the original, Egyptian Passover; פסח־דורות, the Passover of the generations since; and פסח לעתיד לבא, the Passover of the future.

But the same pattern was seen in human history as a whole. It is a movement from here to there; from now to then; from a bad, ugly and miserable present to a good, beautiful and happy future. Human history is seen as what German theologians call *Heilsgeschichte*, redemptive history. The Exodus is a particular historical event which sheds light on all of human history.

That much is clear, but the question remains: how are we to get from here to there? The traditional view is: through the agency of an individual, commissioned by God, known as the Messiah or the Anointed One. But is there any compelling reason why we should accept that view? Some would answer: yes, because the Bible says so. But there are two things wrong with that answer. In the first place, as liberals, we don't feel bound to accept whatever our ancestors, who wrote the Bible, believed. And in the second place, it isn't strictly true that 'the Bible says so'. Yes, it looks forward to a day when an ideal king will sit on the throne of David; and yes, it looks forward to an age of universal peace, when swords will be beaten into ploughshares, and spears into pruning-hooks; and just once these two ideas are combined (Isa. 11:1-9). But nowhere in the Hebrew Bible does the word משיח occur in the sense which the word Messiah came to have later. That concept is essentially a creation of a kind of pseudo-prophecy called apocalypse; and if we are not bound by what the classical biblical writers have to say, still less are we bound by what the apocalyptists have to say.

Nevertheless, the belief in a personal Messiah did pass into normative, Rabbinic Judaism; it has played an enormously influential part, for good and ill, in Jewish life for over two thousand years; and a doctrine of which that can be said should not be lightly dismissed. Let us therefore modify the question and ask: if there is not a *compelling* reason, is there perhaps nevertheless a *good* reason why we should believe in a personal Messiah?

But before we answer that, let us remind ourselves that there are two contrary strands in the tradition. According to one, the Messiah will come when the human situation is at its *worst*. It draws on biblical passages such as Amos saying, 'Why do you desire the day of the Eternal One? It is darkness, and not light' (5.18), and the Second Isaiah: 'For darkness shall cover the earth, and thick darkness the peoples; then the Eternal One will rise upon you, and God's glory will appear over you' (60:2). So the Talmud tells us that, when a heretic asked Rabbi Abbahu, 'When will the Messiah come?', he answered: 'When darkness covers the peoples' (San. 99a). And the Mishnah, in an unusual, apocalyptic passage, tells us that the 'footprints of the Messiah' will be attended by increasing arrogance and famine, heresy and fornication; 'the wisdom of the scribes', it says, 'will stink, those who fear sin will be despised, and truth shall nowhere be found' (Sotah, end).

On the other hand there is a strand which suggests that the Messiah will come when the human situation is at its *best*. At least that seems to be the implication of passages which stress that human beings, by their actions, can *hasten* the coming of the Messiah; passages which so interpret the Psalm verse, היום אם בקולו תשמעו, 'Today the world would be redeemed if you would hearken to God's voice' (95:7); for instance, 'If Israel kept the Sabbath properly even for one day, the son of David would come' (Exod.R. 25:12).

And one Rabbi hedged his bets! That was Rabbi Yochanan, the leading authority of third-century Palestine, who said: 'The son of David will come either in a generation that is altogether blameless or in a generation that is altogether delinquent' (San. 98a).

Which of the two trends, pessimistic or optimistic, is the dominant one? About this opinions differ, but the greatest authority on the subject, Gershom Scholem, had no doubt. 'Jewish Messianism', he wrote, 'is in its origin and by its nature ... a theory of catastrophe' (*The Messianic Idea in Judaism*, p. 7). In other words, when ultimate disaster strikes our planet, the Messiah will come to the rescue.

The case against the belief in a personal Messiah is this, that on the optimistic view, that he will come only when the human situation is at its best, that is, when men and women have already learnt to do God's will and live at peace, he is redundant, there will be nothing for him to do; and on the pessimistic view, that he will come only when the human situation is at its worst, there is nothing he will be able to do; it will be too late. In other words, a personal Messiah is neither necessary nor sufficient! And therefore, not only is there no *compelling* reason to believe in a personal Messiah: there is not even a *good* reason.

But still the question remains whether there is any harm in holding such a belief if, for whatever reason, one is inclined to do so. And I suppose the answer is: it depends. On the one hand it is good to be hopeful, and the less ground there is for hope, objectively speaking, the greater the need for hope to keep us from despair. On the other hand, if it is a *passive* hope, if it is an excuse for sitting back and comforting ourselves with the thought, 'No matter what a mess we make of things, when it comes to the crunch, God will bail us out', and if it therefore becomes a substitute for action, then it is harmful. And if it raises false expectations, as has happened so often in history, whenever the imminent advent of a Messiah has been predicted – as the Lubavitcher are now encouraging the thought that quite possibly their Rebbe, Menachem Schneerson, is the Messiah – then it is positively dangerous, for the disillusionment that inevitably follows destroys the very hope that gave rise to the prediction.

On the other hand, if the belief in a personal Messiah is combined with emphasis on human action to speed his coming, then there is no harm in it; it is merely gratuitous. For then the human action, not the Messiah, is the operative factor.

In short, if the question is asked, whether the Progressive movement has been right to reject the belief in a personal Messiah and emphasise rather the hope for a Messianic Age, brought about by human action in co-operation with the forces of goodness that emanate from God, the answer is surely yes.

In any case, what matters is not the scenario of 'the last days', which none of us can foresee, but simply the hope for a better world, the hope which is the principal theme of this festival – that, and the determination to do what lies within our human power to make the hope come true.

לשנה הבאה בירושלים, 'Next year in Jerusalem', says the traditional Haggadah. לשנה הבאה כל-חי נגאל, 'Next year in a world redeemed,' we add in ours. The quintessential purpose of this festival of Passover is to renew that hope within us, and to motivate us to rededicate ourselves to the task of תקון עולם, the betterment of the world, which it implies.

The darker the world – and today it is very dark – the greater the need to rekindle that hope. The stronger the forces of evil – and today they are very strong – the greater the need to muster the forces of goodness against them. For both reasons, the festival of Pesach has a message for us as relevant and urgent as it has ever been.

❖   ❖   ❖

A Feast of History
Pesach, 4 April 1996

In 1972 Weidenfeld and Nicolson published a beautifully illustrated book by Chaim Raphael entitled *A Feast of History*. I had always taken the title to mean that the study of the historical evolution of Passover and especially of the Haggadah, which is what the book is chiefly about, is an intellectual feast. But then it occurred to me that the title could also be understood in another sense: that Passover is itself a history festival, that history is what it is essentially about.

And in *that* sense the author could have called his book 'The Feast of History', for Passover is in that respect unique among the major Jewish festivals. Admittedly, all of them began as nature festivals, and all of them were eventually associated with historical events, but, with the exception of Passover, never convincingly. And though Passover, too, was originally a nature festival, celebrating the lambing season and the barley harvest, nevertheless, once it became connected with the Exodus from Egypt, that motif became the dominant one.

Passover, then, celebrates a historical event. That is the single most important fact about it. Whether the event happened exactly as the Bible tells it, doesn't matter for our purpose. No doubt the story was embellished as it was told and retold from generation to generation. Most probably the reality was more modest in scale. Quite possibly there was more than one exodus. But that there were Hebrew slaves in Egypt who escaped to re-establish themselves in the land where their Patriarchal ancestors had once lived, is not to be doubted.

We can even be pretty sure *when* it happened. Recently two Cambridge professors have suggested that the volcanic eruption of the Greek island of Santorini in 1628 BCE may very well have caused the seven years of famine in the land of Egypt of the Joseph story, and if the Israelites stayed in Egypt, as the Bible tells us, for four hundred years, that would place the Exodus, as scholars have long thought, squarely in the thirteenth century.

So Passover celebrates in essence, a real historical event, not a fictional one. And not only *a* historical event but *the* historical event: the one that our ancestors regarded as the most significant of all, illuminating the entire historical process in a unique way.

For one of the greatest achievements of our Israelite ancestors was that they evolved a sense of history. By this I don't just mean that they were intensely *interested* in their own past. That was true of other peoples. They each had their folklore, mostly fanciful, about their remote origins, and some of them, like the Greeks, developed serious historiography, though not before the fifth century BCE, with Herodotus, commonly known as the 'father of history'. What I mean is that our ancestors discerned a pattern, a plan, a purpose, a plot, in history. For as they saw it, it was under the guidance of a divine Scriptwriter whose righteous will must ultimately prevail.

Nothing like that is to be found elsewhere in the ancient world. At best, one encounters a *cyclical* view of history, as an endless succession of ups and downs which, like a Samuel Richardson novel, leads nowhere. But mostly there was little interest in history, and little inclination to see any great significance in it.

Even today it is fashionable to pooh-pooh the whole idea of teleology – that is, of purposiveness – in history, and to make cynical remarks about it. What is history? Many will answer, with Macbeth: '... it is a tale / Told by an idiot, full of sound and fury, / Signifying nothing' (Act V, Scene 5). Or with Voltaire: 'Nothing more than a tableau of crimes and misfortunes' (*L'Ingénu,* Chapter 10). Or with Ambrose Bierce: 'An account, mostly false, of events unimportant, which are brought about by rulers, mostly knaves, and soldiers mostly fools' (THQ, p. 34).

Even the great historian H.A.L. Fisher wrote: 'I can see only one emergency following upon another as wave follows upon wave ... only one safe rule for the historian: that he should recognise in the development of human destinies the play of the contingent and the unforeseen' (*A History of Europe,* p. vii).

But Judaism has always insisted that history is not 'just one darned thing after another'; that it is going somewhere; that it is leading, however slowly and painfully, with many a retrogression, towards a grand finale. Admittedly, there is no way of proving it: not, at least, conclusively. Like the belief in God, it is a matter of faith; a hunch, an intuition, a way of seeing reality which can't be forced on those who don't see it but which to those who do see it is, like the 'eureka experience', illuminating and compelling. At any rate, Jews *have* seen it that way ever since the days of the Prophets. And the festival of Passover is the most dramatic expression of it; it is 'The Feast of History'.

The mere fact that on this festival we remember, re-tell and re-live an event that happened so long ago shows an intense interest in history. But it is not the interest of an antiquarian. We celebrate the Exodus, not as an intriguing episode of ancient Near Eastern history, but for what it reveals beyond itself. And what does it reveal? It reveals that there is, or at least that there can be, *movement* from worse to better – or, as the Haggadah puts it, 'from bondage to freedom, from sadness to joy, from mourning to celebration, from darkness to light, from servitude to redemption.'

Because it has happened once, it can happen again. Indeed, it *has* happened many times in human history. The liberation of South Africa from white supremacy is the most momentous of recent instances. And therefore the liberation of every people from every kind of oppression is at least a possibility. But it is more than that: because God wills it, therefore, at least to the extent to which human beings learn to co-operate with the Divine Plan, it *must* ultimately happen. That is the Jewish Messianic Hope.

Admittedly, the hope has expressed itself in several different ways. There is the belief that it will all come about through a descendant of King David, Isaiah's 'shoot from the stump of Jesse' (11:1), later to be known as the Messiah. There is the belief that the Messiah will come when things are at their worst, to deliver us from catastrophe. There is the belief that he will come when things are at their best, to clinch what has been achieved already. There is even the belief, more characteristic of Christianity than of Judaism, but now entertained by some of the more incorrigible Lubavitchers, that he has come already. And there is the belief, favoured by Progressive Judaism, that it will happen gradually, without need of a personal Messiah, through the triumph of good over evil as human beings turn to their Creator and the earth becomes 'full of the knowledge of God as the waters cover the sea' (Isa. 11:9).

But whichever form it takes, it suffuses our understanding of the historic process with hope, a hope expressed again and again in the Seder: when we drink the four cups and fill the fifth; when we eat the Matzah and hide away the *Afikoman*; when we open the door for Elijah; when we recite the Great Hallel; when we sing in the *Chad Gadya* how the Holy One, ever to be blessed, will ultimately slay the Angel of Death; and when we wish each other 'Next year in Jerusalem! Next year in a world redeemed!'

Passover is a messianic festival. To fail to appreciate that is to miss the whole point of it. It celebrates the past, but only as a pointer to the future. And therefore it reminds us that all of us, standing as we do between the past and the future, have a responsibility.

Now I think it needs to be admitted that this messianic consciousness can be overdone. It can become obsessive. For we don't live only in history; we also live in nature. We are not only travellers from past to future; we also live in the present. We should enjoy the legitimate pleasures of every day, and carry out our daily tasks, without always having to think where we have come from and where we are going. And if the thought sometimes crosses our minds that the hope for a golden age which we shall never experience is little consolation for the troubles of the present, it cannot be denied that there is more than a little truth in it.

And yet the greater danger, surely, is the opposite: that we shall 'eat, drink and be merry', and live from day to day with too little rather than too much thought for the part we are playing in a process that transcends our life-span. That is why Passover, the Feast of History, is so important. It reminds us that we are, among other things, agents of history; that, whether we like it or not, we are actors on a stage, and the only question is whether we play our part well or badly; that every day matters – what we do and what we say, how we behave and how we bring up our children – because we are members of a generation which is the sole link between the generations of the past and the generations of the future; because everything we do either hastens or delays the coming of the Messianic Age, or, in kabbalistic language, either repairs the broken vessels of the world or fragments them further.

By all means, therefore, let us lead carefree lives to the extent to which our circumstances and our temperaments permit; but let the consciousness never be far from our minds that we are also engaged on a journey to a messianic destination which, though we shall never see it, nevertheless makes all our efforts and all our sufferings worthwhile; and let the Feast of Passover renew that consciousness within us.

❖   ❖   ❖

Season of Revelation

Civilisation
4 June 1957

The word 'civilisation' is used in two senses. We speak of particular civilisations, like that of the Egyptians or the Romans, which rise and fall. But we also speak of civilisation in general. In this wider sense civilisation is a condition of humanity the opposite of which is barbarism.

Western civilisation is said to be an amalgam of Greek culture and Hebrew morality. But they are not equal partners. Given a moral civilisation, culture is a precious adornment. But no amount of culture can compensate for an absence of morality. The worship of beauty and beautiful things as values superior to, or even on a par with, ethical values, is paganism. From a Hebraic point of view all the plays of Shakespeare, all the paintings of Rembrandt, and all the symphonies of Beethoven, do not compare with one injustice righted, one evil conquered, one act of kindness and of love.

What makes a civilisation great is not culture, still less material comfort or technological efficiency, but righteousness and humaneness. That is the Jewish view, and it is reinforced by experience. For history shows that these qualities, which make a civilisation great, also enable it to endure. The neglect of moral principles leads to social disintegration and ultimately to world war, so that a civilisation which does this will in the end lose all its material assets, as well as its cultural treasures, on a common heap of ruins.

If morality is the true foundation of civilisation, then Judaism is the foundation of Western civilisation. For the ethical values of Western civilisation derive from the religion of the ancient Hebrews. All else – the theology and the ritual – Christianity rejected or transformed. The moral values alone remain. They constitute the true greatness of Western civilisation and hold out hope that, in spite of all the perils that threaten it, it will survive.

Therefore, when on this festival of Shavuot, we recite the Ten Commandments, we do more than perpetuate an old tradition. We proclaim the paramountcy of morality in the life of humanity, and we re-affirm our responsibility as custodians of the Moral Law which is the basis of civilisation.

❖   ❖   ❖

Festival of Conversion
Shavuot, 16 May 1975

That Shavuot is the Cinderella of the Festivals has become a platitude. Nor are the reasons far to seek. And they have very little to do with the fact that Shavuot usually falls on a weekday. For the same is true of the first day of Pesach and the first day of Sukkot, which attract much larger attendances, nor are the synagogues notably more crowded when Shavuot happens to fall on a Sunday.

Obviously, therefore, Shavuot lacks appeal. But why? The answer usually given is that it is deficient in picturesqueness, that it has hardly any of the symbols which make the other festivals popular. There is no Matzah to eat, no Shofar to blow, no Sukkah to build; there aren't even any rousing tunes like the *Kol Nidre* or the *Maoz Tsur*. In other words, Shavuot is like a children's book without pictures.

But can that really be the whole of the explanation? Are we really like children that we can't appreciate a festival unless it has colourful rituals? Should we not consider the possibility that it is the *meaning* of Shavuot that lacks appeal?

Certainly its meaning isn't all that clear. In the Bible it is merely a harvest festival, and that aspect has little significance for us today. The Mishnah calls it *Atzeret*, the concluding feast, which implies no more than that it concludes the seven weeks of the counting of the *Omer* and therefore makes it an appendage of Pesach. Only in the days of the Amoraim, the post-Mishnaic rabbis, did it come to be regarded as זמן מתן תורתנו, the Season of the Giving of our Torah, that is to say, the Festival of the Sinaitic Revelation.

And even that interpretation doesn't make the impact one might expect. For the Sinaitic Revelation is shrouded in mystery. Who knows whether it really occurred at this time of the year? Who can be sure that it occurred at all? And if it did, who knows exactly what happened? Did the people really hear a divine voice? Can there be such a thing as a divine voice if God is incorporeal? And even if the voice was the voice of Moses interpreting God's will, how can we be sure that he interpreted it correctly? And in any case, what exactly was it that Moses proclaimed to the people?

According to the traditional view, it was of course the entire Torah. But that view is no longer tenable, for we know that the Pentateuch stems from different periods. How much of it then goes back to Moses? If we read the works of modern scholarship we find there a great variety of opinions. Which of them are we to believe? And even if we discount the most sceptical of them and assume that at least the Ten Commandments – if not in the form we have them, then in a more rudimentary form – go back to Moses, we are still left with the question whether the Ten Commandments deserve all the praise they have received.

They are, after all, rather elementary. They do not include such lofty teachings as 'You shall love your neighbour as yourself'. They contain that rather dubious phrase about God visiting the iniquity of the parents on the children. They seem to treat the wife as the property of her husband in the same way as his slaves and cattle. And the tenth commandment, 'You shall not covet', seems to counsel an acceptance of the economic status quo which is hardly compatible with modern movements for social justice. In short, even if we could be sure that at least the Ten Commandments were proclaimed on the sixth of Sivan, it is still doubtful whether that assurance would evoke from us any great raptures of enthusiasm.

Of course it would be possible to argue that the historical details don't matter; that it is sufficient to know that Jewish tradition singled out the 6th of Sivan as זמן מתן תורתנו; and even if what happened at Sinai is now nebulous, and even if it marked only a phase in a process of revelation that extended over many centuries, still the fact that the Jewish people *did* receive the Torah, however gradually, is a fact worthy of celebration.

And yet even this line of thought fails to convince. For what is Torah? Essentially, it is a body of laws, and that isn't something we find it easy to get excited about. Why? Partly because not all of them are still valid today. Even from an Orthodox point of view a

sizable proportion – the laws of sacrifice, of ritual purity and of agri-
culture – are, at any rate, in abeyance. And from a Liberal point of
view, not only these but many other laws too are seen as time-con-
ditioned and superseded.

But I doubt whether even that is the main problem. It seems to
me, rather, that the very concept of law has lost much of its flavour.
I may be mistaken, but I suspect that the average Jew today, especially in our section of the community, no longer thinks of religion as
consisting primarily of laws. They think of it, not chiefly as making
certain well-defined demands, but as conferring certain vaguely
understood benefits: at its lowest a sense of comfort and reassurance
that, in spite of all the confusion and upheaval of our time, fundamentally all's well with the world, and at its highest an opportunity
to penetrate beyond the concerns of every-day to the awareness of a
reality beyond, where all is beautiful and serene. To put it over-sim-
ply, the average Jew today thinks of religion as affording a sense of
mystery. If they go to synagogue, that is what they expect to find
there; and if they don't, it is because they doubt whether they *would*
find it there.

This craving for religious experience is not of course to be
debunked. It is an important aspect of Judaism, as of any other religion, and it may well be that we pay insufficient attention to it.
Judaism has a wealth of wisdom relevant to this quest, especially in
the Kabbalah, the tradition of Jewish mysticism, and it may well be
that if we explored this more and laid more emphasis on it, not so
many of our people, especially our young people, would turn to
other disciplines, such as Transcendental Meditation, in search of
inner spiritual experience.

Nevertheless, it is only one side of Judaism, and we must always
come back to Leo Baeck's famous formulation of Judaism as consisting of two parts: Mystery and Commandment. Of the two, it is
the Commandment that is most obviously relevant to Shavuot. And
it is also, I think, the more distinctive of Judaism generally. For if an
individual merely seeks an intense form of spiritual experience, why
should they go to a synagogue? They could indeed find it there, but
they could also find it, perhaps more obviously, in a Christian
Church or a Buddhist Temple. The distinctiveness of Judaism, its
spécialité de la maison, is that it has set itself the task of working out
in every detail what God requires of human beings by way of conduct. The chief distinguishing feature of Judaism is its Halachah,
and unless we become again aware of this, and proud of it, and
excited about it, Shavuot is not likely to elicit from us the enthusiasm it deserves.

Never mind if some of the provisions of the Halachah are now out-dated and need to be revised. The mere attempt to construct a way of life in conformity with God's will is a noble enterprise, indeed the noblest of all enterprises; and if we truly believe this, then the beginning of that enterprise at Mount Sinai, even though it was *only* the beginning, becomes the greatest moment in the history of Judaism.

But now let me turn briefly to another aspect of Judaism which, as we shall see, is closely related to this one. Some time after the completion of the Talmud it became customary to read on Shavuot the book of Ruth. Why, is not at all clear. Several reasons for the practice have been suggested. But the most convincing is that Ruth was a Gentile who became a Jewess, and that her individual acceptance of the Torah parallels the Jewish people's collective acceptance of the Torah at Mount Sinai.

Now why should Gentiles convert to Judaism? For the sake of marriage? Well, that may be a valid motive, though it didn't apply exactly in Ruth's case, since she didn't convert until after her Jewish husband's death. Because they like the Jewish people and their customs? That is all right, too, and it was evidently true of Ruth, but it is more or less fortuitous. Because Jewish worship offers a surer way of apprehending God than any other? That is questionable. Because Jewish theology makes good sense? That is indeed essential since without such a conviction sincere conversion is impossible. But surely there must be something more. What chiefly deserves the attention of Gentiles about Judaism is that it has taken with unique seriousness the task of formulating God's will for all aspects of human life. It is, once again, the Halachah.

But is not the Halachah only for Jews? Not at all! One of the recurring legends in the Midrash is that the Torah was offered to all the nations of mankind. That is why it was revealed in the wilderness, that is, in no-man's-land, and that is why it was revealed in seventy languages.

What I am suggesting, therefore, is that if we wish to revive the observance of Shavuot, it is not sufficient to invent new rituals for it, though that may help. We need also to re-emphasise its essential message. It must once again become the festival of the Torah, but the Torah understood, not as the private property of the Jewish people, its peculiar folk-ways which are only of anthropological interest to others, but as an attempt, unequalled and unparalleled in human culture, to translate the affirmation of a moral God into a way of life for human beings generally. And it is precisely the book of Ruth which can remind us of this broader significance of the Torah. I am suggesting, in other words, that Shavuot should become, not only the

Festival of Revelation but also the Festival of Conversion, of Proselytism; that it should recall to us our duty to share our religious heritage with our fellow human beings. *Of course* that doesn't mean to
foist it on them, or indeed to bring the slightest pressure on them to
convert. Nor does it mean to pretend that Judaism has all the
answers. But it does mean to give them the opportunity of knowing
what Judaism is, and to invite them, if they are so inclined, to join us
in building on what our ancestors have achieved.

If we take this view; if we think of the Torah as given to us, not
only for our own benefit but for the enlightenment and guidance of
humanity, then we too may come to appreciate more keenly its
worth; and then Shavuot may come to be seen by us, not as the least
of our festivals, but as the most significant of all.

❖   ❖   ❖

A Tree of Life
Shavuot, 6 June 1984

The event which this festival of Shavuot commemorates is irretrievably hidden in the mists of antiquity. For though archaeologists may
yet discover one or two relevant inscriptions, and scholars may yet
make new deductions from the available sources, the chances are
that generations hence our descendants will know little more about
what really happened at Sinai than we do.

But then it doesn't really matter. For one thing, whatever happened must have been mysterious in itself, so that even those who
were present would have had the greatest difficulty in verbalising it.
Somehow or other, we must assume they became momentarily conscious, with an intensity they had never experienced before, of the
presence of a Being of immense power and supreme holiness who
demanded their obedience.

For another thing, Sinai was only the beginning. It only set in
motion a process which has continued ever since: a twofold process
which has involved, on the one hand, divine revelation or inspiration
or guidance and, on the other hand, human striving to comprehend
God's will. The mixture has varied. Sometimes, as at Sinai, the divine
initiative of self-disclosure has perhaps been the main factor. At most
times it has been predominantly or even exclusively a human search
with all the fallibility, the partial perception, the proneness to error
and misinterpretation which that inevitably involves.

This process is called Torah. There is indeed another sense in which the term Torah is applied to that which the process yields, the *literature* in which its results are recorded. In that sense it refers most obviously to the Pentateuch, which is indeed known as the Written Torah. But the Pentateuch was always supplemented by an oral tradition interpreting and augmenting it, and in the course of time this Oral Torah, as it is called, grew larger and larger, until it became quite impossible to store it even in the most retentive memory, and it, too, was committed to writing. It became the Mishnah, then the Talmud, then the codes and commentaries and responsa, so that, in this broader sense, the term Torah describes a literature of unimaginably vast extent. And what is more, the literature is still growing, and will continue to grow; and for that very reason it seems best, after all, to think of Torah as a *process* rather than a literature. It is, quite simply, the process of the endeavour to discover God's will; and so understood, it is a process in which we ourselves are called upon to play a part.

But in order that we may be able to do so, there is one inescapable precondition. We must acquaint ourselves with the process as it has been in the past. We may not agree in all respects with what we find there. We Liberals especially are likely to find ourselves in disaccord with whole areas of it, for instance those relating to the sacrificial cult and to the status of women; but unless we know what has gone before, we are not competent to carry the process forward. Then we may still express opinions; but if they are not rooted in the tradition, if they don't grow out of it and have no point of contact with it, then they are just *that*: personal opinions which have no claim on the acceptance of the Jewish people as a whole, and therefore do not qualify as Torah. And therefore to celebrate this festival of Shavuot, *z'man mattan toratenu*, the season of the giving of our Torah, without some kind of renewed commitment to the study of the Torah that has been handed down to us, the study of the literature of Judaism – not *about* Judaism but *of* Judaism – would be, if not an act of hypocrisy, an empty gesture.

Unfortunately, such learning is not something for which Anglo-Jewry is renowned. It has produced remarkably few Jewish scholars, and shown little respect for those, mainly from Continental Europe, who have lived and worked in this country. A case in point is Solomon Schechter, since he came to England from Romania but, finding so little respect for Jewish learning in this country, moved on to the United States a few years later. In his 'Epistles to the Jews of England' published by the *Jewish Chronicle* on the eve of his departure in 1901, he was particularly scathing about the attitudes he found among the upper and middle classes. This is what he wrote:

> Notwithstanding our self-congratulating speeches at the annual distribu-
> tions of religious prizes, it is a fact that ignorance is on the increase
> among our better situated classes. Very few are capable of reading their
> prayers, and less are able to understand what they read; whilst the num-
> ber of those who know anything of Israel's past ... forms almost a negli-
> gible quantity. And he continued: 'The outlook is thus dark; dark
> enough, indeed, to be followed by some great revival or renaissance ...
> Now the Renaissance is usually described as the moment in history in
> which man discovered himself. In a similar way the Jew will also have to
> re-discover himself. This discovery ... can be made only by means of
> Jewish literature, which retains all that is immortal in the nation. (*Studies
> in Judaism*, II, 198f)

Fortunately, there have always been exceptions to that rule.
Indeed, to *some* extent Schechter's hopes for a revival have begun to
come true. Certainly Yeshivah-type learning is flourishing as never
before; but even scientific Jewish scholarship has made some head-
way in the universities, and I think Schechter would have been well
pleased if he had paid a visit to our Synagogue around midnight last
night, and seen us engrossed in the study of medieval Hebrew texts.

Let me in conclusion tell you a little about one of the authors we
studied, because he is himself an illustration of the fact that the history of Jewish learning in England is not an entirely sterile one. His
name was Jacob ben Judah, and he lived here in London in the thirteenth century. His grandfather was known as *Yaakov ha-Aroch*, 'Jacob
the Tall'. Presumably his remoter ancestors had come over from
Normandy with the Conqueror in 1066 or not long afterwards. Like
all or most of the Jews who lived in England at that time, he spoke
Norman French as his mother tongue. But evidently he also received
a good Hebrew education, for he wrote a book in perfectly good
Hebrew. This book he called *Etz Chayyim*, 'The Tree of Life', in allusion to the verse in the book of Proverbs which refers to Wisdom but
was later interpreted to refer to the Torah, 'It is a tree of life to those
who hold it fast, and those who cling to it are rendered happy' (3:18).
It is, in fact, a code of Jewish Law: not one of the greatest and certainly not one showing great originality, for the author relied heavily on Maimonides' code, the Mishneh Torah, which was then only
about one hundred years old, as well as the even more recent *Sefer
Mitzvot Gadol* ('Great Book of Commandments') by the French
scholar, Moses of Coucy. Nevertheless Rabbi Jacob displays wide
learning and makes a number of references to the customs of the
Jews of England and to legal cases that occurred among them.

He mentions, for instance, how *Gittin* (Jewish divorce documents)
were written in London in his time, the location being described as
כאן בלונדרש מתא דיתבא על נהר טמיזא וגלברוק, 'Here in London, the city

which is situated on the rivers Thames and Galbrook' (II, 172) –
which, I gather, is another form of Wallbrook. He also refers to other
Jewish scholars who lived in England in his time, such as Rabbi
Berechiah of Nicole (that is Lincoln) and Rabbi Isaac ben Peretz of
Northampton. Of course he also mentions French scholars, for there
was close contact between the Jewish communities of England and
France. Indeed, in *Hilchot Shabbat*, the section of the book dealing
with the laws of the Sabbath, Rabbi Jacob remarks that it is quite
possible to sail from the land they call *Inglaterra* on a Friday morning
and arrive in Dieppe before Shabbat comes in (I, 281).

In another section of the code, dealing with the Jewish calendar,
the author illustrates his point by quoting the year in which he is
writing. That year was 1287, that is, only three years before the Jews
of England were expelled. What happened to Rabbi Jacob after that
is not known. Let us hope that he had a safe crossing and lived to a
ripe old age on the other side of the Channel.

What happened to the *manuscript* of the book is also not known as
fully as one would wish. But it is known that it amounted to about one
thousand pages of parchment, that it was sold to somebody called
Isaac, that it or a copy of it became the heirloom of a family called
Bick in the fifteenth and sixteenth centuries, that in 1674 it passed into
the possession of a Christian Hebraist, Professor Johann Christoph
Wagenseil, and eventually to the University Library of Leipzig. Its
existence there was brought to the attention of England's Chief Rabbi
Hermann Adler towards the end of the nineteenth century, and he
resolved to publish it, but only made a start on the task, which was
ultimately completed by Chief Rabbi Sir Israel Brodie in 1962, when
it was published by Mosad ha-Rav Kook in three volumes.

Unfortunately, Rabbi Jacob ben Judah of London has very little
to say about Shavuot. Perhaps the festival aroused no more enthusiasm in his time than it does in ours, which would give us a little cold
comfort. More probably, he never got round to completing that section, for there are a number of indications that the book was written,
or completed, in a hurry; and in view of the Expulsion only three
years later, that is hardly surprising. At any rate, Rabbi Jacob does
deal at considerable length with Pesach, even adding a stanza of his
own to the song, *Ki Lo Na-eh*, which may indeed be his composition,
for he was something of a poet. That section is followed by two
chapters about the laws of *Chol ha-Mo'ed*, the Intermediate Days of
the Festivals, and then two chapters about the counting of the *Omer*.
Only at the end of that section is there any mention of Shavuot. It
consists of a single paragraph, and though it doesn't tell us anything
we don't know, nevertheless, since it is all he has to say about the

festival we are celebrating, we might appropriately finish with it. It simply says:

> On the fiftieth day of the counting of the *Omer* is the festival of Shavuot, also known as *Atzeret* (the Concluding Festival), the day on which the Torah was given. And on that day it is incumbent on everybody to rejoice, for it is a Holy Day on which the doing of work is forbidden, as we have explained in the Laws of the Holy Days. And it is customary today to observe it for two days in the Diaspora, but in the Land of Israel it is only one day. (I, 341).

'The Jew', said Solomon Schechter, 'will have to rediscover himself. This discovery ... can be made only by means of Jewish literature, which retains all that is immortal in the nation'. May our observance of this festival of the Giving of our Torah be for us a step in that process of rediscovering the soul of our people, and therefore also of rediscovering the God for whom the Jewish soul has yearned for thousands of years.

❖   ❖   ❖

Torah Truth
Shavuot, 24 May 1996

One of the high points – both metaphorically and, in a sense, literally – of the Shabbat morning service in Orthodox synagogues is the ritual of *hagbahah*, the Elevation of the Scroll, while Cantor and Congregation, with great gusto, sing: וזאת התורה אשר שם משה לפני בני ישראל עלֹ־פי יי ביד משה , 'This is the Torah which Moses set before the Children of Israel at God's command by the hand of Moses.' There are several problems about that verse which we may appropriately discuss on this Festival of Shavuot, *zeman mattan toratenu*, the 'Season of the Giving of our Torah.'

The first problem is that the verse is a hybrid. It consists of two parts which don't really go together. The first part, comprising eight words, comes from Deuteronomy, chapter 4 (v. 44), and the recitation of it when the Scroll is elevated is quite ancient, going back at least to eighth century (Soferim 14:14). The second part (עלֹ־פי יי ביד משה) comes from the book of Numbers, where it occurs twice, in chapter 4 (v. 37) and in chapter 9 (v. 23), and was added on about a thousand years later, in the seventeenth century (B.S. Jacobson, *The Sabbath Service*, p. 269).

It is a clumsy addition since it doesn't make syntactical sense to say that 'Moses' set the Torah before the Children of Israel 'by the hand of Moses'. Why then was the extra phrase grafted on? About that there are two theories. One refers to Numbers 9, which relates how, by God's command through Moses, the Israelites carried the Tabernacle through the wilderness, which it seemed appropriate to recall when the Scroll was about to be carried in procession round the Synagogue (Jacobson, *Sabbath Service*, p. 269).

The other, more sophisticated, theory was put forward quite recently in a brilliant essay by Rabbi Jeffrey Cohen of the Stanmore Synagogue (*Judaism: A Quarterly Journal of Jewish life and Thought*, Vol. 40, No. 4, Fall 1991, pp. 407-18). He takes the tagged-on phrase from Numbers 4, where the context is the census of the Israelites in the wilderness, and suggests that in the liturgy it serves the purpose of reassuring the congregation that, contrary to a deeply ingrained superstition against counting people, it is permissible to count the eight men (including the reader of the Haftarah) who are, by tradition, called up to the reading of the Torah.

But the deeper problem is posed by the first part of the verse, even without the clumsy addition, and it is simply this: what does it mean, at the precise moment of *hagbahah*, to say *v'zot ha-torah...*? It can only mean one thing: that the text of this parchment scroll that is now being shown to the Congregation is identical *verbatim* with the text of the Torah which Moses set before the Israelites in the wilderness of Sinai 3,300 years ago.

But, taken like that, it is untrue! Why? Well, for one thing, we can't be sure that Moses wrote anything. If he did, he probably wrote in Egyptian rather than Hebrew. And if he wrote in Hebrew, he certainly would not have used the script familiar to us, which is really Aramaic, but rather the ancient Hebrew script, which is completely different. But, more importantly, we simply have no evidence that a Hebrew law book of any kind existed during or for many centuries after the time of Moses. The earliest evidence we have dates from the late seventh century BCE, when a law book, which scholars have identified with Deuteronomy, was 'discovered' in the Temple (II Kings 22-23). And of course it is to that book, and not to the Pentateuch as a whole, that Deuteronomy itself refers when it says *v'zot ha-torah ...*

Even before Deuteronomy, the word *torah* was indeed used, but always in the sense of an individual teaching which a prophet believed had come to him from God, and never in the sense of a law book, let alone the Pentateuch. To cut a long story short, the Pentateuch as such dates from after the Babylonian Exile, say, the fifth

century BCE, though it was based on written and oral traditions of
various degrees of antiquity.

Now, all that has been known for at least two hundred years and
is as elementary to Bible study as the theorem of Pythagoras is to
geometry. Of course there are many different theories as well as
changing fashions among Bible scholars, but the belief that the Pentateuch was written by Moses has about as much chance of being true
as the belief that the earth is flat. Yet Shabbat after Shabbat, that
belief is proclaimed, and assented to, in Orthodox synagogues! Such
is the disdain for historical truth among those who want to go on
believing what they have always believed. And when it is pointed out
to them that there are Jews who do accept the findings of modern
Bible scholarship, they ask: but how is that possible? How, in other
words, can you believe both in Judaism and in Bible scholarship?

It is a pertinent question to ask, especially on Shavuot. How
indeed can we celebrate *mattan toratenu*, the 'Giving of our Torah', if
we don't believe about it what our ancestors believed about it? A full
answer to that question would require many sermons. But very
briefly stated, it comes to this. Although the Torah, in the sense of
Pentateuch, is neither as ancient nor as perfect as was formerly
thought, it nevertheless holds a unique and pre-eminent place in the
literature of Judaism. It tells at length the early history of our people,
from Abraham to Moses: no other book does that. It sets that history
in the context of world history, back to the Creation: no other book
does that. It contains the Ten Commandments and the Shema and
'Love your neighbour as yourself': no other book does that. It contains the foundations of Jewish ethics and ritual, including the sacred
calendar: no other book does that. It is the end-product of a process
which, we have good reason to believe, began in the days of Moses
in the Wilderness of Sinai. And it has been so closely studied that the
whole of Jewish literature is to a large extent one gigantic commentary on it.

Isn't that enough? Surely it is *more* than enough! To say that you
can't celebrate Shavuot unless you believe that the Pentateuch as we
now have it was dictated by God to Moses on Mount Sinai, and that
every word of it is good and true and beautiful, is rather like saying
that you can't celebrate a person's birthday unless he or she is at least
one hundred years old and is, moreover, a perfect saint who has
never made a mistake.

But the question goes far beyond Shavuot. For the assumption
that underlies it is this: either you believe all that is traditionally
understood by the phrase וזאת התורה אשר שם משה לפני בני ישראל or else
you have no good reason to believe in Judaism at all. And even

more generally: either you believe that we have in our possession a holy scripture which contains the truth, the whole truth and nothing but the truth, or the bottom has been knocked out of religion altogether. The choice is between fundamentalist religion or no religion – all or nothing. That is the assumption. And therefore the question ultimately comes to this: is liberal religion possible?

And our answer to that is surely yes. Not only is it possible, but for many of us it is the *only* possibility. Indeed, we would say that, in the nature of the case, a full and correct understanding of God and God's will, or anything remotely like it, must be beyond the capacity of human beings. And therefore all the efforts of our ancestors to achieve such an understanding, however magnificent, must necessarily be imperfect. There simply *cannot be* such a thing as a perfect Torah, and those who believe it believe it in defiance of all the evidence. They live in an imaginary world which has no basis in any solid historical reality. They are fully entitled to do so, and to be respected for the beliefs they hold. But what *we* believe about God, and the literature about God, must be in harmony with the truth – every kind of truth, including historical truth. For as the Rabbis said, חותמו של הקדוש ברוך הוא אמת, the very seal – or signature – of God is truth (Shab. 55a).

Is liberal religion possible? Yes, of course it is! But if we change the question a little and ask how liberal religion is doing, we have to admit that it isn't doing all that well. Although there are many millions of liberal Jews, liberal Christians, liberal Muslims, liberal Hindus and liberal Buddhists in the world, their level of conviction and dedication is not, on average, conspicuously high, and all too often they allow themselves be browbeaten by the fundamentalists into an inferiority complex or a loss of nerve. Ultimately, therefore, the possibility of liberal religion has to be demonstrated, not only in theory but in practice, by those of us who subscribe to it: by the seriousness of our commitment to it in our daily lives.

❖　　❖　　❖

Season of Sorrow

Reflections on the Ninth of Av
Tish'ah b'Av, 23 June 1977

עת לבכות ועת לשחוק, 'There is a time to weep, and a time to laugh'. So said Ecclesiastes (3:4). And what he said, we Jews have always known. We have our festivals and our *simchas*. We know how to celebrate, how to rejoice, how to laugh, and our sense of humour is proverbial. But there are other times, when the joy departs and grief takes over. Tonight is such a time. It is עת לבכות, a time to weep. It has been so for over 2,500 years.

Do we need any justification for continuing the tradition? I don't think so. Of course, if we feel no sorrow, there is no point in expressing it, and then the question of justification doesn't arise. But then, too, we lack sensitivity. Indeed, it is one and the same sensitivity which enables us to laugh and to cry. Those who never feel any real sorrow, never feel any real joy. And those who do feel it, who are sensitive, for them that fact alone provides all the justification that is needed. To ask the bereaved, 'Why are you weeping?', is to ask a senseless question.

But why tonight? Well, any other night would do as well. If *Tish'ah b'Av* didn't exist, we should have to invent it, and then the same question could be asked. Perhaps the best answer is: because we can't grieve all the time. Heaven knows, we have enough cause. But it would be intolerable. So we concentrate our sorrow into a single day and try to live with some sort of equanimity during the rest of the year. And if so, why not the day that has already been set aside for the purpose for countless centuries?

Of course we know that the early Reformers had their doubts about *Tish'ah b'Av* and tended not to observe it. But that was because they wished to make a particular point: that the destruction of the Temple, which the traditional *Tish'ah b'Av* liturgy emphasised, was really a blessing in disguise, since it brought to an end the primitive sacrificial cult and enabled the more advanced worship of the Synagogue to take its place. They therefore tended to overlook the human suffering associated with the Babylonian conquest in 586 BCE and the Roman conquest in 70 CE. as well as other tragedies of Jewish history, many of which, like the final defeat of the Bar-Kochba Rebellion in 135 CE, occurred, by a curious coincidence, on or near the 9th of Av.

And they had another reason for overlooking these calamities, for they regarded them as belonging only to the past; they believed themselves to be living at the beginning of a new age of enlightenment and tolerance, of freedom, justice and peace. For that is how they read the signs of the times, the onward march of education and democracy. It was a noble error on their part. But an error it was, and one which, unless we are totally blind, we are not likely to repeat.

For since their time we have experienced the greatest calamity of all. Perhaps the word 'we' should be qualified. There were those who lived through those fateful years at a safe distance from the inferno. Some of them nevertheless suffered mentally with the victims and continue to do so; they are our brothers and sisters in our sorrow. But many never felt the impact of it, or have allowed the intensity of the feeling to fade with the passage of time. And many more, whose number increases from year to year, were born after it happened and know about it, if at all, only from the history books. More and more people, I am told, when they visit the *Yad va-Shem* Memorial in Jerusalem, seem to be seeing and hearing it all for the first time. And now there is in the Gentile world a growing literature which commits the ultimate obscenity of denying that it ever happened at all.

But we who are gathered here tonight, admittedly a tiny proportion of the Congregation, we know. And if others forget, it becomes all the more important that we should not. Those who mourn the martyrs of the Holocaust are yearly diminishing in number. While we still live, let us be among them. It is, alas, all we can do for those who died: to honour their memory. Let us not do less.

For us, then, the Holocaust overshadows all the previous tragedies, but not completely. For pain is pain, wherever it occurs, and however long ago. We remember, too, those who suffered and died in other times and places, who were slain by the Babylonians and the Romans and the Crusaders and the Cossacks. As far as our imagination permits, we give them too a place in our hearts beside those whose names and faces and voices linger more vividly in our memories. And we do so on this day because on it the blood of our people has flowed even more copiously than on other days and because, as I said, we could not bear to do so every day.

But why here? Why as a congregation in the synagogue? Partly because it helps to share our sorrow with those who understand its magnitude, who understand the full meaning of the Bible verse inscribed on the Memorial to the Six Million in our cemetery: הביטו וראו אם יש מכאוב כמכאובי 'Look and see if there is any sorrow like our sorrow' (Lam. 1:12). But partly also in the hope that by being together in this place, dedicated to the worship of God in the name of Judaism, by imbibing here something of the wisdom of our heritage, by praying and meditating together with and without words, we may grope our way towards some kind of understanding of the agonies of the past which may help us, not merely to live with the memory of them, but to understand what is required of us because of them.

There is in all of us a tendency to hold God responsible for what happened. I believe that is a relic of an untenable theology, and that in reality what happened happened not because God willed it but, on the contrary, because God's will was flouted. It was not God who was silent at Auschwitz but humanity. God spoke all right, as God always does, but humanity refused to listen. But if that is so, then our duty is clear. It is to change humanity, beginning with ourselves. It is, negatively, to practise vigilance, and to conquer the prejudice, the intolerance, the aggressiveness and vindictiveness in ourselves and our fellow men and women. And it is, positively, to cultivate those qualities and attitudes and modes of behaviour which make for conciliation, harmony and peace.

The task is daunting. All the more do we need to grasp every bit of help we can get from one another, from our tradition, and from the God to whom that tradition is dedicated, whose power flows unceasingly to those who open themselves to its influx. Because we shall often fail, we cannot be sure that what has happened will not happen again. But unless we try, we have no right even to hope so. And unless we try, we betray ourselves, our God and our martyrs. We cannot undo their suffering, but next to that, their dearest wish would surely be that we should do whatever lies in our power to ensure that their children's children shall not suffer like them. That, when all else has been said and thought and felt, is the task to which the Ninth of Av demands that we should dedicate ourselves. We dare not say that then the death of the martyrs will not have been in vain. But we can say that then our mourning for them will not have been in vain. עת לבכות ועת לשחוק, 'There is a time to weep and a time to laugh'. Through our efforts and with God's help, may the time for laughing come במהרה בימינו, speedily, in our days.

Season of Repentance

Judgment
Rosh Hashanah, 20 September 1971

L'shanah tovah tikkatevu v'techatemu, 'May you be inscribed and sealed for a good year.' So runs the seasonal greeting. It conjures up the strange notion that once a year, at this precise time, God passes judgment on all human beings. Surrounded by angels, the Divine Judge opens the Book of Life and, on the basis of what it records about each individual, determines what their fate shall be, writing down the verdict and, after ten days of grace, setting to it the final seal.

The idea goes back to ancient times. Traces of it can be found already in the Bible (Exod. 32:32, Mal. 3:16, Psalm 69:29). But the classical statement of it is in the Talmud, when it says that 'all are judged on Rosh Hashanah, and on Yom Kippur their sentences are sealed' (RH 16a), and from there it found its way into the liturgy.

The most graphic version is a liturgical poem, or *piyyut*, which begins with the words *U-n'tanneh tokef*, 'Let us proclaim the holiness of this day ...' For many people, its recitation is one of the emotional climaxes of the High Holydays liturgy: partly because of its disturbing words, partly because of its haunting tune, and partly because of the macabre legend with which it is associated.

The legend concerns an otherwise unknown Rabbi Amnon of Mayence who, repeatedly urged by the local Archbishop to convert to Christianity, finally wavers and asks for three days to think it over. Immediately smitten with remorse for his momentary weakness, he fails to appear on the appointed day, is arrested, and asks that, as a fitting punishment, his hands and feet be cut off. So mutilated, he is carried into the synagogue on Rosh Hashanah, recites a *piyyut* (liturgical poem) beginning, 'Let us proclaim the holiness of this day,' then dies. Three days later he appears in a dream to the poet Kalonymos ben Meshullam, and teaches him the words.

It is, of course, merely a legend. Moreover, according to the latest scholarship the *piyyut* is not by Kalonymos but dates from an even earlier period. But whoever wrote it, it is extraordinarily powerful. And it is full of anthropomorphisms. God, sitting on a throne, judges every human being and records the judgment in a heavenly ledger: who shall live and who shall die, who shall die old and who shall die young, who from one cause and who from another.

All these are, of course, metaphors, not to be taken literally. But even if we 'demythologise' them, are we not left with an unacceptable theology? Surely the *U-n'tanneh Tokef* expresses a deterministic philosophy at variance with the emphasis on free will that is generally so characteristic of Judaism!

But wait! Don't judge too hastily. If we look more closely at the *piyyut* we shall notice two facts which put a totally different complexion on it.

First, the author doesn't deny that to a large extent we make our own destiny. On the contrary, he affirms it, as when he says that what is written in the book of records 'proclaims itself, for it bears the signature of every human being'.

Secondly, he doesn't deny that we are free to choose; free at any moment to change course and so to alter our seemingly predetermined destiny. Not only does the author concede this but he emphasises it. Indeed, it is the main point he wishes to make. For the punch-line is: 'Repentance, prayer and good deeds annul the severity of the judgment'. This is what the poet has been leading up to all along. It is true that he begins by dwelling on the inevitability of the process by which human beings, by their past conduct, pronounce sentence on their future. But he does so only in order to make the punch-line all the more dramatic. And so the *U-n'tanneh Tokef*, far from being a surrender to pagan fatalism, turns out to be the very opposite: *it is an ode to human freedom!*

❖   ❖   ❖

To Life
Rosh Hashanah, 25 September 1976

ויעקד את־יצחק בנו, 'And he bound his son Isaac' (Gen. 22:9). From that phrase, the twenty-second chapter of Genesis is known in Jewish tradition as the *Akedah*, 'The Binding of Isaac.' Already the Talmud (Meg. 31a) ordains the chapter to be read on Rosh Hashanah – more precisely, on the *second* day of the festival, as is still the practice in Orthodox synagogues. *Why* it was chosen, we can only speculate. Perhaps simply because it follows on the twenty-first chapter of Genesis which was the appointed Torah portion for the first day of Rosh Hashanah, though the reason for *that* choice is even less clear.

But there is a more interesting explanation, hinted at in the ancient Jewish sources. It points to the 'ram caught in a thicket by its horns' which is substituted for Isaac as the sacrificial offering, and links it with the ram's horn blown on Rosh Hashanah. Thus the Shofar, among its other symbolic meanings, is made to allude to the Akedah (see, e.g., RH 16a). But why is such an allusion relevant to Rosh Hashanah? The answer lies in the doctrine of *z'chut avot*, 'The Merit of the Fathers.' Let me explain.

We Jews, perhaps alone among the peoples of the world, begin the new year, not with bacchanalian revelries, but soberly and solemnly, with a period of introspection and repentance. The crossing of the threshold from the past into the future makes us more than ever conscious of our dependence on God whose good will is not to be taken for granted, but has to be earned. Therefore we implore God's mercy. But even as we do so, we realise that we are not worthy of it. As we say in the *Avinu Malkenu,* חננו ועננו, כי אין בנו מעשים, 'Be gracious to us and answer us, for we have no good deeds worth mentioning to our credit.' Therefore we cast about for other considerations which might conceivably incline God favourably towards us, and one of these is 'The Merit of the Fathers'.

That is to say, the present generation may be unworthy, but we are a people with a past and, so we hope, a future; a continuum in time as well as space; and our people's past, for all its shortcomings, is on the whole a record of loyalty to God. Therefore we say to God: don't look only at us; consider also the generations that have preceded us; on the strength of our past – our distant past if not our recent past – grant us a future; let the historic Jewish enterprise continue; give us a chance to try to emulate the loyalty of our ancestors, to build on their achievements, to carry on their mission.

But in support of this argument, whom shall we cite as the most telling example? Why, of course Abraham, not only because he was the one who set the whole Jewish enterprise in motion, but because, in his readiness to sacrifice his son, he passed the ultimate test, he gave the supreme demonstration of loyalty. Indeed, according to a tradition so ancient that it is found already in the Bible, it was on the strength of that event that the mountain of the Akedah, in the land of Moriah, became Mount Zion, the site of the Temple, worthy to serve as the abode of God's Presence (II Chron. 3:1; cf. Josephus, *Antiquities of the Jews* 1:13:2 and Jubilees 18:13).

The implication therefore is that the blast of the Shofar is not only an appeal to *us*, namely to repent, but also to God, to remember in our favour the loyalty of our ancestors as exemplified by Abraham on Mount Moriah.

But if this explains sufficiently the connection which Jewish tradition has seen between the Akedah and Rosh Hashanah, it still leaves open the question how we should evaluate the Akedah in its own terms. Clearly, it is a superbly written story. The mounting dramatic tension, the staccato sentences, the pregnant silences – these and other features are the marks of consummate artistry and entitle the story to be regarded as one of the masterpieces of human literature. But for a public Scripture lesson on a day as solemn as Rosh Hashanah, something more than literary excellence is needed: it has to be theologically acceptable and appealing; it has to proclaim a universal truth. And in that respect the founders of Liberal Judaism found the twenty-second chapter of Genesis, as also the twenty-first, deficient.

What then was the basis of their dissatisfaction with the Akedah? The answer is obvious. God commands Abraham to kill his son. Admittedly, it is not God's intention that the command shall be carried out to the bitter end. Its sole purpose is to test Abraham's readiness to obey, as is perfectly clear from the outset, for the narrative begins: והאלהים נסה את־אברהם, 'God put Abraham to the test' (22:1). But though it is clear to the reader, it isn't clear to Abraham. For three agonising days he believes, and Isaac increasingly suspects, that the unthinkable is really going to happen. Surely no benevolent deity would devise so cruel a test. Surely to think God capable of doing so betokens a primitive theology. Something like that, one supposes, is what the pioneers of Liberal Judaism thought and felt.

Perhaps they were also afraid that the story, if read solemnly from the pulpit, would be taken literally, as an account of an event that actually happened. If so, their fear was not unfounded, for even today one still meets people who so misunderstand the Bible as to suppose that it is throughout a record of historical happenings. Of course it is not. Of course it contains, not only fictional short stories such as Jonah, Ruth and Esther, but also, especially when dealing with the earliest periods, folk legends. To suppose that the author of Genesis had some supernatural means of knowing in detail what took place in Abraham's life, let alone his mind, is a childish naiveté which we ought to outgrow when we reach Grade 3 or 4 of the Religion School.

So the Akedah is a legend which, like other such legends, may or may not contain a kernel of fact. But to say that is not enough. It is also a myth. A myth is a legend *à la grande manière,* a dramatisation of a people's deepest anxieties and highest aspirations, an expression of its collective psyche, an epitome of its self-understanding and sense of destiny. It is more akin to poetry than to history. It is something like a dream, rich in symbolism, which has to be interpreted with the mind of a psychoanalyst. Therefore the question,

'What does it mean?', is not a simple question. There are many possible meanings: those intended, consciously or unconsciously, by the Biblical author and by the generations of story-tellers who preceded him, and those which have been read into the story, or out of it, with varying degrees of appropriateness and profundity, by the commentators. It is of the nature of a myth that it is pregnant with many possibilities of interpretation, that it can be understood on a variety of levels.

Nevertheless, in the myth of the Akedah, two motifs stand out. The first, which we have already touched on, is the motif of loyalty. Clearly, those who fashioned the Akedah wished to hold up Abraham as an exemplar. He was the progenitor of the Jewish people, the founder of the Covenant, the pioneer of a historic mission which was to devolve on all his descendants. Therefore he must have done something truly remarkable to earn so high a privilege. He must have been ready, in obedience to God, to sacrifice his greatest treasure, his only son. To an ancient story-teller, such an idea would have seemed less far-fetched than it does to us. For child sacrifice was a widespread practice in antiquity, as the Bible itself testifies. Nevertheless, the author of Genesis 22 was plainly aware of the horror of it. Indeed, if it were not horrific it would not serve his purpose, which is to demonstrate that there are no lengths to which Abraham will not go to do God's will.

But is such unquestioning obedience really praiseworthy? Perhaps the most disturbing feature of the Akedah is that God gives Abraham *no reason* for killing his son. To Abraham, therefore, it must seem not only unnatural, violating every paternal instinct, and not only immoral, contradicting every principle of right conduct, but utterly senseless. If Isaac had committed some appalling crime, or if he represented a fatal threat to the fulfilment of God's plan, maybe then it would be comprehensible. But the very reverse is the case. Isaac is Abraham's only son, as the narrator goes out of his way to stress. Everything depends on him. Without him there is no future at all for Abraham's people or the divine promise. To kill him, therefore, would be not only the cruellest act imaginable: it would also be the most senseless. Why then doesn't Abraham question God's command as when, in another famous Biblical legend, he questions God's intention to wipe out Sodom and Gomorrah?

There is a real problem here. We could of course dismiss it as an incidental flaw. After all, every story has its loose ends, and no analogy is perfect. The Akedah is about the depth of Abraham's loyalty. It serves that purpose. If the narrator had wished to raise the question, 'When is it permissible to question God's will?', which is not here his intention, he would have told a different story, like the one about Sodom and Gomorrah.

Or we could go to the opposite extreme and say that what appears to us as the difficulty in the Akedah is deliberate, that the very essence of its message is to teach us that the highest fulfilment of religious duty is to do God's will, not when we understand the reason for it but when we don't. Such a tendency can indeed be found in Jewish tradition, but it is applied only to certain ritual laws which are not readily intelligible; about these it is sometimes said (for instance by Rashi, Ber. 33b) that to obey them is all the more praiseworthy.

However, the tendency is not *characteristic* of Judaism. It is more characteristic of Christianity, and the outstanding exponent of it was the nineteenth-century Danish theologian Søren Kierkegaard. In a famous book, entitled *Fear and Trembling*, he describes Abraham as the 'knight of faith', who is superior to mere 'ethical man' precisely because he puts obedience to God above obedience to any moral code. It is a viewpoint which flows naturally from the tendency of the New Testament to extol 'faith' above 'works'. But it can hardly commend itself to us as Jews, least of all as Liberal Jews.

We may indeed concede that it has a limited validity, as a corrective against the opposite tendency: to equate the demands of religion with those of a comfortable, bourgeois respectability. The ideals of religion are higher and more exacting. They often require a critique of conventional morality, and the failure to realise this has often held back progress. It has made it possible for supposedly religious individuals and societies to condone and justify slavery, class distinction and racial discrimination.

But when that has been said, we must surely reaffirm our conviction that true religion and true morality speak with one voice. Therefore when religion, in the name of an alleged revelation, demands what our conscience unmistakably condemns as wrong, we must question the authenticity of the alleged revelation. And the failure to see this has done immeasurably more harm than any bourgeois morality. To set faith above and beyond righteousness leads to the Inquisition, the witch-hunt, the torture chamber and the 'holy war'.

If that is right, then Abraham's failure to question God's command is indeed a weakness of the story. A Liberal Jewish version of it would have him say: 'Shall not the Judge of all the earth do justly? This command is not just; therefore I must have misunderstood it.' But if it is a weakness, it is largely redeemed by the sequel, which brings us to the other main motif of the Akedah. It is not only about loyalty; it is also about life. For Isaac is *not* sacrificed. The God who has commanded the sacrifice goes on to forbid it. When God commands it, God is described as *Elohim*, a general term for all kinds of deities; when God forbids it, God is referred to as *Adonai*, the God of Israel. Thereby notice is served that the Jewish God, unlike the pagan gods, does *not* require child sacrifice but, on the contrary, abhors and condemns it; and not only child sacrifice, but killing generally. Judaism teaches that life is sacred, so that to destroy life is sacrilege; and the Akedah is a dramatic affirmation of that principle.

Can the same be said about Christianity? Of course, it too teaches, 'You shall not kill.' Of course, it too condemns those who *inflict* death. But on the other hand it tends to glorify those who *accept* death. 'Greater love has no man than this, that he lays down his life for his brother' (John 15:13). The Cross is a symbol of sacrifice, even of child sacrifice, since according to Christian theology it is the 'Son of God' who is crucified. Not surprisingly, therefore, the Akedah is seen in Christian tradition as a prototype of the Crucifixion (Hebrews 11:17f, Romans 8:32) and is therefore referred to, not as 'The Binding of Isaac' but as 'The Sacrifice of Isaac'.

This glorification of sacrifice has undoubtedly inspired many noble acts of martyrdom. But it is legitimate to wonder whether it has not also weakened the Hebraic affirmation of life. Certainly Isaiah's vision of a world at peace was slow to make an impact on Christendom. In the Middle Ages the Crusader and the 'knight in shining armour' was glamorised as a hero. Until much more recent times warfare was regarded as an honourable occupation; to die 'for king and country' was considered glorious; and the Tomb of the Unknown Soldier was a kind of sacred shrine.

Wilfred Owen, in a famous poem about the First World War, made even more famous by its inclusion in Benjamin Britten's *War Requiem*, retold the story of the Akedah and then gave it a twist. After referring to the ram which is to be substituted for Isaac, the poem ends:

> Offer the Ram of Pride instead of him.
> But the old man would not so, but slew his son, -
> And half the seed of Europe, one by one.

But we should be diffident about seeing in Owen's poem a judgment on Christendom alone. We Jews, too, have shed blood, and not always strictly in self-defence. We too have sometimes glorified our military heroes and martyrs. But when Jews idolise their generals rather than their sages, their values are no longer the values of Judaism. Not that Judaism is necessarily pacifist. It accepts that it is sometimes necessary to die, and even to kill. But however noble the courage of those who fight and die, the *need* to do so is always evil. Death, therefore, is never glorious; it is always tragic.

As the world grows more violent from year to year, the need becomes more urgent for a religion which teaches reverence for life as its highest principle. Judaism is such a religion. The God it worships does not desire the death of the sinner (Ezek. 33:11), but begs us : דרשוני וחיו, 'Seek Me and live' (Amos 5:4) and ובחרת בחיים, 'Choose life' (Deut. 30:19). It is a religion which teaches that those who destroy a single life are considered as if they had destroyed the whole world (San. 4:5). It is a religion which yearns, above all things, for the day when swords will be beaten into ploughshares and spears into pruning hooks (Isa. 2:4); whose aim, in the words of a modern Jewish writer, is 'the creation of a human being unable to shed blood' (Zvi Kolitz, *Survival for What?*, p. 183); whose toast is *L'chayyim*, 'To life!' It is the religion of the Akedah, which is a symbol of life, not death, because Abraham is *forbidden* to sacrifice his son. It is a religion whose New Year is a celebration of life and a plea for its continuance: זכרנו לחיים, מלך חפץ בחיים, 'Remember us unto life, for You, O Sovereign, delight in life; inscribe us in the Book of Life, that Your purpose may prevail, O God of life.'

❖   ❖   ❖

The Eternal Now
Rosh Hashanah, 12 September 1977

A few minutes ago we crossed a boundary. It was, of course, an *artificial* boundary. For the Jewish calendar, like every other, is only a human convention. There is no compelling reason, except tradition, why the Jewish year should begin on the 1st of Tishri rather than the 1st of January or any other date. But the tradition is important. It has singled out this day and invested it with a wealth of meaning. In particular it makes us 'poignantly conscious of the passage of time'. Time passes, of course, at every moment. But we do not normally think about it. The 1st of Tishri brings it home to us. It dramatises the passage of time. And therefore, like Janus, the Roman god of the gateway who gave his name to the month of January, it has two faces. It looks to the Past, and it looks to the Future.

The oldest name of this festival is *yom ha-zikkaron*, the Day of Remembrance. That is what the Bible calls it. For it was thought of as the day on which God reviews the deeds of human beings and judges them accordingly. But from an early time it came to be regarded as a day on which we, too, are bidden to remember. We are to make ourselves conscious of the mistakes we have made, the sins we have committed, during the past year, so that we may confess and regret them, and resolve to overcome them.

But it isn't only our private lives that we recall. On this day the whole House of Israel stands arrayed before God. Therefore we call to mind the whole history of our people, ever since the far-off day when our ancestors stood at Mount Sinai and said: 'We will do and obey'. And to give this day a still broader – a cosmic – significance, our tradition asserted that on it the world itself was created. So on this day the whole panorama of the history of our people, and even of humanity as a whole, unfolds before us: its achievements and its failures, its triumphs and its tragedies.

We Jews are much given to remembering. The Bible was the world's first history book. Our feasts and fasts commemorate historic episodes: the Exodus from Egypt, the Giving of the Torah, the journey through the wilderness, the Maccabean Rebellion, the destruction of the Temple. Our ceremonies and customs all evoke echoes from the distant past. And when we recite the Kaddish, we honour the memory of loved ones who have died in years gone by. למען תזכרו, 'That you may remember', is a lesson we have been well taught. And it is good that it should be so. For the past has made us what we are, so that to understand it is to understand ourselves. The past is the source of the wisdom that nourishes us, the purpose that unites us, the vision that inspires us. Without our past we are nothing, and to remember it is therefore not only beneficial, it is *essential* if we are to survive as a community.

But if the past is important, the future is no less important. The Day of Remembrance is also Rosh Hashanah, the 'head of the year'. It is an end, but also a beginning. It opens up new vistas, it raises fresh hopes. And not only that the new year may be better than the old, but that it may bring nearer the fulfilment of the greatest hope of all, for the time of redemption, when good will finally triumph over evil, and the nations will beat their swords into ploughshares and learn at last to live in peace. The Rosh Hashanah liturgy voices that hope again and again. For it celebrates the sovereignty of God and longs for the day when it will become fully operative, when 'the great Shofar will be sounded' to announce the Messianic Age.

If it is true that 'hope springs eternal in the human breast', it is especially true of the Jewish breast. Memories and hopes, these are the staple diet of the Jewish spirit. There is perhaps no people on earth that remembers more faithfully or looks forward more fervently. Past and Future, these are the twin poles round which, it seems, all our thoughts and emotions revolve. But is this polarity all there is? Does Judaism, like Janus, have only two faces. Does it look only backwards and forwards? Does it not also have a Present?

It has often been remarked that the Hebrew language has no present tense, only a past and a future, and though that remark requires some qualification, there is some truth in it. There is indeed a sense in which the Present is only an abstraction. As the Equator has no extension in space but is only an imaginary dividing line between the Northern and Southern hemispheres, so the Present has no extension in time but is only an imaginary dividing line between the Past and the Future. And therefore, as we feel no bump, except an emotional one, when we cross the Equator, so we feel no bump, except an emotional one, when we cross the threshold of a new year.

And yet there is another sense in which the Present, far from being an abstraction, is the most 'real' reality of all. After all, the Past is largely shrouded in mystery; the history books report only selected facts, and interpret these according to the author's point of view; even our own recollections soon become blurred and distorted. And the Future is notoriously uncertain. Who can be sure that the earth will even exist as a habitable place a few centuries hence? But the Present, that is our one certainty. In the words of Abraham Cowley:

> Nothing is there to come, and nothing past,
> But an eternal Now does always last.
> (*Davideis*, Bk. 1, l. 361)

It is this 'Eternal Now' which we Jews are in some danger of neglecting. Many Jews live too much in the past. They cling to laws and customs which have long since lost their validity or their relevance, merely because they are old. To them 'tradition' is a magic word that conjures away the need for intelligent appraisal. There is a story about Rabbi Moses Kraemer, great-grandfather of the Vilna Gaon, that whenever he proposed some innovation, and was attacked for it by the diehards, he would point to a law in Leviticus (19:31) and suggest that it should not be read, אַל־תִּפְנוּ אֶל־הָאֹבֹת 'Do not turn to ghosts', but אַל־תִּפְנוּ אֶל־הָאָבֹת, 'Do not turn to ancestors'; that is, 'Do not rely entirely on what former generations have taught' (Louis Ginzberg, *Students, Scholars and Saints*, p. 126). There *is* that danger in Judaism: a kind of ancestor worship.

But if many Jews are too preoccupied with the Past, many more are too preoccupied with the Future. They are always thinking ahead, saving up for a new house, booking for the next holiday, hiring a hall for the next wedding or Barmitzvah, attending committees to plan the next fund-raising campaign, investing money to make a profit to leave to their children so that they may invest it and leave it to their children; always dreaming of another land where the grass is greener; always saying במהרה בימינו, 'Speedily, in our days, may the Messiah come'. They are always in transit from the Past to the Future. Like the White Rabbit, they are always late for an important date.

It is of course very understandable in view of the historical experience of the Jewish people. Too often we have been compelled to live, literally or metaphorically, in a transit camp. Too often the Present has been for us a time to be endured. But if the Present is only that, it is nothing. The concept of enduring time is akin to the concept of 'killing time'. To kill time is a kind of suicide. And much of the emptiness in our lives stems from such an attitude. As Franz Rosenzweig once wrote in a letter to a friend, 'All our seeming contradictions arise from the equation between the today that is merely a bridge to tomorrow, and the today that is a springboard to eternity' (TJQ, 670.3).

In fact, we can go further. The Present is not merely a springboard to eternity. It is *part* of eternity, and even the most important part, for it is the one part we can be wholly sure of. Today is not *less* significant than yesterday or tomorrow: it is *more* significant. In the words of Israel Zangwill, 'Eternity is only a succession of todays. The whole problem of life faces us today' (TJQ, 670.6).

The Present, therefore, is not a time to be endured: it is a time to be *lived*. It is indeed the *only* time to be lived; if we do not live in the Present, we do not live at all. As Longfellow wrote in his hackneyed but still memorable *Psalm of Life*:

> Trust no Future, howe'er pleasant!
>   Let the dead Past bury its dead!
> Act, – act in the living Present!
>   Heart within, and God o'erhead!

To live in the Present is first of all to *do*, to do things that are worth doing, not only for their consequences, though they are immensely important, but for their intrinsic value. If, for Judaism, the Past is the realm of memories and the Future the realm of hopes, the Present is the realm of the *Mitzvah*, of the morally or otherwise significant deed. That is why it warns repeatedly against the danger of procrastination. חביבה מצוה בשעתה, said the Rabbis; 'Precious is a *Mitzvah* at its time' (Pes. 60b). 'When you have an opportunity to perform a *Mitzvah*, perform it at once' (Mechilta to Exod. 12:17). For as Hillel said, אם לא עכשיו אימתי, 'If not now, when?' (Avot 1:14).

But to live in the Present is not only to do: it is also to *be*. It is to savour the world around us, its sights and sounds and smells; it is to appreciate the goodness in our fellow human beings and to enjoy their friendship; it is to look and to listen, to think and to feel; it is to rejoice in the life that pulsates within us; it is to tune in to the rhythm of nature and the music of the spheres; it is to glimpse the Eternal, Divine Reality that overarches the Cosmos and irradiates the commonplace with sanctity.

We Jews are better at doing than at being. For Judaism is a religion of *Mitzvot*, of overt acts. And doing is important, perhaps more important than being, for it is by our deeds that we shape the conditions of life for ourselves and our fellow men and women. But deeds in themselves are only an expression of righteousness, and though righteousness is nearly everything, it isn't quite everything. Judaism also holds up to us the ideal of *holiness*, and holiness is something more. A righteous deed may be only an expenditure of nervous energy; a holy deed springs from an inner nobility. Holiness is possible only when being and doing are in harmony. Righteousness can be learnt; holiness must be cultivated.

Judaism urges us to cultivate holiness and gives us opportunities to cultivate it: the Sabbath and the Holy Days, the times of prayer and worship and study and quiet meditation. But we are too inclined to neglect them; we are too impatient. We have almost forgotten what it means to nurture the life of the spirit, to contemplate, to experience tranquillity, to respond to the plea of the Psalmist: 'Commune with your own heart upon your bed, and be still' (4:5). And that too is something which cannot be achieved yesterday or tomorrow, but only today.

This day is a Day of Remembrance and the beginning of a new year. It looks to the Past, and it looks to the Future, and both are vitally important. The Past is the source of our strength, the Future is the purpose of our endeavours. But it is in the Present, and only in the Present, that life can and must be lived. Abraham Geiger used to say: *Aus der Vergangenheit schöpfen, in der Gegenwart leben, für die Zukunft wirken*, 'We must learn from the Past, live in the Present, and work for the Future.'

It is the middle clause I wish to commend to you this evening. The new year we have inaugurated tonight will be, after all, only a succession of present moments. Let us resolve to use them well. Let us live each day as if it were the only day that ever was or ever will be. Let us sanctify the Eternal Now.

❖   ❖   ❖

A Heart of Flesh
Rosh Hashanah, 27 September 1984

The growth of intolerance seems like an epidemic sweeping across the world from country to country, respecting no boundaries, and contaminating every aspect of public life, especially the political, but also the religious.

What is the cause of the disease? It is fanaticism, fed by dogmatism, grounded in fundamentalism, namely the unshakable conviction that in your sacred text, whether it be the Hebrew Bible, the Christian Gospel, the Muslim Koran, or the economic theories of Karl Marx or Milton Friedman, you possess the truth, the whole truth and nothing but the truth, with the reassuring consequence that your side is always right and the opposing side invariably wrong.

And what are the symptoms? Self-righteousness and arrogance, intransigence and refusal to compromise, a tendency to lecture rather than to listen, to brandish slogans rather than engage in thought, to distrust the democratic process of rational persuasion, to despise and demonise those who dare to disagree with you, a readiness to resort to verbal abuse and physical aggression, and, more generally, that prideful obduracy which Scripture calls the hardening of the heart.

What then is to be done? Clearly, the first step is to become fully alert to the danger. It is, as I said, a kind of epidemic – or, to vary the metaphor, a baobab. It was, you may recall, the planet inhabited by Saint-Exupéry's 'Little Prince' that was infested with this pernicious seed. 'A baobab', he explained, 'is something you will never, never be able to get rid of if you attend to it too late. It spreads over the entire planet. It bores clear through it with its roots. And if the planet is too small, and the baobabs too many, they split it in pieces ...' (Antoine de Saint-Exupéry, *The Little Prince*, p. 21).

Such is the magnitude of the danger; but the question remains, how to counter it. As always, the most important thing is to begin with ourselves. There is an aggressive tendency in all of us; so we had better make sure that we don't succumb to the disease.

It thrives on two deficiencies. One is a lack of humility before God. For it is only when we are full of spiritual pride, only when we are quite sure that we know all the answers, that we have the presumption to seek to impose our beliefs on others. Therefore it is wholesome for us to remind ourselves how little we really know; that God is a Mystery for ever beyond our finding out; that all the literatures of all the religions, including our own, are only fallible human attempts to comprehend God's nature and to interpret God's will.

The other deficiency on which intolerance thrives is a lack of love for our fellow human beings. It is a failure to respect their integrity, to appreciate the good in them, to see the image of God in them. It is, to say it again, a hardening of the heart: a coronary sclerosis, spiritually speaking. That is why, of all the Scripture verses strung together in our liturgy, none seems more apt than this one from the thirty-sixth chapter of Ezekiel: ונתתי לכם לב חדש, 'A new heart will I give you', ורוח חדשה אתן בקרבכם, 'a new spirit will I put within you', והסירותי את-לב האבן מבשרכם, 'and I will remove the heart of stone from your flesh', ונתתי לכם לב בשר, 'and I will give you a heart of flesh' (v. 26).

Often when we look at the world about us, and hear the cacophany of strident voices shouting 'I am right and you are wrong, I am on God's side and you on the Devil's', and see the cold hostility in people's faces, and sense the anger snuffing out their compassion, driving them to deeds of cruelty which make us ashamed to belong to the same biological species, we know just what George Orwell meant when he wrote, 'If you want a vision of the future, imagine a boot stamping on the human face for ever' (*Nineteen Eighty-Four*, part 3, chapter 3), and we wonder whether his vision of the future is not already upon us, whether our fate is not already sealed, whether it is not already too late. But it never is! שערי תשובה לעולם פתוחים, 'The gates of repentance are always open' (Deut.R. 2:12). The still small voice can still be heard. ותשובה ותפלה וצדקה מעבירין את-רוע הגזרה, 'Repentance, prayer and good deeds can still avert the evil decree' (Ibid). It is not too late, but it is late. There is no time to be lost.

'Sometimes', wrote Saint-Exupéry, 'there is no harm in putting off a piece of work until another day. But when it is a matter of baobabs, that always means catastrophe. I knew a planet that was inhabited by a lazy man. He neglected three little bushes ...' (*The Little Prince*, p. 21).

❖　　❖　　❖

The Middle Way
Rosh Hashanah, 12 December 1988

The more I think about the peril in which present-day humanity finds itself, the clearer it becomes to me that it stems from two quite different, and even diametrically opposed, tendencies.

One of them is totalitarianism; and by that I don't only mean tyrannical, one-party régimes of the far Right or the far Left that demand total subservience from their citizens, I mean intellectual, ideological and spiritual tyranny as well as political tyranny. I mean every closed system of thought which claims to possess the truth, the whole truth and nothing but the truth: every kind of dogmatism, fundamentalism and fanaticism.

Why is totalitarianism, in this broad sense, so dangerous? Partly because it suppresses individual freedom. For the human spirit needs freedom as surely as the human body needs air. Partly because totalitarianism stifles progress. For if the truth is already known, there can be, by definition, no advance beyond it. Then any new idea that does not accord with the received doctrine must be rejected as false, and those who propound it denounced as heretics. When the greatest library of antiquity, the one in Alexandria, was destroyed by fire, the caliph Omar is said to have commented: 'If the books contain that which is in the Koran, they are superfluous. If they contain that which is *not* found in the Koran, they are false and should be *allowed* to burn' (q. by Louis Jacobs, *Jewish Chronicle*, 10 June 1988, p. 29). In the same vein it is said of Moses Sofer, one of the founding fathers of Orthodox Judaism, that his watchword was, 'Whatever is new is forbidden by the Torah' (*Encyclopaedia Judaica*, Vol. 15, p. 78).

Above all, totalitarians are so sure that they are right that they see it as their mission to persuade, cajole or compel everybody else to submit to their views, and they are not always very scrupulous about the means they employ in the pursuit of that aim.

If there is another danger, equally grave, it comes from a tendency which is the exact opposite of totalitarianism and for which perhaps the best term is the Hebrew word *hefkerut*. *Hefkerut* is lawlessness, licentiousness, anarchy. It is permissiveness, unrestraint, a complete lack of moral principles. It is, to use a talmudic phrase, the attitude of those who say לית דין ולית דין, 'There is no justice and there is no Judge' (meaning no divine Judge; Lev.R. 28; Midrash Psalms 47:6; Yoma 72a; B.B. 78b; Targum Jonathan. Gen. 4:8); therefore I can do whatever I jolly well please.

Hefkerut has grown immensely in recent times, as religion has declined in influence; and its constituency is a huge, amorphous multitude of persons who, like the Ninevites, 'do not know their right hand from their left' (Jonah 4:11). It is a creeping cancer that destroys one by one the cells of our moral fibre. It is the cause, or at least a major contributory one, of all the hooliganism and vandalism, the petty pilfering and violent crime, the adultery and child abuse, the alcoholism and drug addiction, which are slowly, insidiously undermining the stability of our society. It makes us too weak to control the *yetzer ha-ra*, the 'evil inclination', especially in the form of sexual temptation and economic selfishness; too feeble to oppose commercial interests that are destroying our environment, or political interests that are whittling away our liberties, and ultimately makes us vulnerable to the very totalitarianism which is the opposite of *hefkerut.*

Totalitarianism and *hefkerut,* then, are the two great destructive forces which threaten to bring the experiment of humanity to an untimely and catastrophic end. If there is any hope for the future, it must lie in a third way which avoids both extremes. It is the way neither of authoritarianism nor of licentiousness but of self-discipline. It is the way of respect for the wisdom of the past combined with openness to the insights of the present. It combines tradition with truth, mysticism with reason, and law with freedom.

In the context of our Jewish community, it is the way of Progressive Judaism. I don't mean any particular brand of it. There is room for many versions, and in our own for much adjustment. But in a *broad* sense it surely must be the Jewish way of strengthening those forces which can help humanity to navigate a safe course between the Scylla of totalitarianism and the Charybdis of *hefkerut* towards the calmer waters of a sensible, tolerant and peaceful future.

❖   ❖   ❖

The Last Trial
Rosh Hashanah, 25 September 1995

As a piece of writing, the story of the Akedah has everything. It has tension and drama, and enough action for a five-act play, compressed into eighteen verses. It is packed with energy like a nuclear reactor. It is a paradigm of Aristotle's catharsis, arousing both terror and pity. It deals with the biggest themes and touches the deepest emotions.

It has everything except one: an immediately apparent, morally acceptable and topically relevant message. That is why, in this Synagogue, we used not to read it, and why some people are still doubtful whether we should. But if the story is problematic, it is all the more *challenging.* It gives us something to get our homiletical teeth into.

And not only us. All through the ages preachers have felt challenged by it. There is more commentary on the *Akedah* than on any other chapter of the Bible. Many different meanings have been read out of it and into it. Let us explore yet another way of understanding it.

But first let us get ourselves a compass to guide us on our journey, and it comes from the book of the prophet Micah. 'With what shall

I approach the Eternal One? How shall I worship the God of heaven? Shall I come before God with burnt offerings ...? Will God be pleased with thousands of rams ...? Should I give my firstborn for my transgressions, the fruit of my body for the sins of my soul? Human beings tell you what is good, but what does the Eternal One require of you? Only to do justly, and to love mercy, and to walk humbly with your God' (6:6-8). There is the essence of Judaism, and any valid interpretation of the *Akedah* must accord with it.

To understand the story we need to distinguish three motifs within it. The most obvious is *human sacrifice*. It may even be the main purpose of the story to repudiate that cruel practice – to make it clear that God will have none of it – for though at first Abraham believes himself to be commanded to sacrifice his son, in the end he is emphatically forbidden to do any such thing: 'Do not raise your hand against the boy, or do anything to him' (Gen. 22:12). It is a plausible interpretation, and accords perfectly with Micah, 'Shall I give my firstborn for my transgressions, the fruit of my body for the sins of my soul?' (6:7b).

Clearly, the repudiation of human sacrifice was a major step forward in the history of religion. Unfortunately, the *concept*, as distinct from the practice of it, persisted for many centuries. Christianity knows the *Akedah* as the 'Sacrifice', not the 'Binding', of Isaac. And even in Jewish literature, as late as the Middle Ages, we find interpretations of it which, contrary to the plain sense of the biblical text, assert that Isaac *was* sacrificed, only his ashes were subsequently revived by the dew of resurrection; and that his blood atones in every generation (see Shalom Spiegel, *The Last Trial*, pp. 15f, 26, 32-37, 44, 57f, 133ff). This shocking notion latched onto a textual peculiarity of the biblical story, that in its sequel only Abraham, not Isaac, is mentioned as continuing the journey (Gen. 22:19), but it derived its sustenance from an undercurrent of paganism which never quite dried up, namely the primitive belief that 'there is no atonement without blood' (Spiegel, *Last Trial*, p. 58). In Judaism this idea attached itself to Isaac, but remained peripheral; in Christianity it attached itself to Jesus and became central (Spiegel, *Last Trial*, pp. 116f). As liberals, we reject it absolutely.

But whereas Micah dismisses not only human sacrifice but animal sacrifice as well – 'Will God be pleased with thousands of rams?' – the *Akedah*, on the contrary, ends with precisely the sacrifice of a ram! Nor is that an incidental detail. For there is reason to think that, though the author rejected human sacrifice, he wished at the same time to affirm the acceptability of *animal sacrifice* as a substitute for it. For a second motif of the story concerns the name of the mountain,

Moriah, on which it takes place, which the author explains as 'the Mountain of the Eternal One', that is Mount Zion; and therefore an incidental purpose of the story seems to be to validate the sacrificial cult of the Jerusalem Temple (see Spiegel, *Last Trial*, p. 73).

Obviously, that is something we reject, for animal sacrifice is also a relic of paganism. But we don't therefore reproach the biblical writer. For we know that the history of Judaism is a history of *development*. The Akedah reflects the historical transition from human to animal sacrifice. That was a big enough step forward. But it was not the last step. Already within the biblical period some of the Prophets, such as Micah, spoke against it, and when the Temple was destroyed the idea was mooted that prayer and good deeds may be as acceptable to God as sacrifice, if not more so.

Nevertheless, two thousand years later, Orthodox Jews still pray daily for the restoration of the Temple, so that sacrifices may again be offered; and though some of them don't mean what they say, which is bad enough, many of them do, which is worse. The latest issue of Singer's prayer book has a whole essay by former Chief Rabbi Lord Jakobovits, attempting to justify such prayers. In Israel today thousands of young men are daily studying the sacrificial laws in readiness for the rebuilding of the Temple. As 'Jerusalem 3000' is celebrated, and as the millennium approaches with its seemingly inevitable concomitant of messianic expectancy, we had better be prepared to hear more of this nonsense. How slowly paganism dies – as we have just been reminded by the ridiculous episode of the Hindu idols supposedly drinking milk!

So now we have considered two motifs of the *Akedah*, the human sacrifice motif and the animal sacrifice motif. But there is a third, which is the most disturbing of all. It is stated right at the beginning of the story: 'God tested Abraham'. The whole thing is a test, and more precisely an *obedience test*: whether Abraham is prepared to go *to any length* to carry out God's command, even if it means giving up what he treasures above all else on earth: 'your son, your only one, whom you love' (Gen. 22:2).

And does Abraham pass the test? Yes, with flying colours! Certainly that is how the biblical writer understands the story, since he makes the angel say: 'Because you have done this, and have not withheld your son, your only one, therefore I will bless you greatly …' (Gen. 22:16f). And that is how it has been understood ever since.

But from our liberal point of view this obedience motif raises the greatest difficulty. Of course we would agree – how could we not? – that God must be obeyed, whatever the cost. But how do we know what God requires of us? Ah, there's the rub!

Abraham hears a voice which he takes to be the voice of God, commanding him to sacrifice his son. But how can he believe that? Presumably because he is not yet wholly emancipated from his pagan background. Because with part of his mind he still lives in a world in which child sacrifice is not yet unthinkable. Because he has not yet fully understood that the God of heaven, whose missionary Abraham is being called to be on earth, is a God of justice and mercy who could not possibly make such a demand. Perhaps, therefore, the voice Abraham hears emanates not from God but from his own, dark, pagan past.

Either way, the mere fact that the idea of sacrificing his son enters Abraham's head creates a test. But the test, let me suggest, is not whether he will obey the supposed command, but whether he will question it, just as, in an earlier chapter, he questioned the threatened destruction of Sodom and Gomorrah, saying, 'Shall not the Judge of all the earth do justly?' (Gen. 18:25. By obeying blindly, Abraham does not pass the test: by obeying blindly, he fails the test! But God is patient. This time Abraham will have to be stopped from sacrificing his son, and a substitute ram provided. Evidently, he and his people need more time fully to grasp what Hebraism, which is the negation of Paganism, means.

Four millennia have passed, and we have not yet learned the lesson! Admittedly, most of us no longer hear voices telling us to do outrageous things. Instead, we have a book which the fundamentalists take to be the voice of God. But to ascribe divinity to anything other than God – even to so magnificent a book as the Bible – is also pagan, and like all forms of paganism, leads to baneful consequences. Under its influence, plans are laid to restore animal sacrifice, women are discriminated against, and antiquated laws perpetuated.

But it is even worse than that. It was a fundamentalist, Dr Baruch Goldstein, who, eighteen months ago, in 1994, walked into a Hebron mosque with an automatic rifle and mowed down twenty-nine Muslims at prayer. 'His grave at the entrance to Kiryat Arba has become a place of pilgrimage for a growing band of admirers' (*Observer*, 10 Sept. 1995, p. 22). Leading Orthodox rabbis have published whole tomes solemnly proving from the Bible that it is forbidden for Israel to relinquish a single inch of the occupied territories, and urging active resistance against any such move. They are the mirror image of the Islamic fundamentalists with their suicide squads. Between them, in spite of the historic agreement that was reached yesterday (24 September 1995), they may yet wreck the Peace Process, and if that were to happen, the consequences could be disastrous, not only for Israel but for the Middle East and the whole world.

Therefore please don't think that the issue we have been discussing is purely academic. It is very much 'for real'. Fundamentalism, along with racialism and nationalism, and especially when combined with them, is the greatest evil of our time. And therefore the question of how to interpret the Bible, is fraught with positively explosive consequences.

Our liberal view is clear. We know that the Bible is not the voice of God but the voice of our ancestors trying, sometimes more, sometimes less successfully, to understand and interpret the mind of God. It is a great book, from which we have learned, and continue to learn, most of what we shall ever know about right and wrong. But God is greater than the Bible, and our only unconditional allegiance is to God, not to this book our ancestors have written about God.

How then do we know what God requires of us? Not just by looking up the book, though that is the best first step, but by using our God-given intelligence to discern the process of development at work within and beyond it. Therefore we know that God does not require human sacrifice. Therefore we know that God does not require animal sacrifice. Therefore we know that what God requires can never be contrary to what is morally right.

From a fundamentalist point of view the Bible, as traditionally interpreted, stands above ethics. From a liberal point of view nothing stands, or must ever be allowed to stand, above ethics.

And so back to Micah: 'Human beings tell you what is good, but what does the Eternal One require of you? Only to do justly, and love mercy, and to walk humbly with your God.' That is the compass which must guide us as we try to understand the Bible. That is the compass which must guide us as we try to strengthen the liberal forces in Judaism, and in the world, so that reason and conscience, justice and mercy, good will and peace may prevail.

❖   ❖   ❖

Contemporary Varieties of Idolatry
Shabbat Shuvah, 24 September 1960

'Return, O Israel, unto the Eternal One your God' (Hos. 14:2). These words sum up the whole significance of this Penitential Season. They are also the recurring refrain of biblical prophecy, which is one sustained admonition to the Israelites to repent of their disloyalty to God. This disloyalty, however, is often described as *idolatry*. And here a difficulty arises. For idolatry is not a sin of which we are aware in ourselves. We can barely imagine what idol worship was like.

Yet we are as guilty of idolatry as any generation, only our idols are subtler and less tangible. For idolatry is an attitude of mind. There is nothing intrinsically wrong with a sculpture representing a bull. It may even be a fine work of art. What makes it an idol is the significance attached to it, the worship accorded to it. Idolatry, like beauty, is in the eye of the beholder.

All of us have one or more overriding aims in life: purposes to which we assign the highest place in our scale of priorities and for which we make the greatest sacrifices. We may not always be conscious of them, but they are the real driving force in our lives, and others can read them easily out of our behaviour. Now, to the extent to which these supreme goals are other than, and unrelated to, the will of God, to that extent we are guilty of idolatry. The neatest definition of idolatry is 'misdirected reverence'.

What are the idolatries of contemporary humanity? One, surely, is *the pursuit of pleasure*. It has long been known that this is the most powerful of human drives. The Rabbis called *yetzer ha-ra*, 'the evil inclination'. Freud called it the libido. But the modern world has made its pursuit particularly rampant. The breakdown of moral restraint; the widespread notion that repression is unhealthy; the constant titillation of our hedonistic impulses by the entertainment and advertising industries: all these play into its hands. Add to all that the insecurity of our time, and it is not surprising that the most widespread of contemporary philosophies is: 'Let us eat and drink, for tomorrow we die' (Isa. 22:13).

Another characteristic idolatry of our time is nationalism, which conquered Europe in the nineteenth century and is now sweeping like a forest fire through the rest of the world. For its devotees national independence and glory is the *summum bonum* to which all else, including individual freedom, human life and common decency, as well as the rights of minorities and the legitimate claims of other nationalisms, must be subordinated. We Jews, too, have caught the fever. I remember a conference of the World Union for Progressive Judaism at which an Israeli delegate remarked that in Israel religion is not as important as in the Diaspora because, for the pioneer who tills the sacred soil, that is in itself an act of worship. Whereupon another Israeli delegate, Shalom Ben-Chorin, rose up and said: 'But, you know, there is such a thing as עבודה זרה, false worship or idolatry!'

Another widely worshipped idol of our time is human achievement. Its priest is the scientist. Its shrine is the laboratory. Its devotees are the millions who see in technological advance the salvation

of humanity. We have achieved so much, they say. We have conquered the earth. Tomorrow we shall conquer outer space. Soon we
shall be omnipotent. What need then is there to worship God? Let us
rather worship ourselves.

All these idolatries have brought us to the brink of disaster. For
they all appeal to our baser instincts and leave our human nature
unchanged. It is only when we revere a Being greater than ourselves
that we rise above ourselves. Only the worship of God transforms
the human heart. 'Assyria shall not save us; we will not ride upon
horses; we will say no more to the work of our hands: you are our
gods; for in You the orphan finds mercy' (Hos. 14:4). That is the fundamental difference which distinguishes true religion from all its sub-
stitutes. Hedonism may make people happy. Nationalism may make
them heroic. Science may make them powerful. But only religion
makes them merciful. Only religion teaches us to do justly, to love
kindness, and to walk humbly with our God (Micah 6:8). And unless
we learn that, there is little hope for our future.

The prophecy of Hosea, therefore, is very relevant in the twentieth century, and if he were speaking today, he might re-phrase it:

> Return, O Israel, return, all humanity, to the Eternal One, your God; for
> you have stumbled to the brink of catastrophe by your pursuit of false
> ideologies. Take with you words of prayer, and return to the Eternal One.
> Say to God: Forgive all iniquity and fortify our fitful impulses of good-
> ness. So, instead of merely performing acts of ritual, we will offer the sin-
> cere promises of our lips and the true devotion of our hearts. NATO shall
> not save us; we will not rely on nuclear weapons; we will say no more to
> the products of our factories, you are our gods. For it is in worshipping
> You, the God of justice and mercy, that we shall learn to act justly and
> mercifully to one another.

❖   ❖   ❖

Season of Atonement

The Quality of Life
Yom Kippur, 6 October 1973

'I call heaven and earth to witness against you this day that I have set
before you life or death, blessing or curse; therefore choose life, that
you may live, you and your descendants' (Deut. 30:19). That verse

sounds the keynote of the penitential season. But it also poses a problem: why does it need to be said? If there is anything that can be
taken for granted, surely it is the love of life. Nothing is more basic
to our make-up than the instinct of self-preservation, implanted in us
by countless millennia of evolution. Why then should we need to be
exhorted to choose life?

One answer may be that the self-preservation instinct is not infal-
lible. In exceptional circumstances it may break down and the death
wish may take over. But the exhortation to 'choose life' can hardly be
understood merely as a warning against suicide.

Another possible answer is that, even when the self-preservation
instinct is intact, we sometimes fail, through neglect or thoughtless-
ness, to take the precautions it demands. In this connection it is interesting to recall a passage in the Talmud which discusses the
obligations of a father to his children. It lists several, with a proof-text
for each. And then it adds: according to some authorities he must
also teach them to swim. And what is the proof-text here? It is our
verse: ובחרת בחיים 'Choose life' (Kid. 29a, 30b, Eccles. R. 9:8).

But even that is not the main point. We come nearer to it when we
remember that love of life is not our only motive. We also have other
desires which may conflict with it. One is the desire for wealth. At
first it may only be a means to an end. We seek it in order that we
may be able to purchase the necessities of life. But then, all too easily, it becomes an end in itself, and at that stage it may run counter
to self-preservation.

This fact was noted already long ago. Consider, for instance, the
words of the Shema: 'You shall love the Eternal One your God with
all your heart, ובכל-נפשך ובכל-מאדך' (Deut. 6:5). These last two phrases
were understood by the Rabbis, not as we translate them, but to mean
'with all your life and with all your wealth.' And then they asked: why
are both mentioned? Surely 'life' says everything! If you love God to
the point of being willing to surrender your life, what more is there to
be added? The answer, according to the Rabbis, is that some human
beings value wealth above life (Sifre Deut. to Deut. 6:5).

Today that danger is very real. We live in an acquisitive society.
Everything conspires to impress on us that making money is the
most important of life's activities. It is drummed into us from the cradle. Parents let it be known to their children that they expect them to
opt, not necessarily for the most fulfilling but for the most lucrative
careers. Education is increasingly viewed, not as an enrichment of
the mind, still less as a training of character, but as a head start in the
hunt for job opportunities. Commercial companies are judged, not
by the excellence of the products they market, but by the profits they

show. Trade unions strike most commonly for higher wages. Succes-
sive British governments have regarded it as axiomatic that Britain's
supreme objective must be to achieve an ever higher rate of economic growth. And the British people, brain-washed by this ideology, yet depressed by their relative lack of success in regard to it, are
rapidly losing their self-confidence and beginning to believe that
they are no longer a 'great' nation.

Paul Johnson, in his book, *The Offshore Islanders*, remarks: 'What
distinguishes the present chorus of self-doubt and criticism is not the
fear of internal chaos, or of external perils ... but a nagging anxiety
about Britain's performance in the international league-tables of
material prosperity. The English, who invented modern competitive
sport, are obsessed by the statistical evidence of their decline in the
world championship, and the impending verdict of relegation to
some lesser category of breeds' (pp. 411f). Nor is it only a British preoccupation. The whole world seems to be engaged in a mad scram-
ble to produce and consume more.

But it is precisely at the global level that the dangers of this mate-
rialism-run-riot have begun to be perceived. We now know that if we
continue as at present we shall sooner or later endanger the very survival of humanity: by using up the earth's non-renewable resources;
by polluting air, land and sea with pesticides and the waste products
of industry; by disturbing ecological balances; and perhaps by bringing about fatal changes in the global weather system. In other words,
we are beginning to realise that the pursuit of wealth may actually
militate against the preservation of life, if not in the immediate
future, then in the more distant future. And perhaps that is what our
Torah verse warns against when it says: 'Therefore choose life, that
you may live, *you and your descendants.*'

Let us, however, suppose that we manage to avoid global catastrophe, that we learn, before it is too late, to put a curb on our present unrestrained exploitation of our environment. That itself is a
big assumption, for it already involves some retrenchment of present policies and attitudes, some abandonment of our dogma that
whatever technology can do is *ipso facto* desirable. But even if we
don't actually destroy the conditions for continued life on this
planet, the question still remains: what *kind* of life? And the fact that
this question is now being asked by more and more people shows
that a great change has begun to take place. If I am not mistaken, it
is during the past year that a new expression has come into vogue:
the quality of life.

It implies that material plenty is not enough. For one thing, its
benefits may not be distributed equitably, and this may lead to

resentment, unrest and strife. That material advance must go hand-in-hand with social reform is not, I think, disputed by responsible politicians in this country, or in Europe. Only this week Michael Shanks, the Director-General for Social Affairs in the Commission of the European Communities, made this point when he spoke in London about Europe's 'unprecedentedly rapid rate of economic growth'. For he went on to say: 'We are no longer so concerned simply with the maximisation of growth. We now have the opportunity to examine what it is that growth has achieved. Has it achieved the better quality of life that traditionally people have expected the economic system to provide?'

However, it goes further than that. We are beginning to realise that all social and economic policies must be judged by their effect on human life. We have come to question the building of high-rise blocks if they make for loneliness and lack of community. We have come to question the construction of motorways and airports if those who live near them are subjected to intolerable noise. We have come to question the value of ever-accelerating urbanisation if people have no countryside to visit for relaxation. We have come to question the need for ever more and faster cars if they fill the air with toxic fumes and cause an astronomically high road-accident rate. We have come to question the merit of all forms of centralisation if the price that must be paid for greater efficiency is a lessening of personal attention to individual human beings.

In short, we are beginning to awaken out of the materialistic stupor which has held us in its thrall ever since the Industrial Revolution. We are beginning to discover, or to rediscover, that there are other values besides material prosperity: human values, cultural values, moral values, spiritual values; that we are not only producers and consumers; that we have other, more fundamental needs, and that the indiscriminate pursuit of wealth may be positively harmful to human welfare. Some people are beginning to think, for example, that the task of Britain may be, not to recover its lost political and economic pre-eminence, nor even to achieve an unprecedentedly high standard of living, but to achieve an unprecedentedly high quality of life; to create a society that shall set an example by the maturity of its political processes, the justice of its law courts, the humaneness of its penal code, the fairness of its wage structure, the compassion of its welfare services, the harmony of its community relations, the excellence of its educational system, the splendour of its culture, the wisdom of its town planning, the love of nature shown in the conservation of its countryside, and the decency of its citizens to one another.

But if these things, rather than mere productivity, are to move into the centre of attention, then religion needs to be taken far more seriously than hitherto. For the quality of life is precisely what religion is about. That is its *métier*, its *spécialité de la maison*. Its whole aim and purpose is to teach the ideals that make for excellence in human life, considered as a spiritual rather than merely a physical process.

That indeed is one reason why it has fared so badly in recent times. In a world dedicated to the worship of Mammon, religion is an irrelevancy, a waste of time. While we sit here in the synagogue we are, from a materialistic point of view, ungainfully employed. We do not produce; we do not even consume; and our bank balance does not improve by one penny. And no doubt there are those who consider us, for that reason, a little eccentric if not downright *meshugge*.

If what I have been saying is correct, then the boot is on the other foot. Then materialism represents a scale of values that is fast becoming discredited. Then it is out of touch with the new mood that is coming over the world, especially the younger generation. If the quality of life is now to be item number one on humanity's agenda, then we are the 'with-it' people. For it is in synagogues and places like them that the values which give quality to life are explored, expounded, inculcated and transmitted.

And so we come back to our Scripture verse: 'Choose life, that you may live.' *Of course* it doesn't refer to physical life alone. *Of course* it doesn't merely exhort us to ensure that there is enough clean air for human beings to breathe, and enough good food to eat, so that their bodies may continue to function as efficient biological organisms. That is important and may be part of the meaning. But chiefly it exhorts us so to develop our spiritual powers, so to conduct our relationships with one another, and so to order society, that human life may realise increasingly its limitless potential for excellence – for goodness, truth and beauty. The point of the exhortation is not merely that we should survive but that we should fulfil ourselves, not merely that we should have life but that we should have it more abundantly. And that is something which no amount of scientific inventiveness, technological ingenuity or economic productivity can achieve, but only submission to the One who is our Creator, our Guardian and our Lawgiver.

❖   ❖   ❖

Beyond Materialism
Yom Kippur, 25 September 1974

Have you ever wondered why the Jewish year begins in the autumn? There are of course historical reasons. But on the face of it, it seems a curious choice. In nature, autumn is not a time of renewal. On the contrary, the days get shorter, the winds blow colder, the flowers wither, the trees shed their leaves, the bleakness of winter lies ahead. A more inappropriate time for making a fresh start can hardly be imagined. And yet this year, more than ever, the autumnal season accords with our mood. For it isn't only nature that is slowing down: the whole world seems to be grinding to a halt.

The immediate cause of this feeling is the state of the economy. But that can't be the whole of the explanation. After all, we have experienced economic difficulties before; indeed, it is hard to recall a time when we didn't. Yet never, for as long as most of us can remember, has there been such a deep and pervasive gloom as there is today.

Why is that? Partly because there is no immediate prospect of any improvement. Yet even that would be tolerable if we could look forward to a brighter future in due course. When Winston Churchill, in 1940, made the famous speech in which he said that he had 'nothing to offer but blood, toil, tears and sweat', the nation responded because, beyond the struggle, it could see victory. And indeed there are those today who try to cheer us with the thought that what we are facing is only a temporary setback: that in a few years' time, when North Sea oil becomes available, or when world prices begin to fall, the economic machine will go into forward gear again. But what if they are wrong? What if there is no light at the end of the tunnel? What if, beyond the autumn, there is only unending winter, without a spring to follow? That is, at any rate, a real possibility, and the mere contemplation of it sends shivers down our spines.

But why should it? What is so terrible about living in a non-expanding economy? After all, human beings have done so before, even for generations and millennia. Besides, nobody suggests that we are in any imminent danger of starving to death.

No, it is the simple realisation that we can no longer be sure of ever-increasing prosperity which accounts for our mood of gloom and foreboding. For it has plunged us, with traumatic suddenness, into a situation for which we were not mentally prepared. It has destroyed at one fell swoop an assumption on which, for years and generations, we had based our whole mode of thinking and living: *the belief in continuous and unending progress.*

It is a belief which grew directly out of the rise of modern science and the exuberant confidence it inspired that human beings would achieve a constantly growing understanding of, and therefore mastery over, their environment. By the eighteenth century it had become a kind of dogma. Almost any European thinker of that time could have written, as Joseph Priestley did: 'Knowledge ... being power, the human powers will, in fact, be enlarged; nature ... will be more at our command; men will make their situation in this world abundantly more easy and comfortable ... and will daily grow more happy ... Thus whatever was the beginning of this world, the end will be glorious and paradisiacal beyond what our imaginations can now conceive' (q. by Sidney Pollard, *The Idea of Progress*, p. 80).

It is true that this wave of optimism about the future of humanity was shattered by the French Revolution; but it soon revived and became even more firmly entrenched, especially in the minds of the rising middle classes, throughout the nineteenth century and into the twentieth. Then it received another rude shock, or series of shocks, with the First World War, the Depression, the rise of Fascism, the Second World War, the Holocaust and the spectre of the H-bomb. Doubts began to be felt about the rationality and the stability of civilisation and indeed the survival of the human race. But somehow we managed to suppress even these doubts in the euphoria of the unprecedentedly rapid rate of technological advance and economic growth which we experienced after 1945. We said to ourselves: 'Yes, there are grave dangers, even of global catastrophe; but of one thing at least we can be certain: that *if* we succeed in avoiding these pitfalls, *then* we may confidently expect to see ever increasing material prosperity, leading to a veritable Utopia of abundance.'

To this assumption we have pinned our faith; on this foundation we have built our hopes. And now it has been swept away from under our feet, and we are left disoriented and disconsolate, like a child whose favourite toy has been taken away.

But you know that Rabbi Akiva's teacher Nachum of Gimzo said whenever he received a piece of bad news: גם זו לטובה 'May even this prove to be a blessing in disguise.' There *can* be a blessing in the rude awakening we have received if it prompts us to revise our assumptions.

What are the lessons to be learnt from it? The first is that material prosperity is not the most important thing in the world. *Of course* there are certain basic needs which must be satisfied: food, shelter, clothing, education, medicine; and there even has to be a certain amount of surplus wealth in a society if it is to be culturally creative. But these minimum requirements are not threatened, at least not in the foreseeable future or in our part of the world. And as long as they are satisfied, not only is there no need to despair, but it is an illusion to suppose that our happiness depends on having more.

But not only does happiness not *depend* on material prosperity: it doesn't even necessarily *result* from it. Priestley's conviction that as life becomes more comfortable, so human beings 'will daily grow more happy', is patently untrue. We are much more inclined to agree with a remark which was once quoted by the late Dean Inge, that 'if it is progress to turn the fields and woods of Essex into East and West Ham, we may be thankful that progress is a sporadic and transient phenomenon of history' (Pollard, *Idea of Progress*, p. 107). And therefore the second lesson we need to learn is that economic progress is one thing and moral progress another, and that they don't necessarily go together. Not only are technologically advanced societies not always the happiest: they are not always the most humane. On the contrary, as we know them, they tend to produce evils distinctively their own: pollution, alienation, loneliness, boredom, bureaucracy, vulgarity and violence. After all, the worst outbreak of barbarism of our century occurred in a country which was one of the most industrially advanced in Europe. And it is significant that writers of science fiction do not generally portray the heroes of the imaginary super-automated future as superior to us in the moral virtues, as gentler and more compassionate, but, on the contrary, as insensitive and ruthless. (See Pollard, *Idea of Progress*, p. 198.)

The first lesson we must impress on our minds is that, far from moral progress depending on economic progress, *the very reverse* is the case. Even the most brilliant schemes of social engineering may founder on the rock of human lethargy and selfishness, depend for their success on the willingness of human beings to act responsibly and co-operatively.

If we muster the moral qualities that are so plainly called for, we *may* surmount the present crisis. The inflation rate may be brought down, massive unemployment may be avoided, the balance of payments may be rectified. But we delude ourselves if we suppose that *even then* a high rate of economic growth would necessarily be once again achieved and sustained for ever. For there are limiting factors. The earth's resources are finite. The population explosion may continue to outstrip food production. The underprivileged nations will certainly demand a larger share of the available commodities. The exploitation of nature exacts its penalties. Scientific discovery and invention become progressively more expensive and, in some areas, more dangerous. It may very well be, therefore, that we shall have to consider ourselves lucky if we manage to avoid economic catastrophe and maintain for an indefinite time to come a standard of living not too far below our present one.

For all these reasons the time has come – it is long overdue – for a fundamental re-appraisal and re-adjustment of our values, priorities and objectives. The dream of an endless vista of ever-increasing material prosperity is finished; and if that alone has seemed to us in the past to make life worth living, then we may succumb to despair. But there are other things worth living for: much more important things, much more precious things, much more satisfying things: the acquisition of knowledge, the contemplation of beauty, the enjoyment of love, the cultivation of friendship, the creation of a just, humane and compassionate society. It is to *these* things that we must now give the attention they have always demanded; it is in *them* that we must henceforth find our meaning and purpose, our happiness and fulfilment.

As autumn descends on the earth and the affluence of nature declines, the High Holydays invite us to give our attention to these things; to cultivate our inner life; to consider, not what we have, but what we do and what we are; to dedicate ourselves anew to the pursuit of goodness, truth and beauty. For the value of the pound may fall, but the value of these things is eternally the same. The days may get shorter, the winds may blow colder, the flowers may wither, and the trees may shed their leaves; but if we respond to God's demands, there need be no winter in our souls.

❖   ❖   ❖

Reconciliation
Yom Kippur, 10 October 1978

What then is required of us? Not that we should become perfect. Of that there is, alas, no chance. But if we have been overly preoccupied with ourselves and our daily tasks, we could give a little more time and thought to others. If we have been offended by friends or relations, we could be a little more forgiving. If we tend to be impatient with other motorists, we could remember that they may be beginners, as we once were, or in a hurry for some pressing reason, as we occasionally are. If we catch ourselves treating the bus conductor, or the shop assistant, as impersonal machines, not even looking them in the face, we could give them a smile and say a friendly word. If we have been quick to condemn those whose conduct displeases us, we could remind ourselves of the teaching of the Rabbis that we should not judge others until we have found ourselves in their position (Avot 2:5) and that even then we should incline the scale of merits and demerits in their favour (Avot 1:6). If we have been rigidly dogmatic in our convictions, we could become a little more flexible and try to see the point of view of others. If we have been abusive in our denunciations of those whose theories we consider wrong, we could moderate our tone and practise the virtue of civility. If we have retailed unsubstantiated rumours, or uncritically espoused opinions for no other reason than that they fit in with our likes and dislikes, whether about the Government or the Opposition, trade unions or employers, law and order, crime and punishment, the effect of immigration on our national life, or the alleged irresponsibility of contemporary youth, we could pause to consider the facts and bear in mind the warning of William James, that 'a great many people think they are thinking when they are merely rearranging their prejudices' (THQ, p. 108). If we have been too wedded to the norms of the past, or too reckless in demanding change, we might recall the remark of Dean Inge that there are two kinds of fool, the one who says, 'This is old, therefore it is good', and the one who says, 'This is new, therefore it is better' (THQ, p. 106). If we have been engrossed in the pursuit of material aims, we could remember that our spiritual welfare is even more important, both for itself and, in the long run, for our happiness. If we have neglected our Jewish heritage, we could resolve to let it play a larger part in our lives.

In all these and countless other matters, it is only a relatively small effort that is required of us; we only need to give ourselves a push sufficient to cross over the boundary from one set of attitudes which are diminishing, stultifying and destructive, to another set of attitudes which are enlarging, enhancing and redemptive: from pride, anger, harshness, abrasiveness, meanness and self-absorption to humility, conciliatoriness, gentleness, courtesy, generosity and concern for others. If we were to take even a modest step in that direction, who knows what a transformation would take place? It would gather its own momentum, for, as the Rabbis said, מצוה גוררת מצוה, 'one good deed leads to another' (Avot 4:2), and we would strengthen the forces in the world that make for reconciliation, harmony and peace. It would be a real atonement, a restoration of our broken relationship with our better selves, with our fellow human beings, with our people and its heritage of faith, and with our God.

Ezekiel said it all: 'A new heart will I give you; a new spirit will I put within you. I will remove the heart of stone from your flesh, and I will give you a heart of flesh. I will put my spirit within you, and teach you to live by my laws' (36:26f). That heart of flesh is all we need. The miracle of Yom Kippur is that it is attainable, not in some distant future, but here and now. In the words of Tennyson's *Ulysses,*

> The long day wanes: the slow moon climbs: the deep
> Moans round with many voices. Come, my friends,
> 'Tis not too late to seek a newer world.

❖   ❖   ❖

The Rediscovery of the Transcendent
Yom Kippur, 1 October 1979

'You stand this day all of you before the Eternal One your God' (Deut. 29:9). These words apply to us, for if we don't feel God's presence here and now, we are not likely to do so in other times and places. But do we?

Of course there is no simple answer, since we are all individuals. But my guess would be this. There are probably some among us whose faith has remained uneroded since childhood. There are probably others who frankly doubt whether God exists at all and who come here only 'for old times' sake', because to absent themselves would be too sharp a break with the tradition of their people, or the expectation of their family, or the habit of a lifetime. Many, I suspect, fall somewhere between: they are not as sure about God as they used to be, or as they would like to be; but they are *inclined* to think that God exists, or they *hope* so.

If that is a fair description of our various states of mind, it should occasion no surprise; for ours is not an age of faith. There are indeed those who live in enclaves of faith, cosy ghettos untouched by the cold winds of modernity. We may envy them; just occasionally we may even feel tempted to join them. But we know that it would be a retreat, like a child longing to return to the warm security of its mother's womb. In Louis Jacobs' phrase, it would be to opt out of the twentieth century. It cannot be our way. We have opted to live in the present, and to look it squarely in the face. If our faith can survive such a confrontation, well and good; if not, it is not worth having. We do not care for a blinkered faith, a faith that preserves itself at the cost of ignoring reality.

Living in the twentieth century, we are aware that the belief in God is open to question on many grounds. According to Samson

Raphael Hirsch, it is guaranteed by the biblical account of the six hundred thousand who witnessed the Revelation at Mount Sinai. Unfortunately, facts are not so easily established. There were no camera crews at Sinai, and we possess no eye-witness accounts of what occurred, only folk memories preserved in writings of a later age. We know that those who wrote the Bible were human and fallible; how then can we be sure that they were not mistaken about the very existence of God? We are told that God created the world; but does not modern science suggest that it evolved fortuitously, in the course of billions of years? We are told that God is benevolent; but how can that claim be reconciled with 'nature, red in tooth and claw', or with the inhumanity of human beings to one another, or with the suffering of the innocent? We may have had what we supposed to be intimations of God's presence; but might they not have been instances of wish-fulfilment? We speak of God as if we knew exactly what we meant by the word; but has it not been shown by one school of philosophy that the proposition that God exists is by its very nature unverifiable and therefore meaningless?

So the arguments against God are formidable, and we may not shut our eyes to them. Of course, there are counter-arguments, and they are weighty too. The Sinai experience made so huge an impact on our people that the spiritual force which it released has not yet spent itself, but affects us still, more than three thousand years later; how then can we doubt that something truly momentous must have happened? The Prophets were indeed children of their age, but they were giants of the spirit; how then can we suppose that they were *altogether* mistaken? The universe is unimaginably old; but is it really likely, even on so vast a time-scale, that all the countless galaxies, and all the infinitely various forms of life, showing so much intricacy, so much purposiveness and so much beauty, could have come about by mere chance? The evil in the world does indeed pose an intractable problem; but the good needs explaining too, and is it not a cogent explanation that it emanates from a Supreme Source of Goodness? Our own religious experiences may be too feeble to count as incontrovertible evidence; but how can we dismiss the great chorus of voices that reaches us from the mystics of every age and people, to whom God was an overpowering reality? The existence of God may not be verifiable in any stringent sense; but is it wise to let our apprehension of reality be straitjacketed by a particular theory of verification?

And so the debate could continue indefinitely, to and fro. Where would it lead us? If the protagonists were of equal ability, perhaps to a stalemate. What then? Some might say: since the argument seems to be more or less evenly balanced, therefore, for the time being at least, I must consider myself an agnostic. And that would be a perfectly honourable position. But to such people we should say: don't let your agnosticism separate you from your community. Admittedly, the belief in God has always been fundamental to Judaism, and we appreciate that at the moment you feel unable to affirm it. Nevertheless, Judaism possesses other merits: a glorious history, a magnificent literature, a splendid ethical code. It is by any standard one of the finest manifestations of the human spirit; and it amply deserves your allegiance on these grounds alone. Maybe you can't subscribe to everything we say in our liturgy. Maybe you can join us only with mental reservations, half participant and half spectator. Never mind. By your presence you are still lending your support to a historic enterprise which is eminently worth preserving.

Yet it doesn't seem quite satisfactory to leave the matter there, for too much is at stake. Consider, for instance, the *consequences* of belief and disbelief. Religion, or at least the higher religions, have undoubtedly been a force for good in human history. Admittedly, that assertion needs to be qualified, for in the name of religion people and nations have done ugly things. They have tended to be intolerant, to persecute dissenters, to restrain legitimate human impulses, to perpetuate unjust laws and foolish customs. But surely these evils show the operation of ordinary human failings – ignorance, prejudice, fanaticism, aggressiveness – which do not derive specifically from religion, and may therefore be regarded as aberrations. At any rate, the monotheistic religions have been predominantly beneficial. Not only have they inspired great art and literature, but they have humanised civilisation, raised the sights of human idealism, and produced lives of the highest excellence.

Where, on the contrary, religion has been suppressed by the State, the result seems to have been a hardening of the moral arteries, a blunting of moral sensitivity, a decline in compassion, in respect for persons, and even in reverence for life. And since atheist societies are a relatively recent phenomenon, we may not yet have seen the full extent of the degeneration.

There are then strong reasons to believe that without religion civilisation would deteriorate, perhaps to the point of doom. In words once found among the graffiti at Camden Town underground station, 'the world is fragile; handle with prayer' (Ronald Higgins, *The Seventh Enemy*, p. 269). And if religion is an irreplaceable redemptive force in human history, then it seems a thousand pities that we should feel compelled to withhold our support from it because of our intellectual doubts.

Therefore, consider this: that the objective evidence is the same for everybody; it is there for all to see. Why then do some people react to it in one way and some in another? Evidently, the key lies, not in the nature of the evidence, but in the predisposition of the beholder. Some people may watch a sunset and be entirely unmoved; others are thrilled to the core of their being. Some may look at a picture and see only splotches of paint; others see an exquisite work of art. Some may listen to a symphony and hear only a succession of noises; others hear melodies and harmonies of unearthly beauty. Some human beings are born colour-blind; but the whole rich world of colour, which they miss, is nevertheless very real. Is it not possible, then, that those who look at the world and fail to see God may lack some perceptiveness or some sensitivity which others have? In the words of George Herbert's famous hymn ('The Elixir'),

> A man that looks on glass,
> On it may stay his eye;
> Or, if he pleaseth, through it pass,
> And then the heaven espy.

If there is such an impediment in the predisposition of many, it is not hard to speculate what may be its cause. For we are all children of our time, products of a particular phase of Western civilisation. We are all imbued with a secular, humanistic, materialistic and mechanistic view of the world; we are all inebriated with the success of our science and technology; and we have all been taught to value reason to such an extent that our other faculties – our powers of intuition and imagination – have become atrophied.

Now reason is indeed sovereign within its proper sphere; we may not ignore it or go against it. But it is only one instrument for the discovery of truth, and not a perfect one. For we are human, and perhaps still at an early stage of our evolution as a species. Therefore we must reckon with the possibility, which is indeed a certainty, that 'there are more things in heaven and earth than are dreamt of' in our rationalistic philosophy. But it is precisely this which our Prometheanism makes us reluctant to admit. We like to think of ourselves as – potentially, at least – omniscient. Therefore what we cannot understand, or demonstrate, or measure, we tend to dismiss as fantasy. We are in no mood to recognise a Mystery beyond our powers of comprehension.

Of course this mood is not all-encompassing. On the contrary, it is already beginning to become old-fashioned. Already there are many signs that the armour of our former self-assurance is starting to crack. As science probes into areas where the old certainties dissolve into uncertainty; as nature, greedily exploited, kicks back at us; as the prospect of unceasing economic growth turns out to have been only a mirage; as happiness is seen to depend on factors other than prosperity; as the malaise of alienation becomes more widespread; as we become increasingly disillusioned with the whole materialistic value system on which our civilisation is founded – so many of us are rediscovering what the greatest scientists have always known: that there is 'a great ocean of truth' which 'lies all undiscovered before us'. Many, therefore, are turning with a new openness to religion, especially the religions of the East, untainted by the secularism of the West, and some to bizarre and fraudulent cults.

Ronald Higgins, in *The Seventh Enemy*, speaks of 'a growing recognition of the absurdity of the modern impatience with the mysterious and the immeasurable and a blunt refusal to accept the impoverished view of man and the world which science, misused as metaphysic, has so damagingly spread' (p. 270). He has a whole section entitled 'The Rediscovery of the Transcendent', which he defines as 'the ultimate spiritual reality which is the source of our being and of all love, beauty and goodness … that final truth which lies behind all religions but which none of them can make captive' (p. 271).

In short, what we have lost but are perhaps just beginning to regain is that confession of ignorance, that humility before the cosmos, that apprehension of mystery, that capacity for reverence, which is the precondition of religious awareness. If we can indeed regain it, then the objective data, which are the same as they have always been, may take on a new configuration. The splotches of paint may become a picture, the disparate notes a symphony, and the universe the handiwork of God.

But don't misunderstand me. I am not saying that then any particular traditional conception of God would automatically be reinstated. There is room for many different ways of conceiving God, and all of them are at best only tentative approximations to the truth. My point is rather that any perception of God at all, any religious feeling, presupposes a willingness on our part to admit our creaturely finiteness, to unstop the valves of our intuition, to let go of our clinical scepticism, and to respond with our whole, integrated selves to the intimations of the presence of an eternal Mystery beyond and above ourselves which overarches our little lives.

Then these 'Days of Awe' may again elicit from us the awe of which we are capable. Then we may again understand the phrase found above the ark of many synagogues, from the dying words of Rabbi Eliezer to his disciples, דע לפני מי אתה עומד, 'Know before

Whom you are standing' (Ber. 28b). Then we may again feel ourselves addressed when we read: 'You stand this day all of you before
the Eternal One your God'.

❖   ❖   ❖

The Scale of Merit
Yom Kippur, 26 September 1982

על חטא שחטאנו לפניך, 'For the sin which we have committed against
You ...' So runs the recurring phrase of the *Viddui Rabba* or 'Great
Confession' which is the most distinctive feature of the Yom Kippur
liturgy. Over and over again we recite these self-accusing words; but
do we really mean them?

Up to a point, yes. We do admit that we are less than perfect. We
have our weaknesses, our foibles, our shortcomings. We have sometimes been a little short-tempered, probably because we hadn't slept
so well the night before. And we have once in a while neglected to
do something which we ought to have done, but only because we
were too busy at the time. So, yes, we do confess to the odd *faux pas*,
the occasional lapse of courtesy or error of judgment. But *essentially*
we think of ourselves as decent, well-meaning, respectable, law-abid-
ing people who would never dream of deliberately doing anybody
any harm.

That being the case, to say *chatanu*, 'we have sinned', is perhaps a
bit strong. It doesn't quite correspond to the reality as we see it. But
then we tell ourselves that words like 'sin' are just old-fashioned religious language, which don't have to be taken all that literally, and
anyway there is just enough truth in them for us to be able to say
them without feeling that we are actually being dishonest.

Or else we may take refuge in the plural. We pray, after all, as a
congregation, and a congregation includes all sorts of people. Therefore, when we say that we have committed this, that or the other sin,
we don't have to take it personally. It only means that *some* of us have.

But when we look at our neighbours, they don't really appear to
be all that different from ourselves. So perhaps we should cast the
net wider. We pray, after all, not only as a congregation, but as members of the House of Israel. That is the real meaning of the pronoun
'we' in our liturgy. Indeed, it goes even further. Especially on these
High Holydays, we think of ourselves as members of humanity as a
whole. And when we enlarge the frame of reference to that extent,

the confession becomes quite appropriate, and we can recite it without mental reservation; for there is not a sin, however monstrous, that is not committed by some human beings, somewhere on earth, at one time or another.

Indeed, only ten days ago, on Rosh Hashanah of all days, the news broke of a crime so horrendous that the shock of it is still reverberating round the world: the savage slaughter of hundreds of innocent men, women and children in the Palestinian refugee camps of Sabra and Chatila in the outskirts of West Beirut.

How can human beings do such things? It seems utterly incomprehensible. And so we are bound to ask ourselves: what sort of people are these who are capable of doing such things? Do they have anything at all in common with us, or are they an altogether different species? Perhaps, if they were creatures from outer space, or savages from the Stone Age, quite untouched by civilisation ... But they were not! They were apparently Lebanese Christians. But they *might* have been Arab Muslims, or Russian Marxists, or German Lutherans, or Irish Catholics, or Israeli Jews, or what you will. For the sombre truth is that human beings of all races and nations, creeds and ideologies have been known to commit barbaric deeds.

Why do they? Surely the cause must be some abnormal, pathological condition. Indeed it is, and the condition has a name: it is called hatred. Surely no human being ever kills another unless they are first so consumed with hatred against that person that all their normal human instincts of pity and compassion, which would otherwise make such an act unthinkable, are for the moment rendered inoperative.

In murder the hatred is directed against an individual; in mass murder – and what is war other than mass murder? – it is directed against a group. Therefore we need to ask ourselves: how does it happen that human groups – nations, for instance – come to feel so passionate a hatred towards one another?

I suppose it begins with a clash of interests or a conflict of ideologies, which develops into rivalry, and the rivalry into enmity, and the enmity into prejudice. Each side forms an unfavourable stereotype of the other. And then the demagogues get to work and exploit the prejudice for their own, political ends. They hold rallies and make speeches and publish pamphlets and pour out a constant stream of propaganda which, by a subtle mixture of truths, half-truths and lies, always manages to prove how wrong the other side is, and how right is your own. The people cheer and applaud, for what could be more welcome than to have, at one and the same time, your pet aversion justified and your self-righteousness boosted? So there occurs an escalation of prejudice, until the enemy is portrayed as wholly evil and therefore dehumanised and demonised. Then the killing can start. For if your opponents are less than human you don't need to feel any compassion for them; and if they are the Devil Incarnate you actually do the world a favour by destroying them. It becomes a noble deed, a holy war. As Pascal once said, 'People never do evil so fully and so happily as when they do it for conscience's sake'.

It is so easy to interpret human conflicts in black-and-white terms, to see the protagonists as, in the language of the Dead Sea Scrolls, 'Children of Light' and 'Children of Darkness'. For one thing, it is intellectually convenient. You don't have to bother your head with nice distinctions and cumbersome qualifications: everybody fits neatly into their pigeon hole. For another thing, it does your ego a power of good to know that you are on the side of the angels. And then it enables you in good conscience to give vent to your resentment against the enemy; it gives you licence to hate – and ultimately to kill.

On the face of it, there is no point of contact at all between ourselves, decent and respectable citizens that we are, and the perpetrators of the massacre in the refugee camps. We are light-years apart, like denizens of different universes. And yet we are members of one and the same human race. So there must be a link. And the link, as I have tried to show, is prejudice. The mass murderers only carry to its logical conclusion a process to which we all contribute whenever we endorse and disseminate an unfair generalisation, a detrimental stereotype, about any human group. It all begins with a slight distortion of the truth, and it ends with the mangled bodies of little children putrefying under the Mediterranean sun in a refugee camp in Lebanon.

Prejudice leads to hatred, and hatred leads to murder, or terrorism, or war. How careful we should therefore be to avoid giving it even the slightest hospitality in our minds! If you desire life, says the Psalmist, 'guard your tongue from evil, and your lips from speaking guile' (34:13). Life itself is at stake! Therefore we had better guard our tongues. The Rabbis taught that, next to idolatry, incest and murder, slander is the gravest of all sins (Arachin 15b).

The truth, which we are always in danger of forgetting, is that the real world is not like the world of the Westerns, consisting of goodies and baddies. According to the Talmud three books are opened before God on Rosh Hashanah, one for the totally wicked, one for the perfectly righteous, and one for the in-between (RH 16a). There may be some human beings who are wicked through and through, and some who are absolutely saintly; but I suspect that the books containing their names are rather slim, whereas the book of the in-

between runs to millions of volumes. The overwhelming majority of
human beings are a mixture of good and bad. But that means there
is *some* good in them, and to deny that is to start the process that
leads to murder.

Perhaps the trouble with the word 'sin' in the 'Great Confession'
is not only that it is remote from our everyday vocabulary, but that
it is too vague and general. Perhaps if we were to focus our minds on
just one particular sin – the sin of aiding and abetting prejudice –
maybe then we should become better able to say in all sincerity:
על חטא שחטאנו לפניך, 'For the sin which we have committed against You
...' And maybe, then, too, we should make a more solemn resolve to
practise the corresponding virtue, by heeding what suddenly comes
to be seen as one of the most important of all moral injunctions: הוי
דן את־כל־האדם לכף זכות, 'Judge every person by the scale of merit'
(Avot 1:6). It would be a good beginning.

❖   ❖   ❖

Self-Respect
Yom Kippur, 2 October 1987

אבינו מלכנו, חנו ועננו, כי אין בנו מעשים, 'Our Divine Parent and Ruler, be
gracious to us, and answer us, for there is little merit in us' – or, more
literally, 'we have no good deeds to our credit'. The self-denigration
expressed in that phrase seems rather extreme, and almost Christian.
It is the Christian confession of sins which speaks of 'miserable sinners' and says 'there is no health in us'. It is Christianity, we have
always been told, which teaches that we are wicked and need to be
saved, whereas Judaism teaches that we are imperfect and need to be
improved.

Yet the *Avinu Malkenu* comes from an impeccably Jewish source.
It was first recited, we learn from the Talmud (Ta'an. 25a) by Rabbi
Akiva. Besides, it is not an isolated instance. Our liturgy is full of
such expressions of self-condemnation. There is no need to give
examples. It is enough if we recall the *Ashamnu,* the Shorter Confession in the form of an alphabetic acrostic. What matters is not so
much the actual sins listed in it, though they are damning enough,
since they are largely determined by the need to get in all the letters
of the alphabet. The device itself is a way of saying: 'We have committed every sin in the book, from Aleph to Tav.' And the Longer

Confession, which is the *Al Chet*, spells out in even greater detail the dismal catalogue of human failings. Some versions of it run to over fifty verses!

To be honest, it does get rather wearisome, and we sometimes wonder whether it isn't all a bit overdone. Sometimes, as we confess one heinous sin after another, we ask ourselves: 'Are we *really* that bad? Have we *really* done all these terrible things? And if not, how can we truthfully say so?'

But to such doubts we have a ready answer, which is that all these confessions are couched in the first person plural, not the singular. We don't say 'I have sinned', we say 'we have sinned', and the word 'we' covers, so to speak, a multitude of sins. For who is 'we'? It is the whole congregation and even the whole House of Israel which is today united in prayer and submits itself – collectively – to God's judgment. Therefore it isn't necessary that I should personally have committed every sin in the book: somebody else is sure to have done so!

Well, there is something in that, but the chances are that we are not as blameless as we imagine ourselves to be. For we are all in love with ourselves – as Oscar Wilde once said, 'To love oneself is the beginning of a lifelong romance' (THQ, p. 217) – and therefore inclined to judge ourselves לכף זכות, with a good deal of charity. 'We do not see ourselves as others see us, still less as God sees us. Self-love deceives us; pride makes us unwilling to admit the truth about ourselves. Our motives, we like to think, are good; our weaknesses excusable; and our misdeeds due to forces beyond our power to control' (ULPS, *Gate of Repentance*, p. 34).

Therefore, before we dismiss this, that and the other sin as applicable to others but not – perish the thought – ourselves, we would be wise to ask ourselves: 'Are you sure?'

Besides, the more religious a person is in the best sense of the word – the more spiritually and morally sensitive – the more likely they are to be critical of themselves but generous in their estimation of others.

There is a story about an eighteenth-century rabbi, Meir of Tiktin. It once happened that a *mochiach* – that is, an itinerant moralistic preacher – came to his town and delivered, as a *mochiach* was expected to do, a fiery sermon, castigating the people for all their many transgressions. As he did so, Rabbi Meir burst into tears, and afterwards he complained to the preacher: 'Why did you have to humiliate me in public? Surely you could have reprimanded me privately, as Jewish etiquette requires!' To which the *mochiach* replied: 'But I wasn't referring to *you!*' Then Rabbi Meir protested: 'But all the congregation are righteous people, so which of them is a sinner except me?' (IT. VI, p. 203, quoting *Shemen ha-Tov* by Shmuel Shmelke Horowitz of Nikolsburg, 1726-1778).

Therefore let us not be too hasty in assuming that the first person plural of the confessional prayers is meant only collectively. It is meant distributively as well. Or, to paraphrase John Donne, 'Never send to know for whom the Shofar blows; it blows for thee!' Besides, it is a misunderstanding of Jewish teaching to suppose that the plural, even when used collectively, merely signifies our identification with a community which includes sinners as well as saints. The operative principle is, rather, כל־ישראל ערבים זה בזה, 'that all Israelites are *answerable* for one another' (San. 27b). It isn't merely that we are not supposed to *dissociate* ourselves from fellow Jews but that we are required to accept a share of responsibility for their actions.

The principle is illustrated by a curious ritual recorded in the book of Deuteronomy. If a murder victim was found in no-man's-land, then the elders and judges of the nearest city were required to take a young heifer into the middle of a field, break its neck and recite over it a prayer beginning, 'Forgive, O God, Your people Israel' (21:8). The ritual is primitive but the concept – of collective responsibility – is sound.

Furthermore, what applies to the Jewish community applies, by extension, to society at large. From year to year we seem to become more conscious of the appalling things human beings, the world over, do to one another and to their environment. Perhaps it is because news travels faster, perhaps because technology has made mistakes costlier, or perhaps there has been a real deterioration in moral standards. However that may be, who can put their hand on their heart and say: 'I have no share of responsibility for the ethos of the society in which these things happen?'

And yet, when all that has been conceded, to say אין בנו מעשים, that we have *no* good deeds to our credit, that there is nothing good to be said for us at all, does seem excessively harsh, and does seem to conflict with Jewish teachings about human nature. How then shall we explain it?

Well, of course, the answer is that it *is* a case of hyperbole, but for a purpose. The purpose is that we should not let ourselves off too lightly. This day, of all days, demands of us 'an unsparing effort to face the truth about ourselves, naked and undisguised' (ULPS, *Gate of Repentance*, p. 155). If that goal is to be achieved, then what is called for is no pulling of punches but outright condemnation: a kind of shock treatment. We do need to be made aware how outrageously humanity has fallen short of God's expectations, and how deeply implicated we all are individually in that indictment; and in that light our good deeds are indeed too paltry to be worth mentioning. Without such an awareness nothing else can be accomplished; the process of *t'shuvah*, of repentance, can't get under way.

But once that 'unsparing effort' has been made, then we may recall that there is another side to the story. We do have, as the Rabbis taught, two inclinations. We have a *yetzer ha-ra*, an inclination to do evil, not indeed for evil's sake but because in our pursuit of selfish aims we tend callously to disregard the rights and needs and feelings of others. But we also have a *yetzer tov*, a good inclination: a conscience and a sense of duty and an altruistic concern for the welfare of others and a compassion for their suffering. That, too, is part of our make-up, as fundamental as the other, and even more so if there is any truth in the Jewish teaching that we are created in God's image.

There is, in short, a *duality* in human nature which is a recurring theme of our liturgy. 'What are we?' asks an ancient Jewish prayer, 'What is our life, and what our piety? What our goodness, and what our strength?' But it continues: 'Yet we are Your people, the children of Your covenant, and You have called us to Your service'.

One of the last sermons preached by Rabbi Israel Mattuck pointed out the same duality. 'It is not only human to feel temptation', he said, 'but it is also human to resist it. It is not only human to feel the impulsion of instincts but also human to rule them with a master's power ... It is human to be weak, it is also human to be strong' (*Liberal Jewish Monthly*, April 1954, pp. 51f.)

If it is the purpose of the Penitential Season to make us conscious of the *yetzer ha-ra*, the selfishness that leads to evil, within us, and ashamed of our tendency ever and again to yield to it, it is no less its purpose to remind us of our *yetzer tov*, our capacity for righteousness as beings created in God's image, and to encourage it and activate it, so that it may enhance the quality of our lives in the year to come.

Self-criticism is essential for our spiritual and moral well-being, but so, too, is self-respect. Perhaps that is what an ancient rabbi, quoted in the Ethics of the Fathers, meant when he said: אל תהי רשע בפני עצמך, 'Do not be wicked in your own estimation' (2:13) – don't condemn yourself completely, leave room for self-respect.

Indeed, loss of self-respect is itself one of the major causes of evil, because it is morally debilitating. That is a point which the masters of Chasidism understood particularly well. They taught, for instance: 'When the Evil Inclination approaches, whispering in your ear: "You are unworthy to fulfil the Law", say: "I am worthy"'. (Louis I. Newman, *The Hasidic Anthology*, p. 186).

Our good deeds may be few, and there may be little merit in us. But *potentially* our merit is very great, *potentially* our capacity for goodness is unlimited. To make the potential actual is the purpose of life, and to help us to do so is the purpose of Yom Kippur.

❖ ❖ ❖

The Last Lap
Yom Kippur, 21 September 1988

The process of aging is not a subject that addresses itself with the same urgency to us all. For we have all reached different stages on the road that leads from birth to death: some still near the beginning, some about half-way, some nearer the end. But we are all travelling along it, and in the same direction, for it is a one-way road; and therefore the last stage of the journey concerns us all. Indeed, it is in some ways the most important, just as for the mountaineer it is the final assault on the summit, and for the runner the last lap of the race, that proves their mettle.

Like every other phase of life, it has its peculiar difficulties but also its peculiar advantages and opportunities.

The difficulties are obvious. As we grow old, our physical powers decline: we may become less mobile, our senses may become less acute, our aches and pains more numerous. Our mental powers also decline: we tend to forget what once we knew, and find it harder to learn new things. Our contemporaries die; our circle of friends grows smaller; our savings may run low; we may need to give up some of our privacy for sheltered housing and increased dependence on others; and there is from year to year less to look forward to.

These difficulties are formidable, but there are compensating advantages. As we grow older, we are less torn by passion, less driven by ambition, less likely to behave impulsively. We gain in experience and knowledge, and though we forget much, we are better able to tell what matters from what doesn't matter. We gain – or we should gain – in composure, discretion and judgment. We may even be respected for our wisdom, and our advice may be sought. We also have more leisure to do the things we always wanted to do, to cultivate old interests and to take up new ones; and though we have less to look forward to, we have more to look back on.

Faced with this mixture of advantages and disadvantages, people react in very different ways. Some grow old gracefully. They become sweeter, gentler, more tranquil in themselves and more considerate of others. Other people become increasingly irritable, resentful, ego-centric, demanding of attention and pity, and tired of living.

Why do some people cope so well, and others so badly, with old age? A large part of the answer must lie in individual circumstances. For the mixture of assets and liabilities is not the same for all. Some are more fortunate than others, and we should never condemn the less fortunate. In this area, more than any other, we should heed Hillel's counsel, אל תדין חברך עד שתגיע למקומו, 'Do not judge your fellow human being until you have been in his or her position' (Avot 2:4).

Indeed, it is perhaps in part because the temptation of the young and strong to criticise the old and weak is so great that the Torah goes out of its way to demand respect for them: מפני שיבה תקום והדרת פני זקן, 'You shall rise before the aged and show respect to the old' (Lev. 19:32).

But that having been said, it has to be added that a great deal depends on *attitude*, and therefore the question needs to be considered: what are the attitudes which we should cultivate within ourselves in order that, when the time comes, we may cope well with the process of aging? About that I have several suggestions to make, but I make them with diffidence, knowing that these things are easier said than done, and that none of us can be sure how we shall acquit ourselves until we are put to the test.

My first suggestion, then, is that we should try to look on growing old not just as something that happens to us, of which we are passive victims, but that it is, like every other phase of life, a challenge, a task to be performed, a job to be done, which can be done well or badly, and which we must *work at* if we wish to do it well.

My second suggestion is that we should cultivate a habit of gratitude for what has been and for what still is. We know, as we grow older, that we have had abilities which are now declining, that we have had opportunities which will never come again, that we have made mistakes which we can no longer put right, and we can conjure up many memories of failure and frustration, of sorrow and pain. But we need not dwell on them. At least up to a point, we can train ourselves to recall the happy times and the beautiful experiences. And though we may no longer be able to do all that we would like to do, still, as long as we can see the trees, listen to music, perhaps read books, and feel the touch of a friendly hand, all these are gifts for which we should give thanks. There is a poem which sums up as well as anything the mood I am commending. It is by Rachel, the Hebrew poetess and early Zionist pioneer:

Is it really the end? The path is still clear.
The mists of life still beckon from afar.
The sky is still blue, the grass green.
Autumn is coming.

I shall accept the judgment. My heart harbours no complaint.
How red were my sunsets, how clear my dawns!
And flowers smiled along my path
As I passed.

(Sidney Greenberg, *A Treasury of Comfort*, p. 79)

My next suggestion is a practical one. We should throughout our
lives develop interests independent of our employment which we
can pursue when we retire. It is a very sad fact that many old people
seem to have no such interests, and a terrible indictment of our society that it encourages us to think that virtually the sole purpose of
education is to make us employable. Education should be for living,
not only for earning a living.

Of course the work we do by way of a livelihood may be of great
value, but if so it is because of its intrinsic nature, not only because we
are paid for it. The idea that life is about work, in the sense of salaried
work, is a tragic error, and the tragedy of it is becoming more and
more apparent as the combined number of the unemployed and the
retired grows into an ever larger proportion of the population.

The Rabbis knew better. They did indeed appreciate the importance of wage earning for a person's dignity. 'Great is work', they
said, 'for it confers honour on the worker' (Nedarim 49b). But they
did not see it as the sole or even the main purpose of life. The main
purpose, according to them, is the study of Torah (Shulchan Aruch,
Orach Chayyim 156:1).

My fourth suggestion is that, as we need to cultivate interests, so
we need to cultivate friendships. The world is full of lonely people
whose greatest need is for human companionship but who make no
effort to obtain it. They think of friendship as something which must
come to them, while they sit, passive, in their arm-chairs. If it does-
n't they complain that nobody cares, and when others do take the
initiative, and visit them, they see it mainly as an opportunity to
pour out their own woes. They forget that friendship is a matter of
giving as well as taking.

Then there is a further problem, which is perhaps the deepest of
them all. Many old people complain, not only that they have few
pleasures and few friends, but that they have no wish to go on living.
If they are in constant pain, that is indeed understandable. Then we
can only feel deeply sorry for them, and throw the problem at the
medical profession. But in other circumstances the wish to die, which

is so contrary to the instinct of self-preservation, is a symptom of a deeper problem. Often it turns out that those who speak in that vein cannot see any *purpose* in living.

But is life *ever* without purpose? Surely not. There are always *mitzvot* to perform, and especially the greatest *mitzvah* of them all, 'You shall love your neighbour as yourself' (Lev. 19:18). Given that *mitzvah*, none of us need ever feel that living has no purpose, or that we are not needed. Life *does* have a purpose, and we *are* needed: so that we may love one another.

❖   ❖   ❖

Are We Religious?
Yom Kippur, 24 September 1993

There is a paradox about the High Holydays which we don't often talk about because it is faintly embarrassing but which perhaps we *should* talk about. And it is this. On the one hand, people often say to me: 'I am not very religious, you know.' Sometimes they say it self-deprecatingly and apologetically, sometimes boastfully and with bravado, and sometimes merely because British etiquette dictates that one must never admit to taking anything serious seriously – except something *really* serious, like football or cricket!

That on the one hand. But on the other, we, the self-same people, flock to the synagogue just on these days, which are the most purely religious of all our festivals. Of course we come here for a variety of reasons, and not the least of them is simply to affirm our Jewish identity. But there are other ways of doing this, and even in the synagogue year there are other occasions when we could pretend that we had really come only to see the Sukkah, or to watch the children process, or to chat with our fellow congregants over Kiddush. But no! Of all occasions, we choose to come here *davka* for the High Holyday services, which, if they are not religious, are nothing at all! Perhaps, therefore we are not as non-religious as we like to make out. Or perhaps we are not altogether clear what we mean by 'religious'. So let us think about that.

When people say that they are not very religious, what do they mean? I suppose two things. First, that they are not sure whether, or with what degree of conviction, they believe in God. Secondly, that they don't much care for ritual, including the ritual of communal worship, which they find largely a waste of time and therefore mostly stay away from, just as people with only a slight interest in music wouldn't often go to a concert.

But of course that is all very superficial. There is a far deeper, far more important sense of the word 'religious'. In that sense it is possible to be religious without being sure about God or keen on ritual, and it is equally possible to be sure about God and keen on ritual without being religious. Let us explore that deeper, more important sense. And let us be clear from the outset that it has little to do with *organised* religion. The record of organised religion is in many ways a dismal one, and hardly a day passes when the part it plays in the suppression of freedom and the inflammation of nationalistic or sectarian passion does not fill us with shame. Of course all that has to be set against the good it has *also* done and continues to do, and it may well be that on balance the good outweighs the bad. But, whether that is so or not, religion is not to be identified with organised religion. Organised religion is merely a receptacle which can contain either true religion or false religion *masquerading* as true religion, as a bottle may contain either medicine or poison.

So what is true religion? It is fundamentally an attitude to reality; a response of the whole of our being – mind, heart and soul – to the world in which we are placed. It is a sense of awe and wonder, an apprehension of the mystery beyond the commonplace, that produces, if only in rare moments, a feeling of joy too deep to be communicated except in music, poetry or prayer. It is what Wordsworth tried to convey when he wrote (in 'Lines composed a few miles above Tintern Abbey'):

And I have felt
A presence that disturbs me with the joy
Of elevated thoughts; a sense sublime
Of something far more deeply interfused,
Whose dwelling is the light of setting suns,
And the round ocean and the living air,
And the blue sky, and in the mind of man ...

Are we religious in that sense? I *hope* we are, at least a little. I know some claim that they are not, and some are so blasé that they can look at a sunset and see nothing but refracted light. There is a 'we-know-it-all', 'we-can-do-it-all' arrogance that stops up the well from which religion springs. But I don't think those who are affected by it are wiser than the rest of us: I think they have stifled in themselves something precious, and are the poorer for it. I think Albert Einstein knew better when he wrote: 'The fairest thing we can experience is the mysterious. It is the fundamental emotion which stands at the cradle of true art and true science. One who knows it not, can no longer wonder, no longer feel amazement, is as good as dead, a snuffed out candle.' I hope we are not snuffed out. I hope we have retained something of that sense of awe and wonder, which stands also at the cradle of true religion. To be religious is to feel reverence: first, towards the cosmos as a whole, and secondly, towards the Mind behind the cosmos which we call God. It is here that some people experience a special difficulty, perhaps because they are still schlepping from their childhood an infantile conception of God which doesn't stand up to critical scrutiny. There are also mature conceptions. But there is no need to subscribe to any precise definition. Indeed, any precise definition of God is bound to be wrong. For in the nature of the case, God cannot be otherwise than a mystery to us – indeed, the greatest mystery of all. The only question is whether, when people have spoken about that Mystery, they have spoken nonsense, or whether they have struggled to express a genuine experience; whether the whole world's religious literature, art and music is about nothing or about something.

Are we religious in that sense? I would think that most of us are, at least to some extent. C.G. Jung once wrote, 'Among all my patients in the second half of life ... there has not been one whose problem in the last resort was not that of finding a religious outlook on life' (q. in Anthony Storr, *Solitude*, p. 192).

To be religious is to feel reverence for the cosmos and its Creator but it is also to feel reverence for humanity. In Judaism at least, to use Leo Baeck's formulation, the Mystery leads inexorably to the Commandment. That is a truth which was not always realised but which the world owes to our Hebrew ancestors, with their perception of a *righteous* God, and of human beings as *created in God's image*, so that the acid test of whether we are religious is in the way we treat our fellow men and women. To be religious is to recognise and to nurture the capacity for good that resides in every individual, and the capacity of humanity collectively to build a just society.

To revere God, says the book of Proverbs, is to hate evil (8:13). To know God, says Jeremiah, is to practise mercy, justice and righteousness (9:23). To love God truly, says a Chasidic teaching, we must love our fellow human beings, and anyone who claims to love God but does not love people is a liar. Therefore to be religious, but to feel no compassion when little children die of starvation in distant lands, or to feel no indignation when the strong oppress the weak or the rich exploit the poor, or to feel no joy when enemies become reconciled and nations make peace: all that is inconceivable in any Jewish sense of the word 'religious'.

Perhaps the greatest enemy of true religion is cynicism, not only about humanity in general, but about individual human beings. For, as the Rabbis said, if you despise your neighbour, you despise a being created in God's image (Gen.R. 24:7). Have you ever made a really nasty remark about somebody, and a moment later tried to pray? Then you know that it is impossible. The capacity for religious experience is a delicate plant. If you pour over it the poison of cynicism it shrivels away.

Reverential respect for the cosmos and its Creator, for humanity and its individual members: these are the marks of a religious person. But to them we must add one more: reverential respect for Tradition. And here we Progressive Jews have a special difficulty which we had better recognise. We have been taught, and rightly taught, to be *critical* of our Jewish Tradition. Not everything it comprises is perfect. Sometimes those who shaped it were mistaken in their interpretation of the Divine Will, and some of their ideas, laws and customs have lost their validity, or their relevance, with the passage of time. It is important to recognise that, but it holds the danger that we may get into the habit of thinking of the Tradition as a whole in negative terms, and to do so is to pull the rug from our feet. For though the Tradition has its imperfections, overwhelmingly it is good and true, and it has made us what we are. Therefore, if, while being critical of some *aspects* of our Jewish heritage, we do not love and cherish it *as a whole*; if we do not stand in awe before Moses and Isaiah, Akiva and Maimonides; if we use the word 'traditional' disparagingly, and when the Sefer Torah is lifted up we do not feel a *frisson* of reverence for what it contains and symbolises; then we shut ourselves off from the chief source capable of nourishing our spiritual life.

To be religious, then, is all these things. Much of what it means can be summed up in the single word 'reverence'. But it doesn't stop there. It doesn't lose itself in mere contemplation. It is also an *active* response to that which elicits reverence. It is not merely a feeling of the heart but a decision of the will, a commitment to a task, a self-enrolment in a great adventure. As Benjamin Cardozo, who was a U.S. Supreme Court judge, once wrote, 'The submergence of self in the pursuit of an ideal, the readiness to spend oneself without measure ... for something intuitively apprehended as great and noble ... some of us like to believe that this is what religion means.'

Are we, then, religious? I hope we are: all of us, at least to some extent. But I also believe that we could become more so, and I think we know that it would be good for us, for our community, and for the world, if we were to do so. These High Holyday services could help us to make a little progress in that direction, and if we let them, our time here will surely have been well spent.

❖   ❖   ❖

The Conquest of Selfishness
Yom Kippur, 15 September 1994

'Cast away from you all the evil you have done, וְעֲשׂוּ לָכֶם לֵב חָדָשׁ וְרוּחַ חֲדָשָׁה, and get yourselves a new heart and a new spirit' (Ezek. 18:31). That verse sums up succinctly what the Penitential Season is about. *It calls on us to change.* If we respond to the challenge, it will have achieved its purpose. If not, it will have been a waste of time. But to say that is to raise the question, '*Can* we change?'

All the evidence – or at any rate most of it – suggests that we can't. That very point is made repeatedly in our liturgy. It was also made long ago by the worldly-wise Kohelet: 'Vanity of vanities, all is vanity … What has been is what will be, and what has been done is what will be done … What is crooked cannot be made straight, and what is lacking cannot be numbered' (1:9, 15).

Let us focus our minds on one particular form in which the sceptical view is commonly expressed. It is said that human beings are fundamentally and unalterably selfish. You only have to look at a baby to see that. It cares for nobody but itself. True, it soon becomes attached to its mother, but only because she is its food supply. As it grows older, it does indeed develop positive relationships with other members of the family and beyond, but only because it learns that they, too, are useful in one way or another. Later still it may come to observe the norms of society, but only because there are penalties for infringing them. Some people, admittedly, go to great lengths to help others; they devote endless time to charitable work, or give away whole fortunes to good causes. But even they are motivated by self-interest: it makes them *feel* good, or they hope to get some reward in this world or in the world-to-come. Their behaviour *seems* altruistic but is really egoistic. Selfishness, selfishness, all is selfishness. And because that is our human nature, therefore, in any fundamental sense, we never change. So the argument runs.

Does it ring true? It should, because to a large extent it is. We smile when we read Oscar Wilde's remark that 'to love oneself is the beginning of a lifelong romance' (THQ, p. 217); but only because the shoe fits. And because we love ourselves, therefore we often deceive ourselves into thinking that we are acting altruistically when in fact we are only pursuing our self-interest in a round-about way.

All that is common knowledge. In Jewish tradition it is expressed in terms of the *yetzer ha-ra*, the impulse to do evil, which, on closer inspection, turns out to be an umbrella word for our self-regarding drives – for pleasure, for power, for property, for popularity, and so forth. How powerful – and how subtle – the *yetzer ha-ra* is, is a recurring theme of Rabbinic literature.

So it is easy enough to make a case for the sceptical view that 'The Selfish Gene' – to quote the title of Richard Dawkins' book – dominates human life, and a sure way to win applause for honesty and realism. As Louis MacNeice wrote about 'The Satirist', 'He can discover / A selfish motive for anything – and collect / His royalties as recording angel' (*The Penguin Dictionary of Twentieth Century Quotations*, p. 246). And it tends to become a self-fulfilling prophecy in a society that positively encourages the unrestrained pursuit of private wealth, extols it as a virtue, and rewards extravagantly those who practise it successfully.

The only trouble is: if selfishness is so ingrained in human nature, and so ineradicable, what hope is there for the future? Since the selfish aspirations of one individual necessarily cut across those of another, the future can only be one of perpetual conflict. And since in the modern world conflicts tend to escalate, and involve the risk that one party or the other may resort to nuclear weapons, the long-term prospect can only be one of global catastrophe.

That being so, let us go back to the drawing board and ask ourselves whether it really *is* true that human motives are always and everywhere entirely selfish. The assertion, as I said, rings true, but it is not based on any scientific evidence. Of course, like other animals, we are born with an instinct for self-preservation. But, like them, we also have an instinct for group preservation – the instinct that drives a mother bird to defend its young; and that is already a first step beyond selfishness. More generally, what scientific studies tend to show is that human motives are not to any great extent inborn but learnt. Whether people behave aggressively and pugnaciously, or co-operatively and peacefully, is largely determined by environmental factors, including the *mores* of the society in question. The simple truth is that we are capable of *both*: selfishness and unselfishness, egoism and altruism.

There are indeed some value systems that advocate altruism to the point of self-denial and self-sacrifice. But that is contrary to nature, and often counter-productive. What is needed, rather, is a proper *balance* of the two, egoism and altruism; and that is precisely what Judaism stands for because it is based on the principle of justice, that every human being is equally precious, so that we have a twofold duty: to seek our own well-being and to seek the well-being of others; not one or the other but both.

Nevertheless, it is the duty to care for others that needs to be emphasised, for though we may assent to it in theory, in practice our selfishness constantly gets in the way. Therefore Judaism reiterates it constantly. 'Love your neighbour as yourself' (Lev. 19:18). 'Let your neighbour's property be as dear to you as your own' (Avot 2:12). 'Let your neighbour's honour be as dear to you as your own' (Avot 2:10). 'Is not this the fast I look for ... to share your bread with the hungry, and to bring the homeless poor into your house?' (Isa. 58:6f.)

Are we capable of responding to these exhortations? Are we capable of acting altruistically? *Of course* we are! It is hard, of course, but it is not impossible. As we have just read, 'This commandment which I command you this day is not too hard for you, or too remote ... It is very near, in your mouth and in your heart, that you may do it' (Deut. 30:11, 14). It is within your capability; you only have to be true to what is best in your own, human nature.

To rise above selfishness, to care for others as well as ourselves: that is precisely what it means to be human. 'If I am not for myself,' said Hillel, 'who will be for me? But if I am only for myself, what am I?' (Avot 1:14). That is precisely what it means to grow up, to become a mature person, as every psychotherapist will tell you. And precisely that is what is needed if humanity is to endure. The selfishness of individuals leads to conflict in society. The collective selfishness of nations leads to war. And the collective selfishness of humanity threatens to destroy the earth for future generations.

The conquest of selfishness is therefore the most urgent of all human tasks. It is quite literally a matter of life and death. 'I call heaven and earth to witness against you this day that I have set before you life or death, blessing or curse; therefore choose life, that you and your descendants may live' (Deut. 30:19).

In the long run, therefore, altruism is in the self-interest of humanity, and consequently of its individual members. In the long run, the paradox applies that it is selfish to be unselfish. In the long run, morality and expediency converge, which is exactly what the Hebrew Prophets taught over and over again. And perhaps we are beginning to learn the lesson. When manufacturing companies make ecologically sound products because it is profitable, and when nations make peace because there is a 'peace dividend' to be won, they act both rightly and expediently.

But to rely on these complex calculations of long-term self-interest would not be safe. It is too easy to manipulate them, and make them tell us what we want to hear. Much better that we should habituate ourselves, from childhood onwards, to control our selfish impulses; to take into account the needs and feelings of others as well as our own; and to do so because we really do care for them, not indeed more than ourselves but as much as ourselves; because we recognise and revere the Divine Image in each and every one of them. Much better that we should let ourselves be moulded by a value system, such as Judaism, which actually trains us in the way of altruism.

So if we ask once more whether we are capable of changing for the better, the honest answer must be: not to any great extent. We are too prone to selfishness; the *yetzer ha-ra* is too powerful. But that is not the whole of the story – not quite. We *do* have also a *yetzer tov*, a good inclination. We *are* able to feel love and concern and compassion for our fellow human beings, and to restrain ourselves so that their rights may be respected and their needs satisfied, as well as our own. We may be 99 percent egoistic and only one percent altruistic, but by that one percent, as by a thin thread, the future of humanity hangs. Our task is to increase it; to strengthen the *yetzer tov* within ourselves. That, in a nutshell, is the whole purpose of the Penitential Season.

❖   ❖   ❖

Season of Gladness

The Autumn of Life
Sukkot, 30 September 1977

There is a paradox about Sukkot which never fails to fascinate me. On the one hand it is זמן מחן תורתנו, 'the season of our gladness'. The fun of building a Sukkah, the sweet fragrance exuded by its foliage, the colourful display of fruit and flowers, the rattling of the palm leaves as we shake the Lulav, and the joyful processions – all these combine with the essential message of the festival, of thanksgiving for the bounty of nature, to produce in us a mood of light-heartedness if not light-headedness.

But on the other hand there is also a sombre note which runs through this festival. Traditionally, the seventh day, known as Hoshana Rabbah, has a solemn atmosphere reminiscent of Yom

Kippur; it is in fact regarded as a day of judgment, the worshippers dress in white, beat the floor with willow branches, and recite endlessly repeated pleas for salvation. And there is a custom of medieval origin to read on the Sabbath of this festival the book of Kohelet, otherwise known as Ecclesiastes, which is anything but joyful, for it dwells on the futility of life, the frailty of old age, and the finality of death.

Whatever the historical origins of this duality may be, it isn't difficult to find a warrant for it in the season of the year. For the autumn has a sombre side. Although it is the season of the harvest, revealing the bounty of nature in all its glory, it is also the season of decay. The flowers fade, the leaves wither, the days grow shorter, and winter is not far away. Inevitably, this metamorphosis inspires melancholy thoughts. It reminds us that all good things come to an end, that nature is subject to an inexorable cycle, and that, because we are part of nature, that cycle governs us too. So we think of the seasons as corresponding to the stages of human life. Spring represents childhood and youth, summer the prime of life, autumn middle age, and winter old age and death. It is a thought which has inspired many poets, including Shakespeare. One of his sonnets begins:

That time of year thou mayst in me behold
When yellow leaves, or none, or few, do hang
Upon those boughs which shake against the cold,
Bare ruin'd choirs, where late the sweet birds sang ... (No. 73)

And that, too, is the dominant theme of the book of Kohelet. It is an autumnal book, written by a man in the autumn of his life who wistfully contemplates his oncoming old age. Especially graphic is this celebrated passage describing in numerous metaphors the physiological processes of growing old:

Remember your Creator in the days of your youth, before the time of trouble comes and the years draw near when you will say, 'I see no purpose in them'. Remember God before the sun and light of day give place to darkness, before the moon and the stars grow dim, and the clouds return with the rain – when the guardians of the house tremble, and the strong men stoop, when the women grinding the meal cease work because they are few, and those who look through the windows look no longer, when the street-doors are shut, when the noise of the mill is low, when the chirping of the sparrow grows faint and the song-birds fall silent, when men are afraid of a steep place and the locust's paunch is swollen and caper-buds have no more zest. For man goes to his everlasting home, and the mourners go about the streets. Remember God before the silver cord is snapped and the golden bowl is broken, before the pitcher is shattered at the spring and the wheel broken at the well, before

the dust returns to the earth as it was and the spirit returns to God who
gave it. (12:1-7).

It is a bleak picture that Kohelet paints, unrelieved by any optimism. He could have taken refuge in the hope of immortality. He
could have said: 'Never mind that I am growing old and will soon die,
for a better world awaits me on the other side'. But he doesn't allow
himself that luxury. The most he will say is that the spirit returns to
God. He could have sought consolation in the thought that he would
live on in the memories of his loved ones. But no, he denies himself
even that crumb of comfort, for he says: 'The wise man is remembered no longer than the fool, for as the passing days multiply, all will
be forgotten' (2:16). But surely his achievements will outlast him and
benefit future generations! No, even that is problematic. For 'what
sort of a man', he asks, 'will he be who succeeds me? ... Who knows
whether he will be a wise man or a fool? Yet he will be the master of
all the fruits of my labour and skill under the sun' (2:18f).

I like Kohelet. He is an honest man who refuses to kid himself.
There is a kind of heroism about his honesty: no pie in the sky, no
rose-coloured spectacles, no comforting illusions. He faces reality,
including the reality of aging and dying, without blinkers. But when
he has done so, what remains? Only pessimism? No, not quite. For
one thing, there is acceptance, and that is not the same as pessimism.
It is a kind of unfretting resignation which comes out in such passages as the famous one beginning: 'To everything there is a season,
and a time for every purpose under heaven: A time to be born, and
a time to die ...' (3:1f). Moreover, as long as we live and have our
faculties, we can enjoy happiness. 'I know', he says, 'that there is
nothing good for man except to be happy and to live the best life he
can while he is alive' (3:12). Therefore we should not fritter away
these possibilities by wasting time or by half-heartedness: 'He who
watches the wind will never sow, and he who keeps an eye on the
clouds will never reap' (11:4); 'Whatever task lies to your hand, do it
with all your might' (9:10).

So there is a good deal in Kohelet that is positive. But the most
positive thing of all is the conclusion: 'The sum of the matter, when
all is said and done: Fear God and obey God's commandments, for
that is the whole of man'. That is to say, the value of human life on
earth does not depend on whether there is an after-life, or whether
we shall be remembered when we are gone, or whether our achievements will endure; it depends on its intrinsic quality.

The quality of life is what counts. And that is something which is
attainable regardless of whether we are young or old, whether we are

in the spring, the summer, the autumn or the winter of our lives. Indeed, there is a sense in which it does, or should, become *more* attainable as we grow older. For though we become less agile, alert and energetic, we should become wiser, more experienced, more discriminating; better able to understand ourselves and our fellow human beings, and so to use our aptitudes and opportunities to the best advantage.

Not all grow wiser as they grow older; but those who do acquire a composure, a tranquillity, a gentleness and a contentment which have their own beauty, just as the leaves of the Sukkah give forth their sweetest fragrance as they begin to decay.

That is not the only lesson of Sukkot, but it is one of them, and not the least important. Sukkot remains זמן שמחתנו the 'season of our gladness'. But the gladness changes in tone as we grow older, from exuberance to serenity. And the autumnal, mellow quality of serenity has its own charm. In Shelley's words (from 'Hymn to Intellectual Beauty', VII):

The day becomes more solemn and serene
    When noon is past – there is a harmony
    In autumn, and a lustre in the sky,
Which through the summer is not heard or seen,
As if it could not be, as if it had not been!

❖   ❖   ❖

Say it with Flowers
Sukkot, 15 October 1978

'Say it with flowers.' I don't know who first coined the phrase: probably some florist with a flair for advertising. However that may be, Jews have been 'saying it with flowers' for three thousand years if we may use the word 'flowers' loosely to include the Lulav and Etrog as well as the foliage and various species of vegetation with which we decorate the Synagogue and the Sukkah at this season.

But what exactly do we say with the 'flowers' of Sukkot? To answer that question would be like trying to explain a joke, to translate poetry into prose. For flowers have their own language. They can say many things, for instance, 'Thank you for a nice dinner' or 'I wish you a speedy recovery' or 'I love you', but in a manner different from mere words. So, too, the language of Sukkot is visual rather than verbal, which creates a problem for the preacher. Sometimes I think that the best Sukkot sermon would be silence, merely to feast our eyes on the sights of the harvest produce, and to inhale its fragrance. However, let us attempt to decode the message of the flowers of Sukkot.

First and foremost, they exemplify, and so remind us of, the beauty of the world. Do we need reminding? Of course we do! For, as town dwellers, the scenery of our daily existence is dominated by mortar and brick and machinery; the tempo of modern life is such that we rarely pause to contemplate what natural beauty intrudes into it; and even when we do, we tend to take it too much for granted. So once a year we bring the beauty of the countryside into our cities, our homes and our synagogues and thrust it into the centre of our field of vision. A peculiar custom, maybe, but one that requires no justification beyond itself, any more than going to an art gallery or a concert hall. To those, if such there are, who think it futile, there is no answer. We can only pity them and say, with Wordsworth, 'Dull would he be of soul who could pass by/ A sight so touching in its majesty' (from 'Composed upon Westminster Bridge').

Secondly, if we are at all inclined to be religious, the beauty of the world stirs in us a sense of admiration for, and gratitude to, its divine Creator. Admittedly, atheists can accuse us of being selective. They can point to aspects of nature which are not so pleasing: the apparent cruelty among animals, the diseases and natural disasters that cause pain and death: Tennyson's 'nature, red in tooth and claw'. That, too, is part of the evidence. But though it would be wrong to gloss over it, and to pretend that it does not pose a grave problem, it would be equally wrong to let it mesmerise us and so overlook the positive side, the abundant evidence that nature is predominantly beautiful and bountiful. After all, it need not have been so. It is true that if the earth's atmosphere did not contain just the right mixture of gases, and sufficient water, it could not sustain life at all. But there is no law of logical necessity which makes essential the infinite variety of species, each more exquisite in form and colour than the next, with which our world is crowded. It is therefore almost impossible to resist the conclusion that the Creator delights in the creation of beauty, and desires us to share the sheer joy of it.

But the more we contemplate nature, the more we become aware of a paradox: on the one hand, that we are part of it; on the other hand, that we differ from it. Like all other creatures, we eat and drink, we wake and sleep, we reproduce and we die. But there is more to human life than that. We think, we create, we transmit culture, and we are free to choose. We live in another world besides the world of nature: the world of history.

So the flowers of Sukkot remind us also of our past: of our ancestors who 'dwelt in booths' in the wilderness of Sinai, of the pilgrims who thronged Jerusalem in the days of the Temple, of the journey of our people 'from Egypt until now', of the journey of humanity from the dawn of civilisation to its consummation in the messianic age. And in this world of history there are laws different from those that govern nature: moral laws which must be obeyed if human life is to achieve its potential, and even if humanity is to survive at all. Not that Sukkot draws our attention to all of these laws. There are other festivals for that, such as Shavuot. But it does call to our minds one area of the moral law: that which concerns our relationship with nature.

For instance, Judaism teaches us to respect it. There is a law in the Torah which says, 'You shall not destroy' (Deut. 20:19). Originally it referred only to the destruction of fruit trees when besieging a city in time of war. Later its application was extended to include any kind of wanton destruction. There are also laws concerning the humane treatment of animals. Even the laws of *Shechitah* derived in part from that motive. At any rate, it is clear enough that Judaism requires us to treat nature with respect.

It is also clear that it requires us to share it. We may not simply grab from it whatever we desire. We must also take into account the needs of others. But the *context* in which this sharing has to take place has been gradually enlarged. At first it was only the family, then the tribe, then the whole nation. That is the biblical stage. The Pentateuch legislates for the community of Israel. That is the purview of all its laws for the tithing of agricultural produce and for the maintenance of the poor. Ancient Israel was, in intention at least, a welfare state.

But that is not enough. Just as no individual exists in isolation, so no nation exists in isolation. Already in the Bible, especially in the writings of the Prophets, there are evidences, remarkable for their time, of a universalistic perspective. God, we read, 'is great beyond the borders of Israel' (Mal. 1:5). God cares for other nations, too, and desires that in the messianic future all nations shall live together in harmony and co-operation, sharing the bounty of the earth. This theme too is present in Sukkot. For the prophet Zechariah looks forward to the day when this festival will be observed by all the nations of the world (14:16-19), and various ancient sources inform us that during Sukkot it was customary in the Temple in Jerusalem to offer seventy sacrifices in supplication for the welfare of the seventy nations that comprise humanity (e.g., Midrash Psalms on Psalm 109:4). Today this universal ideal has become an urgent necessity. For we realise, as no previous generation realised, the interdepen-

dence of all peoples. We are therefore beyond the stage of appreci-
ating only the need for equitable distribution within any one country.
There has to be equitable distribution internationally if humanity is
to achieve peace and to endure. There has to be, not only a welfare
state, but a welfare world. And therefore to speak of free enterprise
and free trade as sufficient to solve the problems of the world is to
live blindly and obstinately in a past that has long ceased to correspond to reality.

Yet a further insight has dawned on us in recent times: that just as
the bounty of nature must be shared between individuals, and just as
it must be shared between the nations at any one time, so it must be
shared by humanity as a whole with the generations of the future.
For if we exploit it too greedily we shall destroy the conditions able
to sustain human life on this planet in the centuries to come. The
danger signals are becoming daily more unmistakable. So now there
opens up before us a whole new set of moral imperatives, epito-
mised in the word 'conservation', of which previous generations had
hardly an inkling, and the ancient Jewish teaching that human beings
are, by God's appointment, 'stewards' of the earth, acquires a new
dimension of meaning. That, too, must from now on be part of the
message of Sukkot.

These, then, are some of the things we 'say with flowers' during
this festival. For the rest, let the flowers say it themselves, in their
own language. It is more eloquent than speech.

❖   ❖   ❖

The Secret of Sukkot
Sukkot, 22 September 1983

בסוכות תשבו שבעת ימים, 'In Sukkot shall you dwell for seven days' (Lev.
23:42). This is the verse we must explore if we want to get at the
essential meaning of the festival we have come here to celebrate.

Why dwell in booths? Well, there's always a difference between
the 'real' reason and the 'good' reason for anything. The real reason
for the Sukkah isn't known and must therefore be guessed. But it isn't
particularly hard to guess. For it only has to account for two facts.

First, what a Sukkah in itself is. Now there is ample evidence from
the Bible that a Sukkah was some kind of a simple, rough-and-ready
shelter. For instance, we are told in Genesis that Jacob, after his
encounter with Esau near the ford of the Jabbok, journeyed on to a

place called Sukkot – not to be confused with an Egyptian town of the same name which we read about in the story of the Exodus (Exod. 12:37) – which he so named because there he built *sukkot* for his cattle (33:17). Obviously, these *sukkot* were shelters. And what did Jacob's cattle need to be sheltered from? Partly, perhaps, predatory wild animals, but chiefly the scorching heat of the midday sun. I say 'chiefly' because the word *sukkah* comes from a verb, סָכַךְ which means 'to cover' and suggests *overhead* protection, as indeed the noun סְכָךְ has come to refer to the material for the *roof* of the Sukkah; but also for another reason, that the prophet Jonah built himself a Sukkah for the very purpose that it might afford him shade (4:5).

So that's what a Sukkah is: a makeshift shelter from the sun. But we also have to account for a second fact: that the festival in question is a *harvest* festival. In all probability, therefore, the Sukkot of the festival had their origin in the shelters which the farmers built for themselves at this season, so that they might stay out in the fields all day long while they were gathering in the produce, yet have a little respite from the sun during the hottest part of the day. In fact, the prophet Isaiah seems to refer to such a harvester's shed when he says that 'the daughter of Judah is left as a *sukkah* in a vineyard' (1:8).

Since, moreover, the harvest celebrations would originally have taken place, not in the towns, but in the fields, it makes perfectly good sense to assume that these harvesters' shelters, which at first served only a utilitarian purpose, later became a ceremonial feature of the festival itself.

Something like that must surely be the 'real' reason for the Sukkah. But much more important for our purpose is not the 'real' reason but the 'good' reason; and that, according to the Bible, is 'that your generations may know that I made the children of Israel dwell in *sukkot* when I brought them out of the land of Egypt' (Lev. 23:43).

There is, however, something rather odd about that, as has often been pointed out, since *davka* in the wilderness the Israelites would hardly have dwelt in Sukkot, as we understand the term, since the required materials would have been conspicuously unavailable to them. It is much more likely that they would have made themselves tents. So the 'good' reason is apparently not such a good reason, after all.

Precisely that is, presumably, why Rabbi Eliezer, as we are told in the Talmud (Suk. 11b; Sifra to Lev. 23:43), interpreted our verse to refer, not to *sukkot* in the literal sense, but to the so-called 'clouds of glory', that is, the columns of smoke, mentioned several times in the Exodus story, which accompanied the Israelites on their journey through the wilderness as a token of God's presence and protection.

But then what are we to say of Rabbi Akiva who opposed Eliezer in this dispute? Did he really believe that the Israelites had the wherewithal in the wilderness to build *sukkot* in the usual sense of the term? Surely not! My guess, therefore, is that in Akiva's view the *sukkot* of our verse are indeed to be understood in a material, not a symbolic sense, and yet not in a slavishly literal sense. In other words, he took our verse to mean: 'You shall dwell in makeshift shelters for seven days, that you may remember the makeshift shelters (never mind what they were made of) in which your ancestors dwelt in the wilderness'.

So understood, the 'good' reason turns out to be quite acceptable, after all. But of course it raises further questions. *Why* should we recall the shelters of the wilderness, and why should we do so particularly at this time of the year? It is to this twofold question that the Jewish commentators in the main address themselves; and what I should like to do now is to give you some of their most typical interpretations. From these, we shall find, one main theme will emerge.

We begin with Philo, the Jewish philosopher who lived in Alexandria in the first century of the common era. Among the reasons he gives for the custom of dwelling in *sukkot* during this festival is that 'it is well in wealth to remember your poverty, in distinction your insignificance, in high office your position as a commoner, in peace your dangers in war, on land the storms at sea, in cities the life of loneliness' (*De Specialibus Legibus*, 2:208f).

If the relevance of that remark is not quite obvious, it becomes much clearer in the Bible commentary of the Rashbam, that is Rabbi Samuel ben Meir, a grandson of Rashi, who was born in a little village called Ramérupt, near Troyes, in France, towards the end of the eleventh century. Commenting on our verse, he wrote: 'We leave our houses, full of good things, at the time of ingathering, and dwell in frail booths, so that we may remember that in the wilderness we had no possessions, and no houses to dwell in. And for this reason God decreed that the feast of Sukkot should be observed at the time of ingathering from the threshing floor and the wine vat, so that our hearts may not be lifted up in pride at our houses full of good things, and so that we may not say, "Our hands have gotten us this wealth" (Deut. 8:17)'.

About half a century later, Moses Maimonides, writing in Cairo, Egypt, had this to say: 'The moral lesson derived from these feasts is this: we ought to remember our evil days in our days of prosperity. We will thereby be induced to thank God repeatedly, to lead a modest and humble life ... We leave our houses in order to dwell in makeshift shelters, as inhabitants of deserts do that are in want of comfort. We shall thereby remember that such was once our condition' (*Guide of the Perplexed*, III, 43).

Our next witness is Isaac Aboab, who lived somewhere in Spain in the fourteenth century. He refers to a comment on our verse, quoted in the Talmud (Suk. 2a), by the fourth-century Babylonian rabbi Ravah, which is an interpretation of the meaning of the Sukkah: צא מדירת קבע ושב בדירת עראי, 'Leave your permanent abode and dwell in a temporary abode', and then makes this observation: 'The purpose of this commandment concerning the Sukkah is to teach us that we should not put our trust in the size or the strength or the beauty of our house, even though it be filled with the best of everything; nor should we rely upon the help of any human, not even the owner of the land. But we should put our trust in the One whose word called the world into being, for God alone is mighty and faithful ...' (*Menorat ha-Maor*, 3:4:6:1).

Finally, let us hear Judah David Eisenstein, who was born in Poland but at the age of eighteen emigrated to the United States where he died, aged 102, in 1956, having written a number of very useful Hebrew encyclopaedias. In one of them he gives his own summary of the essential meaning of the Sukkah, basing himself on the same Talmud passage, about leaving our permanent homes to live in a temporary shelter. 'This', he says, 'is to remind human beings that they are only wayfarers and not permanent residents in this world, and that their greatest hope is the world to come. And in this respect the custom may be compared with that of eating unleavened bread, which is called "the bread of affliction", at Pesach ... Both the dwelling in the Sukkah and the eating of the bread of affliction apply equally to rich and poor, so that the rich may not become proud and boastful of their wealth, and look down on the poor, but by virtue of the way of life represented by the eating of unleavened bread during the seven days of Pesach and dwelling in a Sukkah during the seven days of Sukkot, they may learn to understand what it is like to be poor, and will therefore have compassion on the poor and support them out of their wealth' (*Otzar Dinim u-Minhagim*, 285a-b).

All these comments, spanning nearly two thousand years, stress, in their different ways, one main motif. The essence of the Sukkah – never mind for this purpose exactly how it is constructed – is that it is, as the Talmud says, דירת עראי, a temporary abode, a makeshift shelter, a fragile structure not built to last. The purpose of it is to remind us of the journey of our ancestors through the wilderness of Sinai. As a matter of fact, 'remind' is too weak a word. 'Re-live' would be better. Just as at Pesach we are supposed to imagine ourselves participating in the Exodus, so at Sukkot we are supposed to imagine ourselves camping in the wilderness, and in the most effective way possible, by actually simulating the experience. For the idea of the Sukkah is, or at least originally was, that one should actually live in it for seven days, not just enter it briefly for Kiddush or the occasional meal (Suk. 28b, 26a; Yad, *Hilchot Sukkah* 6:6; O.Ch. 639:2). It was only when Jews settled in Northern Europe and found that the Sukkah, though it might afford good shelter from the sun, provided very little protection against the weather conditions they had to face at this season, that they took advantage of an escape clause in the Talmud to the effect that, since Sukkot is supposed to be a joyful festival, one is not obliged to eat in the Sukkah when one's meal is likely to get spoilt by the rain (Suk. 2:9; Suk. 25b; O.Ch. 639:2, 5).

By living, at any rate as much as possible, in the Sukkah, we are supposed to re-live the experience of our ancestors in the Wilderness; and though of course their journey, lasting for forty years, encompassed all the seasons, we re-enact it at *this* season because it is at this season, when the harvest has just been gathered in, that it is most salutary for us to be reminded of it. As Philo said, 'it is well in wealth to remember your poverty' (see above), and as Maimonides put it, 'we ought to remember our evil days in our days of prosperity' (ditto). Why? So that we may not become too proud of our own achievements but remember our ultimate dependence on nature, and therefore on God; that we may remember the privations suffered by our ancestors in the past and by many of our fellow human beings in the present, and may therefore be induced to share our prosperity with them; that we may be all the more grateful to God for our good fortune; and, most profoundly of all, that we may be reminded that life itself is a kind of journey, so that not only are the things we possess perishable, but we are mortal and therefore the very earth we live on is for us, like the Sukkah, only a temporary abode.

But now one final thought. There is, as these interpretations have brought out, a great paradox about this festival. On the one hand there is a kind of asceticism about it. For the Sukkah, although we decorate it so beautifully and thereby to some extent disguise the fact, is basically a symbol not of luxury but of hardship. It is, as Eisenstein so illuminatingly remarked, this festival's equivalent of Pesach's 'bread of affliction' (see above). And the thoughts it inspires about the impermanence of everything material, and even the transience of our own lives on earth, are not exactly cheerful. And yet Sukkot is the harvest festival, when we surround ourselves with evidences of our blessings, and feast our eyes on tokens of the beauty and bounty of nature; and it is *z'man simchatenu*, the season of our gladness.

In this paradox lies the secret of this festival of Sukkot with its curious bitter-sweet flavour. It teaches us to see ourselves as part of nature, to recognise our creatureliness, and to accept the limitations which that implies. Yes, life, like the cycle of the seasons, has its fluctuations, its times of harvest and its lean periods; and like all creatures, we have a life-cycle: there is, as the Bible says (I Chron. 29:15), אֵין מִקְוֶה, no abiding for any of us. But these are the only terms on which life is offered to us at all: it is that or nothing. And therefore everything good we experience is a bonus. Every day we live is a gift from God, every leaf and flower a token of God's generosity which we have no right to expect. If we can learn to accept our limitations, then within these limitations we may find our true happiness. Then the bitterness will dissolve in our acceptance, and only the sweetness will remain. So may it be for us.

❖ ❖ ❖

For all Humanity
Sukkot, 26 September 1988

On the High Holydays we think in cosmic terms; we imagine all humanity standing before its Creator. The 'Low Holydays', by contrast, commemorate particular episodes in the history of a particular people – ours. The scale is reduced. Nevertheless, Sukkot has always been a universal-human and only secondarily a particular-Jewish festival. There are three reasons for thinking this.

The first is simply stated. It is that Sukkot is a nature festival, and nature belongs to all humanity, not only to the Jewish people. Now it is true that the other two Pilgrimage Festivals also began as nature festivals. Pesach originated in an ancient shepherds' festival, celebrating the lambing season, which was amalgamated, because it coincided, with an ancient farmers' festival, celebrating the first barley harvest; and Shavuot not only *began* as a purely agricultural festival but remained so throughout the biblical period. Nevertheless both of these festivals were successfully reinterpreted as commemorations of historical events. For the last two thousand years at least Pesach has been for Jews first and foremost the festival of the Exodus, and Shavuot of the Sinaitic Revelation. But with Sukkot it is different. Although it, too, was reinterpreted as a historical festival, and indeed, unlike Shavuot, already within the biblical period, namely as recalling the Journey through the Wilderness, nevertheless *this*

attempt at reinterpretation was never very successful: it was too artificial, too obviously superimposed.

In short, Sukkot, much more than Pesach and Shavuot, has remained obstinately a nature festival; and nature, to say it again, is
universal.

My second reason is that Jewish tradition itself shows a recurring
awareness that what we celebrate at Sukkot is of concern, not only to
the people of Israel, but to all humanity. An early example of this is
a verse in the book of the prophet Zechariah which is all the more
significant because it occurs in the Haftarah traditionally read on the
first day of Sukkot. The passage is an apocalyptic one which
describes in lurid terms all the terrible things which God will do to
Israel's enemies in the end of days, but then goes on to say: 'And it
shall come to pass, that every one that is left of all the nations that
came against Jerusalem shall go up from year to year to worship the
Sovereign, the God of hosts, ולחוג את־חג הסוכות, and to celebrate the
feast of tabernacles' (14:16). In other words, Sukkot will ultimately
become quite literally, a universal festival, observed by all humanity.

But what I chiefly have in mind is a tradition which keeps on crop-
ping up in Rabbinic Literature to the effect that in ancient times,
when the Temple still existed, seventy bullocks were sacrificed during
the festival of Sukkot, and that they were offered on behalf of the seventy nations of the world. This tradition requires a little explanation.

First, why seventy bullocks? The Talmud informs us that on the
first day of the festival they offered thirteen bullocks, on the second
twelve, and so on for the seven days of the festival, reducing the number each day by one, so that on the seventh day seven were offered.
Since these numbers, from thirteen to seven, average ten, the total
number is seven times ten, which is seventy. (See Suk. 5:6; 55b.)

And why seventy nations? Partly because seventy is a good round
figure. But there is a bit more to it than that. For one thing, the so-
called 'Table of the Nations' in the tenth chapter of Genesis lists,
according to Rabbinic computation, seventy supposed progenitors
of the races of humanity. For another thing, the forty-sixth chapter of
Genesis informs us that 'the souls of the house of Jacob who came
into Egypt numbered seventy' (v. 27), and if you read that verse in
conjunction with a verse in the thirty-second chapter of Deuteronomy, which says that when God portioned out the earth, 'He set the
borders of the peoples according to the number of the children of
Israel' (v. 8), it follows, according to the Rabbinic interpretation, that
the number of nations in the world is the same as the number of individuals who constituted the original Israelite settlement in Egypt, in
the time of Joseph, and equals seventy. Hence it is taken for granted

throughout Rabbinic Literature that there are seventy nations – or, as it is sometimes expressed, seventy languages – in the world (e.g., Targum Jonathan Gen. 11:7, 32:8; Sotah 7:5; Shab. 88b).

But the question still remains, why during the seven days of Sukkot Jewish priests in the Jewish Temple should have offered sacrifices for the Gentile nations of the world. The usual explanation has much to do with the fact that in the Near East the autumnal equinox inaugurated a season of the year in which there must be substantial rainfall if the next year's crops were to be assured; and therefore the whole observance of Sukkot had in ancient times a strong undercurrent of praying for rain. But since the other nations did not even acknowledge the true God, there was always a danger that they might anger God into withholding the necessary rainfall, in which case Jews and Gentiles alike would suffer, and it was therefore a matter of enlightened self-interest for our ancestors to offer sacrifices not only on their own behalf but on behalf of the pagan peoples as well. As Rashi comments on the key passage in the Talmud, the motive was לכפר עליהם הגשמים שירדו שירדו בכל־העולם, 'to make atonement for them, so that rain might fall throughout the world' (Suk. 55b).

More specifically, though, the tradition that the seventy bullocks were offered for the seventy nations is usually stated in relation to a rather strange verse in Psalm 109 which says: 'In return for my love they are my adversaries; but I am all prayer' (v. 4); the comment being: 'Although the nations hate us, nevertheless we continue to pray for them' (Num.R. 21:24; Cant. R. I, 15:2, IV, 1:2; Midrash Psalms 109:4; PRK 28:9). In one of these passages, which Rashi possibly had in mind, the point is explicitly made in the name of a fourth-century Palestinian rabbi (Pinchas) that the reason was 'so that the world may not be depopulated in punishment for their sins' (PRK 28:9).

However, the tradition is older than that and can be traced back all the way to Philo, the Alexandrian Jewish philosopher of the first half of the first century. In a remarkable passage, after describing the robe of the High Priest, which, he says, was richly decorated with symbols of all the elements of nature, he goes on to say: 'Among the other nations the priests are accustomed to offer prayers and sacrifices for their kinsmen and friends and fellow-countrymen only, but the high priest of the Jews makes prayers and gives thanks not only on behalf of the whole human race but also for the parts of nature, earth, water, air, fire. For he holds the world to be, as in very truth it is, his country, and in its behalf he is wont to propitiate the Ruler with supplication and intercession, beseeching Him to make His creature a partaker of His own kindly and merciful nature' (*De Specialibus Legibus* I, 97; *Loeb Classical Library*, Vol. VII, p. 155).

So there you have two reasons for regarding Sukkot as a festival with a universal significance. But there is a third, which is perhaps the most important of them all, and it can be expressed in one word: conservation. If this festival of Sukkot has always taught humanity's dependence on a bountiful nature, that lesson has been brought home to us with immensely increased force by recent revelations of the extent to which humanity's activities on earth are destroying the very environment on which its survival depends. In these circumstances, the commandment בל־תשחית, 'you shall not destroy', which Jewish tradition derives from a prohibition in Deuteronomy against the destruction of the fruit trees of a besieged city (20:19), assumes a proportion never before envisaged. It makes it clearer than ever that we and the rest of humanity share a common destiny. It also makes it clear that it makes no sense to *pray* for rain if at the same time we destroy the forests on which adequate rainfall depends, and, more generally, that it is not sufficient to *hope* for the avoidance of ecological disaster: we must actually work to prevent it.

❖   ❖   ❖

Back to Nature

Sukkot, 30 September 1993

What is the most obvious but also the most problematic fact about this festival of Sukkot? It is quite simply that it is a *nature* festival. And what is so problematic about that? Doesn't every religion celebrate nature? Yes, but *davka* in Judaism there is a difficulty about that because in the ancient Near East in which it grew up, the celebration of nature was closely associated with paganism. And that meant two things. On the one hand, the pagan fertility festivals involved idolatry and cruelty, including child sacrifice and temple prostitution. On the other hand, paganism was amoral: it failed to address the issues of personal morality and social justice which were to Judaism all-important.

And to these points we may add another, related one. As constituents of nature, human beings are not essentially different from other animals. What distinguishes them is the fact that they live not only in nature, but also in another world, the world of culture: of thought and speech, of history and literature, of moral judgment and social structure. It is in civilisation that human beings demonstrate their unique status as bearers of the Divine Image, and hence their dignity.

For all these reasons, Judaism was never very comfortable with too much emphasis on nature, but always anxious to change the subject as quickly as possible to history, the realm of human relations, of right and wrong, and of the working out of the divine plan and purpose. That is especially evident in the case of the festivals, which the Israelites largely took over from the Canaanites among whom they lived, but then transformed from nature festivals with their fertility rites, marking the seasons of the pastoral and agricultural year, into historical festivals, commemorating great events in the annals of the Jewish people. So the festival of the newborn lambs and the festival of unleavened bread were combined to become the annual celebration of the Exodus from Egypt, and the festival of the wheat harvest became, though only in post-biblical times, the anniversary of the Sinaitic Revelation.

Even the great autumn festival was historicised when the harvesters' booths were declared to be reminders of the makeshift dwellings of our ancestors on their journey from Sinai to the Promised Land. The explanation is of course quite unconvincing, since it fails to explain either how the Israelites could have obtained the materials to make Sukkot in the Sinai desert or why the festival should be celebrated in the autumn rather than some other time of the year. But the very fact that such an unconvincing explanation was offered only goes to show all the more clearly how anxious Judaism was to move away from the celebration of nature pure and simple.

Which is not to say that the biblical writers had no interest in nature, or were not perceptive observers of it. Especially in their poetical writings they refer often enough to the sun and the moon, the stars and constellations, the mountains and rivers, the fauna and flora of their region; and they mention by name some scores of different species of plants and animals: enough to fill whole biblical zoos and botanical gardens in Israel and elsewhere.

Yet, on closer inspection all that turns out to be something less than a celebration of nature in its own right. Nearly always, these things are mentioned as pointing to something beyond themselves. They are adduced to illustrate the greatness of the Creator, or portrayed as singing God's praise. They feature in fables and parables, teaching various moral lessons, and as metaphors symbolising various human qualities, as when the righteous are said to flourish like the palm tree (Psalm 92:13), and when the sluggard is advised to go to the ant (Proverbs. 6:6). The biblical writers don't really seem to be interested in nature for its own sake, either from a scientific or from an aesthetic point of view. What matters about the heavens is not their expanse or their beauty, but that they declare the glory of God (Psalm 19:2).

So there *is* great nature poetry in the Bible, especially in the book of Job, in the Song of Songs and in the Psalms, but there is always that obliqueness about it; nature is never the primary focus of attention, and human beings are rarely depicted as simply part of nature, but as having at best one foot inside nature and one outside it.

Interestingly, the chief exception to that rule occurs in the very book which provides the hagiographic reading for this festival: the book of Kohelet or Ecclesiastes. Only there do we find a frank acknowledgment that, from one point of view at least, human beings are part and parcel of nature, and subject to its laws. 'I said in my heart with regard to human beings that God is testing them to show that they are but animals. For the fate of humans and the fate of animals is the same; as one dies, so dies the other. They all have the same breath, and humans have no advantage over the animals; for all is vanity. All go to one place; all are from the dust, and all turn to dust again' (3:18-20).

But that, as I said, is an exception. In general, what Judaism emphasised to its people was not their place in nature but their place in culture: the loyalty they owed to their community and to their tradition; the book learning they must acquire and teach to their children; the laws and commandments they must obey; the part they must play in the struggle between good and evil, which is what history is all about.

This unconcern with, and consequent estrangement from, nature became even more marked in post-biblical times, as Jews were uprooted from their land and turned to occupations that involved little contact with the soil. It is hard to imagine a rabbi of the talmudic period bird-watching or even walking in the countryside just to enjoy its beauty. As a matter of fact, there is a well-known saying in the Ethics of the Fathers (3:8) which expresses the strongest disapproval for anyone who interrupts their study of the Mishnah to admire a beautiful tree.

This alienation from nature continued more or less through the Middle Ages. Jews still built their Sukkah at this season, but only as a reminder of the Wilderness period, and into it they invited, in their imagination, the Patriarchs and other worthies of the ancient past. They still held in their hands the four species of the Lulav and Etrog, but only as symbols of different kinds of Jew, or different parts of the human body. Sukkot was drained of its original meaning as a nature festival.

All this continued until the period of the Haskalah. Only then did Jews wake up to, and protest against, their age-old alienation from nature. It became a major theme in the poetry of Bialik, not least in his long poem *Ha-Matmid*, about the perpetual Talmud student, imprisoned in the house of study, yearning for the sights and sounds and smells of the countryside. Zionism was and is, in one of its aspects, a back-to-nature movement. And what about us? I think it is good that, as Jews, we should live primarily in the world of civilisation; that we should concern ourselves with history and learning, right and wrong, and the struggle for social justice. But not *all* the time! For that is surely the way to become neurotic. Sometimes we must take a rest from worrying about civilisation. Especially after the strenuous exertion of the High Holydays, our intense concentration on what we need to do to improve ourselves and the world, we need to relax. And that is the great value of this festival of Sukkot – or can be, if we allow it to become again what it originally was: a nature festival.

Just for these seven days, let us forget about the dynamics of history and the struggles of the political world. Let the Sukkah be to us again a harvester's booth. Let the Lulav be just a palm branch with twigs of myrtle and willow, and the Etrog a mere citron. Let us simply contemplate nature, and rejoice in it, and think of ourselves as part of it, feel its rhythms, and yield ourselves acceptingly and gratefully to its cycle of growth and decay, of life and death.

❖ ❖ ❖

Festival of Ecology
Sukkot, 9 October 1995

The 'Wallflower Festival' is what Rabbi David Goldberg has called Sukkot. It is an apt name because, apart from featuring flowers, it does suffer from proximity to the more solemn High Holydays, and therefore tends to be ignored. At best, it provides a little light relief after the strenuous exertion of the penitential season.

At least, that is how it was until recently. But now it grows in importance from year to year both in itself and as a necessary follow-on from Yom Kippur. Why? Because if the penitential season is about our relationship with human beings, Sukkot is about our relationship with nature, which is just as important, and, furthermore, the two are closely inter-connected.

What then *should* be our relationship with nature? Let us explore the various possibilities.

One possibility is to *worship* it, or some part of it; to invest it with divinity, and humble ourselves before it. That, in its most primitive form, is the way of *animism*, and in a more sophisticated form, *pantheism*. In either case it is paganism, and therefore something to which Judaism has always been diametrically opposed.

Another possibility is to see nature as one big continuum which includes human beings along with animals and plants and everything else, so that we are not essentially different from them but part and parcel of them. This view, that we are 'of the earth, earthy' (I Corinthians 15:47), brothers and sisters of the buffalo and the grasshopper, is one which one associates with the Native American religions, and perhaps also with Shakespeare's Caliban, so that, for want of a better word, we might call it *Calibanism*.

In Jewish tradition it is to be found almost exclusively in the book of Kohelet or Ecclesiastes, which is traditionally read on this festival. Here is a key passage: 'The fate of humans and the fate of animals is the same; as one dies, so dies the other. They all have the same breath, and the superiority of humans over animals is nothing; for all is vanity. All go to one place; all come from the dust, and all revert to dust' (3:18-20).

Admittedly, this passage, like much of Kohelet, is written in a devil's-advocate, tongue-in-cheek kind of way, for ultimately the book comes to a more positive conclusion.

I am not sure to what extent the same can be said for a writer who rejoices in the name of Felipe Fernandez-Amesto, author of *Millennium*, who wrote an article in The *Independent* recently. In it, he showed how in the past human beings have often considered themselves *inferior* to animals, whose qualities they envied – hence the prehistoric cave drawings, and expressed his own view when he wrote: 'The very attempt to distinguish ourselves from animals is a delusive form of self-flattery' (11 September 1995, p. 11). Indeed, he went even further and compared human beings unfavourably with *vegetables*. 'We may not have to await the day of triffids', he wrote, 'to be judged inferior to plants'. To a visitor from outer space it may well 'look as if they have cunningly manipulated mankind for their own propagation and distribution ... The conservation movement has made us worry about the durability of the natural world, as if nature could not last without mollycoddling by us. Trees, lichens, weeds were here before us. They will be here after we are gone' (ibid.).

That, surely, is the ultimate in human self-deprecation! Judaism has typically gone to the opposite extreme. It has exalted human beings far above the rest of nature and declared that they alone are created in God's image. To the scepticism of Kohelet it has replied that 'the superiority of humans over animals' is immense!

But that perception, in turn, has often encouraged an attitude to nature in which the key word is 'dominion' and which we may therefore call *Domination*. It can all too easily draw support from the Creation Story, where God says to Adam and Eve, 'Be fruitful and multiply; fill the earth and subdue it, and have dominion over the fish of the sea, the birds of the air, and all creatures that crawl on the ground' (Gen. 1:28). And from Psalm 8: 'You have made us little less than divine, and crowned us with glory and honour. You have given us dominion over the works of Your hands; You have put all things under our feet' (vv. 6f).

How dangerous such human triumphalism can be! How easily it can lead to the ruthless exploitation of nature! That is something we hardly realised a few years ago, but we are well and truly aware of it now! And when we read that God has put all things under our feet, we can hardly help adding: 'Yes, and how we have trampled on them'. There is, I am sure, no need to give facts and figures. It is the kind of thing we read about almost daily: how many square miles of natural habitat are being destroyed every day; how many species have already become extinct; how grave are the dangers of global warming; and how nuclear waste, already buried in the earth, is likely to remain radioactive for ten thousand years.

Of course nothing like that was ever foreseen, let alone intended, by the biblical writers. On the contrary, what they had in mind was that human beings should exercise *responsibly* the powers over their environment which God had given them. God placed Adam in the Garden of Eden, we read in Genesis, 'to till it and to keep it' (2:15). So here is another possible way of understanding our relationship with nature: the concept of *husbandry*, that, like good farmers, we should cultivate the earth prudently, so that it may continue to yield good produce for ourselves and our children.

A number of biblical laws are clearly related to this purpose: for instance, the injunction to let the land lie fallow every seventh year, so as not to exhaust the soil (Exod. 23:10f).

And here, too, it becomes apparent that we can't divorce our duties to nature from our duties to our fellow human beings. For by ill-treating nature, we hurt them, if not immediately, then in time to come. Moreover, the self-same failings, of selfishness, greed and aggression, which spoil our human relationships, are also what drives us recklessly to exploit our environment, and therefore hurts our fellow men and women yet again, and not only our contemporaries but future generations as well. The Prophet Hosea saw this interconnection when he said: 'There is no truth, nor mercy, nor knowledge of God in the land. Swearing, lying, and murder, stealing and adultery break out; bloodshed follows bloodshed. Therefore the land mourns, and all who live in it languish; together with the wild animals and the birds of the air, even the fish of the sea are perishing' (4:1-3).

Of the four attitudes we have considered, clearly it is this concept of husbandry, or stewardship, which comes nearest to defining what our relationship with nature should be. Yet even that is no longer adequate. For it is anthropocentric. It assumes that nature exists only for the benefit of humanity. But what we are now learning, or learning again, from the conservationist and animal welfare movements, is that other species have their own rights; they serve all kinds of purposes in the Divine Scheme which we may or may not fully understand, and are to be respected, not only for their usefulness to us, but for themselves.

It is this concept of 'deep ecology', as it has been called, which now needs more than ever to be emphasised. Of course it *includes* the concept of stewardship, for we do have enormous power over our environment, and it is therefore vitally important that we should exercise it responsibly. In a sense, we do have to 'mollycoddle' nature. But often the best way to do that is not to manipulate it at all, but to leave it alone. And that will only happen if we learn to respect it for itself.

Precisely that, as we now realise, is, and has been all along, the message of Sukkot. As the High Holydays teach us to respect our fellow human beings, so Sukkot teaches us to respect our natural environment. It is a message perfectly symbolised by the Four Species. For they have little practical value from a human point of view. The palm may provide us with dates, but we don't often sit in the shade of a myrtle or a willow, and I for one have never tasted an Etrog in my life. Therefore, if we think of Sukkot merely as a harvest festival, it may seem silly to single out just these four species, and perform rituals with them. But if we understand that Sukkot is much more than a harvest festival, that it is a celebration of nature in its own right, then the very lack of utilitarian value of the Lulav and Etrog only reinforces the message.

From now on, therefore, let Sukkot be for us the Festival of Ecology, teaching us to respect nature as the penitential season teaches us to respect one another, and renewing our hope for the day when humanity will be at peace with nature, and nature with itself, and Isaiah's prophecy will be fulfilled: 'They shall not hurt or destroy in all My holy mountain, for the earth shall be full of the knowledge of God as the waters cover the sea' (11:9).

❖   ❖   ❖

Simchat Torah

Simchat Torah, 2 October 1980

Already in the Bible we read that the seven-day festival of Sukkot is to be followed by a one-day festival called *Atzeret*, a word which, for no good reason, is usually translated 'solemn assembly' but which, much more probably, means 'conclusion' (Lev. 23:34ff).

Although tagged on to Sukkot, it is really a separate festival, which 'concludes' not only the harvest festival but the whole series of autumn festivals beginning with Rosh Hashanah; it is a kind of grand finale rounding off the entire, religiously eventful twenty-two day period with which the Jewish year begins.

In Rabbinic times it became known as *Sh'mini Atzeret*, the 'eighth day of conclusion', and that is how it is usually referred to in the Jewish liturgy.

In the same period, like all the other Holy Days except Yom Kippur, it was extended by one further day. But that was owing to a calendrical uncertainty which affected only the Diaspora and was therefore never applied in the Land of Israel.

Until the Middle Ages, this extra day, the 23rd of Tishri, had no special name, any more than the second day of Rosh Hashanah or Shavuot; it was just יום טוב שני של שמיני עצרת, the 'Second Holy Day of the Eighth-Day Festival of Conclusion'. But then, from the age of the Crusades onwards, we find it referred to as Simchat Torah. The question, then, is how that came about.

Obviously, it must have been connected with the public reading of the Torah. But regarding that, practice differed. In the Palestinian synagogues the reading was spread over a three-year period, concluding every third year at the beginning of Adar on account of a tradition that the death of Moses, which is the subject of the last portion of the Torah, occurred on the seventh day of that month. In the Babylonian synagogues, on the other hand, the practice developed of reading the entire Torah in one year, by making the weekly portion three times as long on average. And when did the Babylonian Jews complete their one-year cycle? On the second day of *Sh'mini Atzeret*. So we are informed already in the Talmud (Meg. 31a).

So the possibility arises that some kind of Simchat Torah, although not under that name, may already have been celebrated in talmudic times: either by the Palestinian Jews every third year in the month of Adar or by the Babylonian Jews every year on the 23rd of Tishri, or both. For it is likely enough that the completion of the cycle of Torah readings, whether annual or triennial, would have been regarded as an occasion for rejoicing. But is it only a likelihood or can we actually prove it?

I think we can, by referring to a Midrash on the Song of Songs, known as *Shir ha-Shirim Rabbah*, which was probably compiled in the Land of Israel in the sixth century. Since the Song of Songs begins by claiming to be the work of Solomon, the Midrash initially concentrates on Solomon's proverbial wisdom. In that connection it refers to the well-known story in the third chapter of the First Book of Kings which tells how God appeared to Solomon in a dream and said, 'Ask what I shall give you', and Solomon asked for an understanding mind, and his wish was granted. The story ends: 'And Solomon awoke, and behold, it was a dream. Then he came to Jerusalem, and stood before the ark of the covenant of the Eternal One, and offered up burnt offerings and peace offerings, and made a feast for all his servants' (v. 15). And at this point the Midrash comments: 'Rabbi Eleazar said: From this we learn that a feast is made to celebrate the conclusion of the reading of the Torah' (1:1:9).

The argument depends, of course, on the identification of wisdom with Torah, which is frequently found in Rabbinic Literature. Then it runs: just as Solomon celebrated his acquisition of knowledge of the Torah by giving a feast, so do we. But it is not the argument that matters, but simply the evidence that already in Rabbi Eleazar's time – which, if he is the Rabbi usually referred to by that name, brings us back to the second century CE – there existed a custom of celebrating the conclusion of the reading of the Torah.

This ancient custom made it almost certain that when, in the Age of the Crusades, the Palestinian three-year cycle was finally abandoned and the Babylonian one-year cycle adopted by all Jews, the day of the completion of the one-year cycle, now universal, would become more than ever one of rejoicing and develop into Simchat Torah as we know it. But one more ingredient was necessary, namely that on that day, not only should the reading of the Torah be concluded, but immediately begun again. That practice, too, sprang up, so far as we know, in the early Middle Ages; and one of the first to mention it is Jacob ben Asher who, with his famous father Asher ben Yechiel, a disciple of Meir of Rothenburg, migrated from Germany to Spain round about the year 1300. In his codification of Jewish law, the Arba-ah Turim, this is what he says: 'We call this day Simchat Torah because on it we complete the reading of the Torah, and it is appropriate to rejoice upon its completion. Furthermore, it is customary to begin the book of Genesis immediately so as not to give an opening to Satan to accuse us by saying, "They have completed the reading of the Torah, and now they don't want to read it again"...' (O.Ch. 669).

To complete the story, it is only necessary to add that Progressive Jews, even in the Diaspora, do what Jews of all kinds have always done in the Land of Israel: they combine *Sh'mini Atzeret* with Simchat Torah, so that it serves a double purpose: to conclude the autumnal festival season, and to celebrate the completion and re-commencement of the Torah cycle. And why do we, as Progressive Jews, do that? Because, although we don't share the view of the Orthodox that the Torah contains the truth, the whole truth and nothing but the truth, we do see it as a marvellous attempt on the part of our ancestors to comprehend the will of God, an attempt which is the basis of all subsequent attempts and may therefore fittingly symbolise the entire enterprise. We rejoice in the Torah, then, because, like Solomon, we do not set the highest value on riches and honour, but on wisdom to discern between good and evil. We give thanks that we have inherited such wisdom from the generations of the past, and announce our intention to continue to study the literature containing it, so that it may teach us the art of living, and that we may be spiritually, morally and intellectually equipped to pass it on to the generations of the future.

❖   ❖   ❖

Season of Dedication

Nationalism and Religion
Chanukkah, 6 December 1975

What is nationalism? Basically, it is the will of a people to maintain its identity and to ensure its survival. There is nothing dishonourable in that. On the contrary, it is praiseworthy, and it plays an important part in the Chanukkah story. The edict of Antiochus which provoked the Maccabean Rebellion demanded that the Jews of Palestine should give up their distinctive way of life and conform to Hellenism. It was therefore an assault on their identity, and since, if they had yielded, they would have disappeared from history, a threat to their survival. In these circumstances the defiance of Mattathias – 'Even if all the nations that live under the rule of the king obey him ... yet I and my sons and my brothers will live by the covenant of our fathers' (I Macc. 2:19) – was noble and may serve as an example to us. We too have a duty to maintain our identity and to resist, if necessary by force and at the cost of martyrdom, any attempt to destroy it.

But nationalism, as normally understood, goes further. It is about means as well as ends. It maintains that *in order* to preserve its identity and ensure its survival, a people must have a territorial base and exercise sovereign control over it. That was not at first the aim of the Maccabees. If Antiochus had revoked his edict, if he had left the Jews alone to 'do their own thing', most of them would probably have been willing to remain under Syrian rule. But the craving for independence soon asserted itself, and within a generation, the successors of Mattathias, taking advantage of the declining power of the Seleucid empire, managed to establish an autonomous Jewish State. In that there is nothing ignoble either; and if it was justified then, it is more justified today. For the intervening two thousand years have demonstrated all too clearly the need of the Jewish people for a country they can call their own, so that its doors may always be open to those who need a refuge from persecution. It is this, the humanitarian aspect of Zionism which makes it both more legitimate and nobler than most nationalisms – this and its other creative achievements: the redemption of barren deserts and marshes, the establishment of a progressive economy and a democratic government in a backward region of the world, the revival of the Hebrew language, and many more.

Unfortunately, the pursuit of territorial independence often compels nationalistic movements to resort to the use of arms. It was so in the case of the Maccabees, and in view of the repressive policies which provoked their rebellion, it was probably justified. But we must also remember that Zionism always hoped to attain its objective without fighting. The methods it employed were fund-raising, land-purchase and political diplomacy. It was only when their State was attacked that they replied in kind. Their wars have been wars of self-defence. And therefore, if we are not out-and-out pacifists, we may also applaud their heroism; it was certainly not less remarkable than that of the Maccabees.

But what has been said about capitalism is also true of nationalism: that it can have, though it need not have, an 'unacceptable face'. For nationalism is, by its nature, self-regarding. Therefore it tends to disregard the interests of other nations and even to become chauvinistically hostile to them.

The tendency of nationalism to degenerate into chauvinism is not, we must confess, entirely absent from the story of Chanukkah, for the Maccabean victory generated a militancy that is readily discernible in the literature of the period. It inspired the book of Daniel, which gloats over the downfall of Babylonia – that is to say, Syria; for Nebuchadnezzar read Antiochus – and the book of Esther, which dwells at length on the vengeance executed by the Jews against their Persian enemies, as well as other books of the same ilk, such as Judith among the Apocrypha.

But even when it does not descend to chauvinism, nationalism tends to do something else: it tends to stifle spirituality. This is not to say that nationalism and religion cannot go together. They often do. The Maccabees were deeply religious, and drew their support chiefly from the Chasidim, the most devout of the people. Mattathias's rallying call was: 'Let every one who is zealous for the Torah … come out with me' (I Macc. 2:27). The first action of his son, Judah, when he had won his victory, was to cleanse and re-dedicate the Temple; and to its credit, the Chanukkah liturgy stresses this aspect of the story far more than the military one.

But nationalism also tends to stifle the religious spirit in more intangible ways, by the whole atmosphere it generates. It tends to take the view that the end justifies the means, whereas religion insists that the means be proper. It tends to rely on political skill and military strength, whereas religion, especially Prophetic religion, asks us to trust in God and the ultimate triumph of righteousness. It tends to be cynical about human motives, whereas religion teaches us to believe in the possibility of altruism. It tends to be strident and acrimonious, whereas religion would have us be serene and conciliatory. It tends to indulge in self-pity and self-congratulation, whereas the characteristic religious mood is one of self-criticism and humility. The values of nationalism tend to be sectional; the values of religion are universal.

The festival of Chanukkah, too, loses the essence of its message if it is observed only in a nationalistic vein. And the creators of our liturgy, as if aware of that danger, ordained long ago that its chief prophetic lesson should be the passage from Zechariah which contains the great verse: 'Not by might, nor by power, but by My spirit, says the God of hosts' (4:6). Exactly how it was meant is not perhaps quite clear. But it was probably intended as a rebuke to Zerubbabel for having sought to re-establish the Davidic monarchy by some kind of military insurrection. To us it has a broader meaning: that the Kingdom of God cannot be built by secular means alone, but only by a power greater than that of any *Realpolitik*, the power of the spirit of God, the power of truth and justice and compassion; and that that power is available to us if only we have the faith to trust in it and the courage to harness it.

❖   ❖   ❖

Religious Activism

Shabbat Mi-ketz and Chanukkah, 18 December 1981

'Don't just sit there, *do* something!' That is how one might roughly translate what Jacob says to his sons (Gen. 42:1). His actual words are: למה תתראו, 'Why do you stare at one another?' But the meaning is clear: there is a famine in our land; our food supplies are running out fast; if we do nothing we shall all starve to death; in Egypt there is still grain to be had; go and buy some, שנחיה ולא נמות, 'that we may live, and not die' (Gen. 42:2).

There speaks a man of action. But he does not typify all religious people. Many, in the face of impending catastrophe, have tended to adopt a passive role; to leave it all to God; to rely on God's providence; to throw themselves on God's mercy; to 'wait patiently for God' (Psalm 40:1).

Activism versus passivism. The conflict between these opposing tendencies is illustrated by the Chanukkah story. It begins with passive resistance to the attempt of the Syrian king, Antiochus, to enforce Hellenism throughout his empire. At first the faithful among the Jews merely refuse to comply; they continue to study the Torah, to circumcise their sons, and to observe their dietary laws, in defiance of the king's decree, and many of them are martyred for their defiance.

Mattathias, too, begins with civil disobedience. When the king's officers come to his village of Modiin, he bluntly refuses to perform the token act of idolatry which they demand of him, and we recall his stirring words: 'Even if all the nations that live under the rule of the king obey him, and have chosen to do his commandments, departing each one from the religion of his fathers, yet I and my sons and my brothers will live by the covenant of our fathers. Far be it from us to desert the law and the ordinances. We will not obey the king's words by turning from our religion to the right hand or to the left' (I Macc. 2:19-22). But he soon realises that it is not enough, and with the battle-cry, 'Let everyone who is zealous for the Torah and supports the covenant come out with me!' (2:27), he goes over from passive to active resistance.

Even then the conflict is not entirely resolved, for the immediate sequel tells us how at first the Maccabean guerrillas refused to defend themselves if attacked on the Sabbath, so as not to desecrate it, saying, 'Let us all die in our innocence' (2:37). Only when it became obvious that such a policy amounted to mass suicide did Mattathias and his friends formally revoke it, saying, 'Let us fight against every man who comes to attack us on the sabbath day; let us not all die as our brothers died in their hiding places' (2:41).

From this point onwards the story of the Maccabees is unequivocally one of activism, but, it must be emphasised, of *religious* activism. They did not fold their hands and wait for a miracle to happen. They knew that they must give God a helping hand. But their motive was essentially religious. They saw themselves as acting in partnership with God, but God was decidedly the 'Senior Partner'. It was for God's sake that they took up arms; it was God's Torah which they resolved to defend; it was God's Temple which they intended to purify and rededicate; and it was from God that they drew their strength and courage. Later tradition regarded the name Maccabee as an acronym made up of the words, מי כמוכה באלים ה', 'Who is like You among the gods, Eternal One' (Exod. 15:11): an unfounded theory but which conveys well enough the religious spirit that animated the Maccabees in the early stages of their rebellion.

But it didn't last! Having achieved their war aim, of freeing Jerusalem and reconsecrating the Temple, they didn't stop fighting. For by this time they had become a highly efficient army, and other glittering prizes lay within their grasp. Flushed with success, they made a bid for political independence, personal power and national glory. They gave themselves royal titles, embarked on a programme of territorial expansion, and even imposed Judaism on the conquered populations, as Antiochus had tried to impose Hellenism on them. In other words, they behaved like any pagan ruler. They were still activists, indeed more so than ever, but no longer on behalf of God. George Santayana once said: 'Fanaticism consists in redoubling your effort when you have forgotten your aim' (THQ, 168). In that sense the Hasmoneans became fanatics, and with results which a prophet, if there had been one around, could surely have predicted. The sequel is a story of moral decline and corruption, of intrigue and internecine strife, not unlike the story of the Borgias, and it was only a matter of time before the Hasmonean State was bound to collapse. About a hundred years after the first Chanukkah, it became a Roman province.

However, of all this most Jews during the last two thousand years have known little, for it is related in books like the Apocrypha and Josephus which have not been readily available to them. They have known about the Maccabean Rebellion from the liturgy of the Synagogue, which says nothing at all about the later stages, and even as regards the first stage, puts all the emphasis on God's initiative. Mattathias and his sons did what any loyal, self-respecting Jew was bound to do. After that, God took over, causing the few to triumph over the many, and performing the miracle of the oil. With the rededication of the Temple, the story ends, for there is nothing, at least nothing significant or edifying, left to tell.

Just as God, not Moses, is the true 'hero' of the Passover story, so God, and not Mattathias or Judah is the true 'hero' of the Chanukkah story. This point is further emphasised in the words of the Hallel, traditionally recited throughout the eight days of the festival, for the 115th Psalm begins: לא לנו, ה׳, לא לנו, 'Not to us, Eternal One, not to us, but to Your name let glory be given'; and the 118th Psalm adds: 'This is the God's doing, and it is wonderful in our eyes'. Furthermore, the Haftarah which Judaism chose long ago for recitation on the Sabbath in Chanukkah is the Zechariah passage which not only contains the description of the golden candlestick, linking it with the legend of the oil, but includes the great motto, לא בחיל ולא בכוח כי־אם ברוחי 'Not by might, nor by power, but by My spirit, says the God of hosts' (4:6), which is a rebuke to Zerubbabel for his attempted insurrection against the Persians and therefore, more generally, a warning that the messianic kingdom is to be brought about by moral, not military means.

Two centuries after the Maccabean Rebellion the conflict between activism and passivism surfaced again. Messianic fervour ran high, but it took different forms. At one extreme were the Essenes, who were convinced that God would intervene supernaturally, and dreamt apocalyptic dreams. At the other were the Zealots, always itching to fight the Romans, always saying to the people: 'Don't just sit there, *do* something!'

In view of the festival our Christian neighbours have been celebrating, we might ask ourselves, incidentally, where Jesus stood in this dispute. The answer seems to be that he had much in common with, and was perhaps torn between, both of the extreme positions. Obviously he expected some kind of direct, supernatural, divine intervention. On the other hand one comes across in the Gospels such tell-tale sayings as this: 'You must not think that I have come to bring peace to the earth; I have not come to bring peace, but a sword' (Matthew 10:34). I say 'tell-tale' because it is surely quite inconceivable that the Evangelists would have invented such remarks. On the contrary, their interest must have been in suppressing them, since they wished to commend to the Gentile Church, not a Jewish national liberation movement leader but a divine saviour. That such teachings were nevertheless preserved and reported makes it virtually certain that they are genuine, and that Jesus was closer to the Zealot position than has generally been admitted. The fact that one of his disciples, Simon, *was* a Zealot, may be of some relevance here.

At any rate, the Zealots ultimately won the argument, and with disastrous consequences. State and Temple were destroyed, and the last flare-up of that kind of activism, under Bar-Kochba, some sixty years later, achieved only a short-lived success.

After that the Jewish people settled, by and large, for passivism. They allowed their destiny to be largely determined by the good-will or, more frequently, ill-will of the nations among whom they lived. Only in the last century or two has Jewish activism re-asserted itself, and in two ways: first, in the demand for Emancipation, and then, when that failed to put a stop to anti-Semitism, in the demand for a State of their own.

Zionism is the supreme example of Jewish activism in modern history, but it has not, for the most part, been a *religious* activism. Many of the founders and followers of Zionism have been secularists, and they have therefore tended to interpret the Chanukkah story in secular terms, to emphasise the human rather than the divine dimension of it. To them, it is the story of a national victory in which the military exploits of the human heroes, especially Judah the Maccabee, receive great praise.

A good example of that new spirit, diametrically opposed to traditional Jewish piety, is the popular song, מִי יְמַלֵּל גְּבוּרוֹת יִשְׂרָאֵל, 'Who can recount the mighty deeds of Israel?' Of Israel, please note, not God! Judah the Maccabee is referred to, not only as גִּבּוֹר, 'hero', but as מוֹשִׁיעַ וּפוֹדֶה, 'saviour and deliverer', both terms which are traditionally applied to God, not to humans. And the song ends by calling on the Jewish people, not to wait to be redeemed by God, but לְהִגָּאֵל, to redeem itself.

Self-redemption is indeed what Zionism is all about, and it is precisely for this reason that it has been, and continues to be, so bitterly opposed by extreme fundamentalist groups such as the Natorei Karta who insist that God alone is the Redeemer.

And where do *we* stand? We are not passivists. We are too modern for that. We do not think in terms of supernatural divine interventions in the normal course of human history. We know that we are responsible for our own destiny. To that extent, the Zionist concept of self-redemption commends itself to us. But we are *religious* Jews as well as modern Jews, and therefore to us any proposed act of self-redemption must pass the test of being in accord with God's will. To put it another way, the idea that appeals to us most is that we are God's מְשׁוּתָּפִים, partners; that redemption is a process in which God and humanity must work together.

Applying that criterion, many of us would endorse the basic aims of Zionism: to obtain by political means a homeland for the Jewish people; to defend it by military means when it is attacked; and above all, by spiritual means to establish in it an ideal society. Many of us believe that these aims are in accord with God's will, and that the extraordinary courage which the builders and defenders of the State of Israel have displayed in the pursuit of these aims has derived to some extent, like the courage of the ancient Maccabees, from God's part in the redemptive process. But some of us are also gravely afraid that the present leaders of Israel may repeat the mistake of the Hasmoneans, that they may be pursuing aims, like territory, power and glory, which go beyond the point at which they cease to have God's approval, and that in so doing they may court disaster. At such a time it is more than ever necessary to emphasise the words of Zechariah, 'Not by might, nor by power, but by My spirit, says the God of hosts', and to understand them to mean that a policy of self-redemption is doomed to failure unless the redemption it seeks is the kind which God intends for us, and unless the means which it employs to achieve it are in harmony with God's will.

❖   ❖   ❖

The Truth about the Pharisees
Chanukkah, 30 December 1989

> Yours the message cheering
> That the time is nearing
> Which will see
> All men free
> Tyrants disappearing

With these stirring words from 'Rock of Ages' by Marcus Jastrow and Gustav Gottheil we shall conclude our service. They remind us that the overthrow of tyrants is a cause for rejoicing only because it brings nearer the time 'which will see / all men free'. But even *freedom* is only that which makes *democracy* possible. And even democracy is not an end in itself, but merely the system that offers the best chance of achieving *a just and humane society*.

Let us keep these thoughts in mind while we recall once more the events of over two thousand years ago which Chanukkah commemorates. For three years the Maccabees fought a gruelling guerrilla war against the tyrant of their time, Antiochus Epiphanes. But while they were giving their attention to the enemy *without*, something was happening *within* Judean society which proved ultimately even more significant. I am referring to the emergence of the Pharisees, as they later came to be called.

Exactly how or when it happened we don't know, but it must have been round about the time of the Maccabean Rebellion. Why? First, because from that time onwards (but not before) we hear a great deal about the Pharisees; and secondly, because both of them, Maccabees and Pharisees, seem to have emerged out of the same section of Judean society: a group of people called Chasidim or 'pious ones'. These people were particularly staunch Jews and devout practitioners both of Scripture study and of prayer. They were strongly opposed to Hellenisation and, more than any section of the population, ready to resist when Judaism came under threat. From them, therefore, the Maccabees drew their keenest recruits. So we learn from the First Book of Maccabees (2:42), which also tells us, however, that, once religious freedom had been regained, the same Chasidim had no further interest in military action but were then ready to make peace with the Syrians (7:13).

So there developed a rift between the Chasidim and the Maccabees, which grew even wider when the latter assumed royal honours and established a hereditary dynasty, that of the Hasmoneans, which not only usurped the Davidic throne but became pretty tyrannous itself.

However, there also developed a rift between the Chasidim and the *priests*, who claimed descent from a priest of the time of King David called Zadok, so that they and their supporters became known as *Tz'dukim* or Sadducees. For one thing, they tended to be Hellenisers. For another, they claimed as exclusive an authority over the nation's *religious* life as the Hasmoneans did over its *political* life. For they presided over the Temple, which was the only permitted place of worship, and they considered themselves the sole custodians and interpreters of the Torah. The Chasidim, who knew the Torah as well as the priests, and better, must have resented that. Especially after the Maccabean war, in which they suffered the heaviest casualties, they might well have argued: 'If we are good enough to die for the Torah, then we are good enough to study and to teach it'.

So there sprang up a movement which challenged the concentration of religious authority in the hands of a hereditary priesthood, and sought to spread it more widely: a *democratising* movement which, by establishing synagogues where all classes of Jews could worship as equals, and making education accessible to rich and poor alike, tried to transform Judaism into a people's religion.

In their new capacity as leaders of this movement, the Chasidim called themselves *Chachamim*, wise ones, that is to say, lay scholars.

However, their opponents, the Sadducees, called them *P'rushim*, which means 'those who separate themselves', a derogatory name which they *never* applied to themselves (see Ellis Rivkin, 'Defining the Pharisees', in *Hebrew Union College Annual* Vols XL-XLI, 1969-1970) but which, in its Latinised form 'Pharisees', has stuck to them ever since.

That is an unfortunate fact because it has led to all sorts of theories of how the Pharisees kept aloof from the common people, which is not only untrue but the *reverse* of the truth, for, unlike the Sadducees, they were drawn from the common people and beloved of the common people. What is even more unfortunate is that the Gospels portray them as hypocrites, and that most Christians accept the Gospel caricature, and persist in doing so even though by now scores of scholars, Christian as well as Jewish, have demonstrated that it is historically false.

A shocking example of that persistence occurred in October 1989, when the Archbishop of Canterbury, who should know better, in an interview in *The Director*, described as 'Pharisees' the people who, having achieved success in Thatcherite Britain, have become self-righteous and judgmental towards the unsuccessful – the poor and the unemployed. To which I replied in The *Independent* that, while the Archbishop's social critique might be justified, his disparaging reference to the Pharisees was not. For, as I said, 'far from being inclined towards self-righteousness, the Pharisees taught "Be humble before all men ...", and far from being judgmental, they urged "Do not judge your fellow man until you are in his position"' (4 October 1989). Similar rejoinders appeared in other papers. For instance, Rabbi Dr Jonathan Sacks, Principal of Jews' College, wrote in *The Times* that the Pharisees should be seen, on the contrary, as 'Jewish architects of a responsible, caring society' (4 October 1989).

And that, we hoped, had set the record straight. But almost immediately the Prime Minister, to get her own back on the Archbishop, declared that most people in this country were not at all as he had described them. On the contrary, she said, three out of every four are caring people, like the Good Samaritan, and only one in four is uncaring, like the Pharisees. Poor Pharisees! Dr Runcie and Mrs Thatcher are in complete agreement that they were nasty people, and only differ as to whether most of us are, regrettably, like them or, happily, unlike them.

I don't know whether anybody came to the defence of the Pharisees on that occasion, but now a third incident has raised the issue yet again. In her Christmas Day broadcast, Her Majesty the Queen commended to all her subjects both the Golden Rule of 'You shall love your neighbour as yourself', as taught by 'Jesus Christ', and, like Mrs Thatcher, the parable of the Good Samaritan.

But what is the truth? Well, we all know that the Golden Rule comes from the Torah, which Jesus merely quoted. But there it is only one of *many* commandments, and doesn't stand out with the same prominence as it does in the Gospels. Jesus singled it out for special emphasis. But then so did the Pharisees! According to Hillel it is the very essence of the Torah (Shab. 31a). According to Rabbi Akiva, it is the greatest of all the commandments (Sifra to Lev. 19:18). Admittedly, Christians wouldn't generally know that. But the Gospels themselves, which they do know, record an incident from which it emerges quite clearly that, whatever Jesus and the Pharisees may have disagreed about, they agreed about the pre-eminence of the Golden Rule.

In fact, the story occurs three times. In Mark, which is the oldest version, a scribe asks Jesus, which is the greatest commandment. Jesus answers by quoting, first, from Deuteronomy (6:4f), 'Hear, O Israel, the Lord is our God, the Lord is One; and you shall love the Lord your God with all your heart ...', and then from Leviticus (19:18), 'You shall love your neighbour as yourself'. The scribe applauds the answer – it is evidently just what he would have said himself; Jesus in turn compliments him, and they part in perfect harmony (12:28-34). In Matthew, where the questioner is identified as a Pharisee, the atmosphere is chillier, and the mutual compliments are omitted (22:34-40). In Luke the questioner is a lawyer. But Jesus throws the question back at him, so that it is he who supplies the answer, and Jesus who applauds it (10:25-28).

It is at this point that Luke introduces the parable of the Good Samaritan, which, as most scholars agree, had originally nothing to do with the incident. It is furthermore doubtful whether it was originally about a Samaritan at all, for the sequence 'Priest, Levite, Samaritan' is incongruous, whereas the sequence 'Priest, Levite, Israelite' occurs very frequently in Jewish literature. Again, considering that the parable is supposed to answer the question 'Who is your neighbour?' for the purpose of the Golden Rule, you would expect the answer to be the victim of the mugging, whereas it is the Samaritan who comes to his aid (10:29-37).

So the story is a bit confused, but it nevertheless makes the point effectively enough that good neighbourliness consists in helping those in need, whoever they may be. But of course that is a point the Pharisees would have heartily endorsed! Indeed, it is most probably from the Pharisees that Jesus learnt it in the first place. (There are in fact quite similar stories in Rabbinic Literature; see Israel Abrahams, *Studies in Pharisaism and the Gospels*, First Series, p. 110, and Second

Series, p. 39). For not only did they emphasise the commandment, 'You shall love your neighbour as yourself': they urged particularly its practice towards the weaker members of society – orphans, widows and strangers, and above all the poor. 'Let the poor be members of your household' (Avot 1:5) is just one of many typically Pharisaic teachings. But unlike the Prophets, and unlike Jesus, the Pharisees did not content themselves with merely *preaching* concern for the weak: they actually *legislated* for an equitable social order. So whether the leader of a government under whose legislation the gap between rich and poor has grown ever wider, and the problem of homelessness ever graver, is in a strong position to criticise the Pharisees for their supposed lack of concern for the unfortunate is a question to which it is not easy to think of a polite answer!

The historical truth is that the Chasidim and their successors, the Pharisees, were champions of freedom, champions of democracy, champions of neighbourly love, and champions of social justice. Therefore we, who are their heirs, have every reason to be proud of them, especially during this festival of Chanukkah which recalls the period of their origin, and if this country, during the 1980s that are now about to end, had made a serious attempt to live up to the ideals they taught and practised it would undoubtedly be a more just, compassionate and humane society than it is.

❖   ❖   ❖

Season of Levity

The Wars of the Eternal One
Shabbat Zachor and Erev Purim, 14 March 1987

Tonight we can let our hair down but not yet! For we still have some remembering to do, today being *Shabbat Zachor*, the Sabbath of Remembrance.

The name comes from a short paragraph, of only three verses, which occurs in the fifteenth chapter of Deuteronomy and is traditionally read on the Sabbath before Purim from a second Scroll. It begins, זכור את אשר עשה לך עמלק, 'Remember what Amalek did to you', and ends, 'Therefore you shall blot out the memory of Amalek from under heaven; לא תשכח, you shall not forget' (vv. 17ff).

But what *did* Amalek do? The incident in question is related in the seventeenth chapter of Exodus. Evidently, the Amalekites were a marauding tribe who periodically attacked, plundered and slaughtered any people within their reach, and the Israelites, on their way out of Egypt, became the target of such an attack. In the event, they counter-attacked successfully; but for some reason the memory of the battle impressed itself with unique bitterness on their consciousness – perhaps because the attack was a peculiarly unprovoked and vicious one; we don't really know.

What we do know is that from that time Amalek became in the minds of our ancestors a symbol of all that is wanton, cruel, merciless and anti-Semitic. That perception is already present in the way the incident is related. It is no ordinary military skirmish. Though Joshua commands the troops on the ground, the operation is conducted by Moses from a hill-top, and whenever he raises his hand, Israel prevails. There is something supernatural going on. The battle is not between two Near Eastern peoples. It is between cosmic forces. That becomes quite clear in the concluding phrase and punch-line of the passage: מלחמה לה' בעמלק מדר דר, 'The Eternal One will have war with Amalek from generation to generation' (v. 16).

This concept of a cosmic war between the forces of good and the forces of evil is a recurring one in our tradition. The Bible even mentions a book – one of the lost books of ancient Hebrew literature – with the title ספר מלחמות ה', the 'Book of the Wars of the Eternal One' (Num. 21:14); in the Middle Ages the Provençal scholar Gersonides wrote a work of Jewish philosophy under the same title; and among the Dead Sea Scrolls there is a book entitled מגילת מלחמת בני אור בבני חשך, 'The Scroll of the War of the Children of Light against the Children of Darkness'.

So that is what *Shabbat Zachor* is all about. We are to remember the cosmic struggle between good and evil. The question of course remains: why? Why drag up the past? It is a question being asked a great deal at the present time, particularly in relation to the Holocaust, which is for us not only a painful memory of relatively recent times but has become for us a paradigm of evil in much the same way as was the attack of the Amalekites for our ancestors.

With so many reminders assailing our consciousness, we hardly need a Sabbath of Remembrance. If anything, there is *too much* remembering going on. That, at least, is how many people feel. Gentile commentators see in our preoccupation with the Holocaust a token of Jewish vengefulness and lack of the Christian virtue of forgiveness, and even Jews, especially young Jews, sometimes scream at us: 'For heaven's sake, give the subject a rest!'

They have a point. The preoccupation *can* be morbidly obsessive; it *can* damage our health, like an old wound too frequently reopened; the remembrance can become unbearable. Perhaps that is one reason for the feast of Purim. Just once a year we are allowed to forget. We are allowed to dull our senses. We are allowed to drink, as the talmudic saying goes, עד לא ידע, until we no longer know the difference between 'Blessed be Mordecai' and 'Cursed be Haman' (Meg. 7b). But only once a year, and only for twenty-four hours. With that one exception, we are to remain cognisant of reality, however painful it is. No escapism for us during the rest of the year! And especially on the Sabbath before Purim we are to listen to the stern demand, לא תשכח, 'You shall not forget'.

And if we again ask why, the answer is surely that that is what reality is like. Evil does not exist only in our morbid imagination: it exists out there, in the real, all too real, world. It is easy to forget about it while we are secure, as it is easy to forget what it feels like to be ill when we are well. But it is there, doing its destructive work, hurting, maiming and killing, and for the sake of its victims today and tomorrow we had better not turn a blind eye to it. There *is* a war going on between the forces of light and the forces of darkness, and we may not look on from the sidelines.

Of course, we may not oversimplify the battle either. There is a constant temptation, which becomes especially acute in times of conflict, to do that: to see humanity as divided into two camps, the goodies and the baddies; to construct a mental scenario in which 'we' are on the side of the angels and 'they' are on the side of the devil. But the world isn't like that. The distribution of good and evil is a whole lot more complex.

Is there such a danger of oversimplification in the stereotype of Amalek? Yes, of course there is, and especially in the book of Esther, which is the ultimate statement of the stereotype. That is indeed one of the stock objections to the book. But the objection is serious only if the book is taken seriously, which of course it should not be! For one thing, it is a work of fiction. It has all the hallmarks of a fictional short story, and is instantly recognisable as such if one is familiar with that genre of literature.

But it isn't only that. We have to add that the book is a fairy-tale which dramatises the cosmic struggle between good and evil. It is to be compared, not only with the apocryphal book of Judith or with the Arabian Nights, with both of which it has striking resemblances, but with Cinderella and with Punch and Judy. It is not only an oversimplification but a *deliberate* oversimplification, stylised and allegorical, extravagant, grotesque and funny. The line of battle is clearly drawn, and there are no ambiguities. As in an old-style Western, we are never left in any doubt who are the heroes, and who the villains.

It is not to be thought, therefore, that it was the events related in the book of Esther which supplied the impetus for the institution of the feast of Purim. It is the other way round. First came the felt need for a feast like Purim; then the book of Esther was written to provide the script. And the need requires little explanation. Just as the suffering of humanity is unbearable if we must contemplate it all the time, without ever a moment's respite, so the reality of evil is too complex for us always to keep in mind the subtle distinctions. The feast of Purim provides a means of escape both from the suffering and from the complexity. Such escapism would be dangerous if we indulged in it all the time, or normally; but just once in a long while it may be therapeutic to imagine a world in which goodies are goodies and baddies are baddies, and the goodies always defeat the baddies, and the more resoundingly the better! In such a context, the vengeance wreaked by the Jews on their enemies towards the end of the book is not to be seen as a lapse of good taste on the part of an insensitive author: it is part and parcel of the *genre*. You are not supposed to feel sympathy for the crocodile as Punch hits it over the head; you are supposed to find it hilarious!

It is all harmless good fun, and a salutary way of letting off steam, provided that you only do it once in a long while, and that you know what you are doing. It is when the book of Esther is taken in dead earnest, and when its cowboys and Indians mentality is carried over into real life, and becomes a basis of judgment in actual political conflict, it is only then that it becomes dangerous.

Let me give the kaleidoscope one more twist. There is also the opposite danger, of perceiving so many complexities, and making so many allowances, that in the end all moral distinctions become blurred, and we come to pretend or, worse, to believe that there really is no difference between 'Cursed be Haman' and 'Blessed be Mordecai', or, in the words of the prophet Malachi, we cease to discern 'between the righteous and the wicked, between those who serve God and those who do not' (3:18). Good and evil are real enough, though it is not always easy to identify them, or to know how best to assert the one and defeat the other. Life is full of ambiguities, but the battle of good against evil is nevertheless a real battle, and to remind us not to remain aloof from it, but to engage in it, is, I take it, the message of *Shabbat Zachor*.

So tonight let us let our hair down. Just for twenty-four hours let us enter the fairy-tale world of make-believe, where right is clearly recognised as right and wrong as wrong, and the victory of the children of light over the children of darkness is instantaneous and over-whelming. And when Purim is over, let us come down to earth and strive, in spite of all the ambiguities and complexities of the real world, patiently to bring the fulfilment of that vision a little nearer.